LESSONS FOR LIFE 3

LESSONS FOR LIFE 3

JILL MASTERS

THE WAKEMAN TRUST * LONDON

THE WAKEMAN TRUST
(UK Registered Charity)
5 Templar Street
London SE5 9JB

LESSONS FOR LIFE 3

First published 1993

ISBN 1 870855 15 9

Cover design by Andrew Sides

Visual aid drawings by Alan MacGregor
with graphics and presentation by Andrew Owen

Scripture quotations are from the Authorized (King James) Version, unless otherwise indicated.

Printed in Great Britain by The Alden Press, Osney Mead, Oxford.

CONTENTS
Book 3

USING THIS BOOK

This is the third of a series of lesson books providing a four-year scheme (set out on pages 250-251). Take-home leaflets (in 'master' form for local photocopying) to accompany the lessons in this book, are also published. The address for enquiries is shown on page 252.

These lesson notes have an evangelistic aim, using Bible portions which clearly include an evangelistic application. Each lesson seeks to confront children with those truths and arguments which, by the Holy Spirit, could lead to conversion. Alongside this, the lessons are designed to give a good outline knowledge of all the Scriptures.

The syllabus has been arranged to present biblical events in an orderly manner, worthy of the Word of God. The Old Testament is mainly dealt with chronologically, so that the pattern of God's dealings with mankind before Christ are known and appreciated. Series of Old Testament lessons are interleaved with series based on the Gospels and the *Book of Acts.* Both children and teachers prefer this method of following a basic historical plan, to an approach which jumps from one part of the Bible to another with such frequency that perspective is lost. Parents (unbelievers as well as believers) will appreciate that their children are receiving a biblical education.

Experience has shown that teachers are the best people to adapt the lessons to an individual class. These notes therefore contain material which can be adapted to the needs of all age groups, from Beginners (pre-school age) to the teenage Bible Class. A range of suggested applications and guidelines is provided so that teachers may utilise the particular points most suited to their age group. Teachers of older classes often use the complete lesson outline, while those teaching younger classes select fewer points. In the many years this scheme has been in use in Sunday Schools, no teacher has ever complained that this has presented a problem.

This lesson system is tailored to fit around the Sunday School year. Most Sunday Schools, like day schools, divide their programme into three terms a year. Most suspend programmed lessons at such times as Christmas, New Year, Easter and other holidays and special occasions. Speakers usually choose and prepare their own subject on these Sundays, and it is assumed, therefore, that a maximum of 46 lessons per year is required. The lessons are grouped into series, and individual Sunday Schools may use these in any order to suit their Sunday School year. However, the Old Testament series should be kept in chronological order, whereas New Testament series may be fitted into the year according to choice.

In these volumes the aim is to offer the children a great and varied Gospel challenge as they set out on life's journey. Prayerfully, our concern is that it will lead them to the Saviour in early years, but if not, it will plant in their minds and hearts a knowledge of the Lord which can be used by His Spirit in later years to prick their consciences and lead them to seek the Saviour.

The promise of the Lord that His Word will not return to Him void *(Isaiah 55.11)* provides a great incentive to continue through weeks of patient toil. In days of irreligion and apathy amongst the adult population, it is extremely touching to witness large numbers of children gathering together, and to see the Lord still preparing His praise out of the mouths of even the youngest *(Matthew 21.16)*.

He that goeth forth and weepeth, bearing precious seed, shall doubtless come again with rejoicing, bringing his sheaves with him (Psalm 126.6).

Series 12
Mark's Gospel (Part III)
GAINS AND LOSSES IN FOLLOWING JESUS

27:04:03

93 – Preparing for the Saviour

John the Baptist announces the coming of the Messiah. He urges the men and women of his day to sincere and practical repentance. Are we ready to change our minds and our ways in response to the Saviour? John also spoke about the Holy Spirit Who can bring about these changes in the hardest heart.

04:05:03

94 – Leaving All to Follow Jesus

Four fishermen immediately leave their boats and nets to follow Jesus. What can we learn from their example? Years later Peter wrote in his second epistle about – *the knowledge of him that hath called us to glory and virtue.* Nothing in this life is worth holding on to by comparison with knowing and walking with the Lord Jesus.

11:05:03

95 – The Value of a Soul

The Lord Jesus never made false promises. Near to Caesarea Philippi He warns His disciples of the cost of following Him down to Jerusalem, where He must suffer greatly. He explains what they will gain.

96 – The Currency of Heaven

This confident young ruler imagines that he can easily 'buy' his ticket to Heaven, but when he discovers the real cost, he goes sadly away. What can he teach us? Jesus suggests that it is easier for little children to follow Him. Have we grasped the opportunity?

97 – The Cost of Our Salvation

In the Garden of Gethsemane we catch a glimpse of what it cost the Saviour to redeem His people. When we consider what Jesus suffered, is there anything we would refuse to do for Him?

98 – Gaining from Loss

Peter weeps bitterly when he realises that he has denied his Friend and Saviour three times. What relief he feels later as the Lord Jesus receives his three assurances of love. What gladness he experiences as he is restored and made useful to his Lord once again. All repentance is painful but it teaches us to appreciate how much we have been forgiven.

99 – Profit or Loss?

Many children hear the kind invitation of the Lord. What keeps many of them from following Him to the end? Jesus outlines four categories of hearers in this parable of a sower. In which category do you belong?

100 – Revision

This lesson provides an opportunity for us to check our accounts and to consider our ways. Are we ready to suffer the loss of all things, and regard them as rubbish, in order to gain Christ? Those who have found Him never hesitate to recommend this step to others.

Teachers' Introduction to the Series

This selection of lessons, which completes our survey of Mark's Gospel, notes a common theme. In one way or another the lessons emphasise the great and eternal benefits gained by those who follow Christ. They also speak plainly, as the Saviour did, of the cost. Mark tells us that Christ began His work in

Galilee by calling on men and women to *repent . . . and believe the gospel (Mark 1.15).*

There is always a tendency among teachers to major on the benefits of the Gospel without speaking of the necessity of real repentance. Many materials produced for children's work have been heavily influenced by the fun culture around us. Songs replace hymns, quizzes replace lessons, and children are often given the impression that becoming a Christian is more-or-less the same as joining a secular club.

These lessons will enable us to give a correct balance between benefits and cost. They emphasise that following Christ is a most serious matter which involves heartfelt repentance of sin and a total yielding of heart and life to the Saviour – without suggesting that these endeavours earn salvation. Children respond well to an honest approach, and it is vital if any true work of the Holy Spirit is to take place. Those large numbers of childhood 'conversions' associated with a diluted Gospel disappear as quickly as they appear. (They belong to the second and third categories of the Sower parable.)

Preparing for the Saviour (93)
John the Baptist Points the Way

Mark 1.1-15

Aim: To so describe these early events at the beginning of Mark's Gospel, that the children will be challenged about their own response to the coming of the Lord Jesus Christ.

Teachers' Introduction

We long that every child in our care should be moved to seek the Lord, and we hope that He will call them while in our class. How can we prepare them to hear? John the Baptist prepared the people of Judea for the coming of their Messiah. We can learn much from him.

Three mistakes to avoid. (1) The first mistake to avoid is to give the impression that repentance is a 'good work', or a way of *earning* salvation. John the Baptist urged repentance as a fitting preparation for the visit of the Saviour, Who alone could reform the heart by a work of the Holy Spirit.

(2) The second mistake is to make the lesson too solemn. Repentance is certainly solemn, but we teach it here in the context of glorious 'gains'. The occasion of John's plea for repentance was the great coming of the Lord, so long and eagerly awaited. Parting with our sinful ways is nothing when compared with the privilege of knowing the Saviour and His blessings. The Lord Himself pictured this in the parable of the Pearl of Great Price.

(3) The third mistake to avoid is the one which John himself pin-pointed – to close the lesson with John and his mission, instead of with the Lord and His work *(Mark 1.7)*.

Lesson Outline

Preparing for visitors. Arrest the children's attention by describing the way in which preparations are made for special visitors. Older classes may like to consider how account sheets have to be prepared and checked before the arrival of the auditor. Younger children will have experienced the tidying up and the laying out of special displays at school when a parents' evening is due. Remind the class of the frantic preparations when world leaders visit one another's countries, requiring military parades and state banquets to impress the guest.

Preparing for a royal visitor. Then take the children back in time to a journey of a royal person. Explain that in those days Eastern kings, accompanied by their servants, had to travel across deserts with a train of camels and pack animals to carry all their belongings and gifts. All kinds of problems could arise to delay their arrival by weeks and even months. There were no telephones to advise the hosts of their expected time of arrival. It was the custom therefore for a royal or special visitor to send a messenger ahead to announce his approach. The townspeople would be warned in time to make the necessary arrangements for the arrival of their visitor.

A Saviour is coming! Remind the class that ever since the beginning of the world, when Adam and Eve first sinned and were sent out of the Garden of Eden, God had promised to send a Saviour to take away sin, and restore people who believed in Him back to God. Throughout the Old Testament days He renewed this promise – to Abraham, to Moses, to King David, and then in even more graphic detail to prophets like Isaiah and Malachi.

A messenger is promised. So great and important would be the coming of the Saviour that God promised to send a messenger to prepare His way. Isaiah predicted that this messenger would appear, not in royal courts, nor even at the palace of a Jewish king, but in the wilderness. He prophesied that the messenger would be a lone voice calling people to make ready for the coming of the Lord and urging them to make straight paths for Him. Then tell the children that although Isaiah spoke some 700 years before the birth of Christ, this was exactly what happened.

John the Baptist appears. Describe how, shortly before the Lord Jesus began His public work, His cousin John appeared as a lonely messenger in the wilderness country outside Jerusalem. He had been prepared by God alone for his special work. He did not come from the ranks of the religious leaders of those days, nor had he been trained in their college. Instead an angel had announced his birth to his elderly father, Zacharias. The angel had predicted that John would know the Lord from birth and that his life would be set aside for the special task ahead. He would live an austere life in the wilderness, reminding Jewish people of the prophet Elijah *(Luke 1.13-17)*. This strange figure, wearing a camel-hair garment fastened at the waist with a leather belt, and living on desert food (locusts and wild honey), came suddenly on the scene, preaching to great crowds of people who flocked to hear him from the towns and villages, and from the capital, Jerusalem.

Preparing for the Saviour. Ask the children what they would expect John to say to these great crowds. Did he tell them to refurbish the palace, or to hang out special decorations for the coming of the Messiah? If the Lord Jesus had been an earthly king such a welcome might have been appropriate, but He was the King of Heaven. He was not concerned with outward trappings. Indeed, He had been born in a poor stable, and His cradle had been an animal feeding trough. His concern was the condition of people's hearts. Remind the children that one of Christ's names is the *Sun of righteousness.* When the sun comes out, it puts to shame all the dirt and darkness of the winter months, and shows us it is time to spring-clean. When the Lord Jesus appears He shines into hearts, showing up all the selfishness and sin, and making men and women ashamed of their ways.

They repented. This was how John's hearers responded when he announced the approach of the Saviour. They felt ashamed and unprepared for such a guest. The people of Judah and Jerusalem knew that their God was pure and holy, and that the coming of His Messiah would mean that they must repent and turn away from their sins. John made some very practical suggestions to people showing them how they must change their ways and give up dishonesty, oppression, selfishness and hypocrisy *(Luke 3.11-14).*

They were baptised. Many people took John's words very seriously, and as a pledge of their intentions were baptised in the River Jordan. Explain that this was a very good picture of repentance, a word which has two clear aspects: (a) sorrow for past sin, and (b) a determination not to continue in it – to confess and forsake. Baptism pictured the need to be washed clean, and to stay clean in the future.

They looked for the Saviour. Explain that John taught the people that while repentance and baptism were essential signs of a right attitude, yet these had no power to bring about their forgiveness. Mere water could never wash away sin. Good intentions could never bring about a real change of heart. He urged them to look forward to the coming of the Person Who alone would be able to wash away their sin, and Who would give them a new heart and life. He, the Lord Jesus, would baptise them with His Holy Spirit Whose special work this was.

They must eagerly await His coming, for He would soon arrive.

The baptism of the Lord Jesus. Tell the children that it was in this atmosphere of repentance and expectation that the Saviour arrived and was Himself baptised, a lowly act which teaches us what a wonderful person our Saviour is. It shows us:

(1) His obedience. Explain how the Lord Jesus came from Nazareth and joined the crowds listening to John. He also asked to be baptised, a mark of His obedience and humility. How different from the proud Pharisees! They used religion to bolster their standing and importance without any real desire to please God. He was willing to obey humbly every law and command of God.

(2) His kindness. The Lord Jesus, Who had no sin of His own to wash away, submitted Himself to this outward, lowly act alongside guilty, selfish people who needed His forgiveness. Help the children to appreciate the kindness of the Saviour. Few friends on earth are willing to identify with us when we are in trouble and under correction.

(3) His divinity. So unassuming was He that not even John the Baptist realised that this Jesus from Nazareth was the promised Messiah, until He came up out of the water, the heavens opened, the Spirit of God descended on Him, and a voice came out of Heaven saying, *Thou art my beloved Son, in whom I am well pleased.* (The Gospel accounts do not mention that the crowds witnessed this event. Mark says only that the Lord *saw the heavens opened,* and John, in his Gospel, says John the Baptist did not recognise Christ until he saw the Spirit descend on Him – then he told others.)

(4) His readiness to die at Calvary. The same love which led the Lord Jesus to identify with repentant sinners as they were baptised in the River Jordan, led Him also to Calvary. There He humbled Himself even further and became obedient even to the point of death. Nailed to the cross between two thieves, jeered at by the crowds, and bearing the shame of all His people's sins, the King of Glory suffered in agony – all because He loved us so.

A message for you. Remind your class that this same Lord Jesus is soon to return. Are they prepared for that great day when He will come to judge the world? Suggest that you, as a Sunday School teacher, have a similar role to play as John the Baptist. Like him, you must urge children to face up to their unfittedness to face their God, to recognise their sinfulness with shame and sorrow, and to look to the Saviour Who gave Himself that they might be washed clean and pardoned.

Visual Aid

Make or show a clear and colourful map of the Holy Land in the time of Christ. (A simple outline can be copied from VA 9 on page 159.) Mark in particular the River Jordan where the disciples heard John the Baptist and met the *Lamb of God.* Mark Jerusalem and Bethlehem. Use the bottom corners of the map to add relevant pictures, adding interest.

Leaving All to Follow Jesus (94) 04:05:03

Four Fishermen Obey Christ's Call

Matt 4.12-22 Lk 5:1-11

Mark 1.14-20; see also 2 Peter 1.3-4 Jn 1:35-42

Aim: To show in plain terms what repentance means and to testify to the wonder of Christian conversion.

Teachers' Introduction

It is the duty of a Sunday School teacher to be both evangelist and pastor to children. This lesson provides a very graphic and down-to-earth picture of what is entailed in following the Lord. It will enable us to counsel children as to how they must seek to become Christians. Each teacher needs carefully to consider what repentance will mean to the group he or she teaches. Even small children have sins or idols. While these may seem insignificant to us, they are important to *them*, and must be sacrificed for the Lord. With older classes the items due for surrender may be more obvious.

It is at times such as these that our interest in the children and their lives out of Sunday School will be put to the test. Do we know how they spend their evenings; what books and magazines they read; where they go on Saturdays? If we are to be proficient fishermen, we should know the habits of our fish. Only then can we expect to catch them for the Saviour. Only then will our pleadings carry real conviction, and lead to conversions. As Sunday School teachers it may be our great privilege to witness boys and girls noticeably altering their ways, and deliberately parting with old activities or friends as an expression of their desire to follow the Lord. Such practical steps of repentance speak of a genuine work of the Spirit in a child's heart. They are to be valued above mere words of profession, however dramatic.

Lesson Outline

Begin by telling the class that you want to answer a very important question – 'How exactly does someone become a Christian?' Remind the class that we must go to the Bible for the answer to such a question. God's way is the only way. How did the Saviour tell people to seek Him? What did He expect of them? What does He expect of us?

The fishermen –

(1) Their background. Describe these four men who had their fishing business on the Sea of Galilee. Often we see them pictured with long robes, which makes us think of them as rather soft, gentle people who enjoyed a simple life, catching fish from picturesque boats on a beautiful lake. In fact they were very tough, hardened men who had to shoulder the responsibilities of a business and handle the rigours of a physically demanding job. The Sea of Galilee is comparatively small, but it frequently changes from being a tranquil lake into a raging tempestuous sea in a matter of minutes. In the days when there were no engines in boats, and no winching gear to move sails and anchors, men depended on physical strength to combat the elements.

Storms were not their only worry. Sometimes they would fish all night and catch nothing and then they had to bear financial worries. Sometimes they took only a few hours' rest before returning to their labours hoping for a better catch. If they had no 'luck', then they and their family had to go without, a point which needs to be emphasised in a day and age of state benefits. Because those who follow Christ do not shout and brawl, foolish and scornful people may regard them as soft and gentle too, but Christians are rather like the fishermen-disciples. Many Christians do very tough jobs, and cope with very hard circumstances in their lives; but when they were converted, they received a new nature and new strength, which enables them to be calm and resilient in all circumstances.

(2) Their respect for God. The fishermen of our lesson did not imagine for a moment that the world came about by chance or accident. They were familiar with the enormous power of the wind and sea, and they knew the nightly pattern of the stars. They were convinced that an almighty power and intelligence lay behind these, and they believed it to be the Lord God, of Whom they read in their Scriptures. Encourage your class to respect the Lord, for the Bible tells us that this is the starting point, and the beginning of wisdom.

(3) Their facing up to sin. Your class may be surprised to learn that at least two of these men travelled to Judea to hear John the Baptist preaching about the coming of the Messiah. Their consciences had been stirred as they listened to the Lord's forerunner exposing sin in all its ugly forms. They demonstrated their desire to forsake sin by joining the crowds who were baptised. Suggest that any child who is sincere about wanting to become a Christian should first face up to personal sinfulness. Only then is anyone ready to find the Saviour.

(4) Their willingness to listen to the Lord. Tell the children how John the Baptist had pointed the disciples to the *Lamb of God, which taketh away the sin of the world (John 1.29)*. Describe their sense of privilege at being asked to the home of Jesus, and their conviction by the end of the day that He was the long-awaited Messiah. They must surely have been the first to go and listen to Christ when He returned to Galilee to preach. They were in the position of many children in Sunday School who have heard about the Lord Jesus, believe that He is the Saviour and are ready to listen to His message. Tell the children how glad you are that they come to Sunday School. Encourage them to attend regularly for it is so often here that the Lord graciously comes to call children, one by one, to follow Him.

The losses involved –

(1) They left their nets. While the fishermen were enthusiastic to hear Jesus' preaching, they were soon to learn what it would cost them. One day Jesus approached as they were casting one of their hand-nets into the sea. He asked them to leave their fishing and to come with Him so that He could make them *fishers of men.* This was a very big step for them to take. They were now accustomed to their way of life and they may have had plans to expand their business and improve their standard of living. They surely valued their independence. Must they forfeit all this to be followers of the Lord? They began to realise that if they were to enter His school they must step down from being 'boss' in their lives, and accept His orders. If they were to enter His service they must sacrifice their personal plans and ambitions.

Help the class to appreciate the great privilege of being called by the Son of God to follow Him. Help them to see that to become a Christian means giving the Lord ourselves, our lives, our hopes, our all. It means belonging to Him and being ready and willing to be used in any way He may choose. It means acknowledging – as Peter was soon to do *(Luke 5.8)* – that we are sinful people, unworthy of His interest and care. It means being amazed at the Lord's mercy in calling us and bestowing on us the privilege of being disciples.

(2) They left their comforts and 'security'. When Jesus called the four fishermen to make this hard decision, they did not fully understand what *fishers of men* were. What hours would they have to work? Where would they live or stay? What would they be expected to do? What opposition would they meet? Where would their money come from? Would they have to leave Capernaum? The answers to these and other questions were unknown. Jesus called, and they had to trust Him. When we today hear the call of Christ, to repent and turn over our lives to Him, we have no idea what it will feel like to be converted, or how the Lord will arrange our future lives. We also must respond to His call by trusting Him.

(3) They left straightaway. Having put their trust in the Lord, the fishermen obeyed straightaway. It could not have been a normal, easy thing for them to drop their work and immediately go off with Jesus, but this is what they did. His command was so clear, and His presence so compelling, that everything else paled into insignificance. His instructions were far too important to be put off for another day.

Explain that some boys and girls, sadly, do not act with such urgency and haste. They hear about the Saviour and His call, but they delay any real response. They think they will wait until they are older before committing themselves to the Lord. They imagine there are more important things to be done today. Warn against such an attitude.

(4) They left everything. Following the Lord meant giving up a great deal for Peter, Andrew, James and John. In a later chapter of Mark's Gospel we read that Peter claimed – *We have left* ALL, *and have followed thee (Mark 10.28)*, in response to Jesus' words. They had to spend long periods away from home. They had little or no time for recreation. They had to leave the security and comfort of home, and travel with a Saviour Who had *not where to lay his head (Luke 9.58)*. They had to bear the suspicion and hatred of the religious leaders who hated the Lord Jesus.

Ask the class what things they would have to give up if they were to follow Jesus. First, they would have to give up their sins. Then they would have to give up their time and be ready to see their lives, powers and possessions as not theirs, but the Lord's. They would have to surrender their ambitious day-dreams and plans for life and seek His guidance. They might have to change their whole timetable, especially their out-of-school programme.

At this point in the lesson teachers could describe the talented musician Philip Bliss, who turned down the opportunity to direct one of America's leading orchestras, so that he could devote his life to taking the Gospel message to as many people as possible. We may not be called upon to give up anything as dramatic, but we should be just as willing.

The gains received –

(1) They escaped the disappointments of this world. Use an illustration along the following lines. A young lady (or man) planned to marry. She told her family what a wonderful man she had found and sung his praises continually. He was clever. He was rich. He was good-looking, etc. Plans were well advanced for the wedding, when suddenly she discovered something terrible – he was already married. Indeed, she found that he was a criminal, and very violent. In tears the young lady called off the wedding, but before long she began to realise what a narrow escape she had experienced. Had she married, her life would have been a tragedy. She would have been beaten, taken advantage of and then abandoned. A year later she was married happily to a really fine man.

Show that in a way, this is how Christians feel when they look back at their decision to leave the world and follow the Lord. At first it seems like making a great sacrifice, because the world seems so wonderful with so much to offer. But soon they see everything another way. Peter wrote years later in his second epistle (older classes could read *2 Peter 1.3-4*) of *having escaped the corruption that is in the world.* Since the days of being a fisherman he had known difficult days as he travelled with Jesus, frightening days, tiring days, but these trials seemed only minor and not worth consideration compared with *the knowledge of him that hath called us to glory and virtue (2 Peter 1.3).*

(2) They experienced wonderful privileges. Remind the class of the privileges enjoyed by these fishermen which made their sacrifices pale into insignificance. They saw Christ's miracles firsthand; they heard His parables and their meanings;

several were eyewitnesses of His transfiguration (a sight they never forgot; *2 Peter 1.16-18*); they were amongst the first to know that He had risen from the dead; and they experienced special sign-gifts from the Holy Spirit at Pentecost. The letters of Peter and John, two thousand years after they were written, are still being used of the Lord to bring human 'fish' into the Lord's 'Gospel net', and to help Christians in their lives.

Tell the class that all those who are prepared to part with everything this world holds dear, soon discover that their old life is worthless compared with knowing Christ. They wonder how it ever held any fascination for them. Following Christ may sometimes involve trials and sacrifices but these are nothing compared with knowing Him.

(3) They left darkness and found light. Peter described conversion as being called *out of darkness into his marvellous light (1 Peter 2.9)*. The Lord Jesus promised Peter that he would receive a hundred times as much as he had left, in the present age, AND *in the world to come eternal life (Mark 10.30)*.

Close the lesson by explaining, perhaps with personal testimony, that becoming a Christian may involve us in a great struggle, but once we belong to the Lord, and have made our vows to Him, then we experience His forgiveness of our sins and lovingkindness day by day and can say with the hymn-writer:

O happy day, that fixed my choice
On Thee, my Saviour and my God!
Well may this glowing heart rejoice,
And tell its raptures all abroad.
Philip Doddridge

Visual Aid

Use the map prepared for the previous lesson (93). Mark the Sea of Galilee and Capernaum, near to which this incident occurred. Use a corner of the map to illustrate the kind of fishing boats used by these men.

The Value of a Soul (95) 11:05:03

Plain Speaking at Caesarea Philippi

Matt 16:13-27
Lk 9:21-26

Mark 8.27-38; Philippians 3.7-11

Aim: To contrast the false promises of this world with the plain speaking of the Lord. To convince the class that it is worth the loss of all things for the excellency of the knowledge of Christ Jesus as Lord.

Lesson Outline

The Lord Jesus has unlimited power. Explain that the Lord did many amazing things after He called the fishermen to be His disciples. He demonstrated His power not only over illness and disease but also over nature, death and the hearts and lives of hopeless men and women. Describe the vast crowds that gathered wherever the Lord went, to hear His teaching. They would walk miles rather than miss His unique parables which, though so clear and simple, were so rich in meaning. People like Peter, who lived in close proximity to Him, testified that He – *did no sin, neither was guile found in his mouth (1 Peter 2.22).* How remarkable! What power over His own life! Yet the Lord Jesus never boasted of His powers, and often asked people to tell no one about Him at that time.

'Thou art the Christ!' Many people had come to believe that Jesus was John the Baptist returned to life, or Elijah the prophet, or even a new prophet sent from God. However, when asked by the Lord, Peter announced that he believed that Jesus was none other than the promised Messiah *(Mark 8.29).* At this stage it was not surprising that the disciples, and many other Jews, wanted to follow the Lord, because they had been taught by Jewish leaders that when the Messiah came He would soon set up a great kingdom and wield great power. The disciples thought that the Lord would do this, and then make them His closest advisers *(Mark 10.37).*

'The Son of man must suffer.' Instead of allowing His disciples to continue in this mistaken dream, the Lord turned to them and solemnly told them that the opposite would be the case. Soon, He said, He would travel to the capital, Jerusalem, where He would endure suffering and shame, not power and glory. He would be rejected by the religious authorities, and their hatred would lead to His early and cruel death. Mark tells us that – *He spake that saying openly (Mark 8.32).*

Peter was so shocked that he argued with the Lord, thinking that all this could not happen. But the Lord rebuked him for his objections, saying that they were of Satan – not God. It was Satan who would have given anything *(Matthew 4.8-9)* to prevent the Lord Jesus going to the cross of Calvary where He would suffer and die in order that men and women, boys and girls might be saved. Peter was silenced very firmly.

Soon Jesus summoned the crowds as well as His disciples and spoke to them very clearly. We will follow His words, phrase by phrase. He said:–

(1) 'Whosoever will come after me . . . ' If the Lord Jesus had been only a man, like our politicians, pop stars or business tycoons, He would have taken advantage of His high rating in the 'opinion polls' to lure a great crowd of followers to Jerusalem, and then sought to make His debut in the capital. He would have encouraged the disciples to imagine that He would set up an earthly kingdom in which they would share His great power. He would have accepted the support of all who followed Him, whatever their motives or understanding.

(2) ' . . . let him take up his cross, and follow me.' Far from exciting the crowds with rosy promises, the Lord turned to the people and warned them that they must be willing to pay dearly in order to follow Him. The terms seemed very hard. They must be willing to deny themselves, take up their cross, and follow Him. Explain that a man carrying his cross to the site of his execution was not an uncommon sight in the Roman Empire. Christ's meaning was clear. Those who would follow Him down to Jerusalem must be ready to forget their own interests and prepare to face much suffering as His followers.

(3) 'For whosoever will save his life shall lose it.' The Lord proceeded to explain His hard words. Ask the class to follow them carefully. He warned that people who put themselves and their own plans and pleasures first, and kept their lives all for themselves, would lose their eternal souls together with the forgiveness of their sins and their place in Heaven. But, He went on –

(4) 'Whosoever shall lose his life shall save it.' The only way to save their *real* lives (their eternal souls), would be to lose their present earthly lives – in other words, to give them up, or surrender them to the Lord. All who would say, 'Lord Jesus, take over my life, my plans, my home comforts, my pleasures, and I will come with You to Jerusalem where there will be many trials,' would receive a new, eternal life.

No doubt there were some hearers who thought they could have *both* lives – present earthly pleasures, *and* eternal life. They wanted to follow the Lord's programme with interest and sympathy, but they would not cut themselves off from their normal lifestyle. However, the Lord Jesus was very clear. He said it must be one or the other; they must be either for Him or for the world. Explain that this is the issue laid before us too. If we surrender our lives wholly to the Lord, then we shall gain real life. If we live only for the here-and-now, to get what we can for ourselves in this world, then we shall lose our souls.

Give the children an example along these lines. Supposing someone was going for a job – an exceptionally good job – and was sat before an interview panel composed of very important people. Would the candidate suddenly say, 'By the way, can I still keep my present job too? After all, this new job is not really that difficult and I can easily fit it in alongside.' Is it likely that he would be offered the new job? Of course not. In the same way we must be willing to give up every selfish plan, all our sins, and the government of our own lives, in order to follow the Lord. He can never be only a part-time choice. The surrender of our lives does not earn or deserve our salvation, but it is an essential part of true repentance.

(5) 'For what shall it profit . . . ?' *For what shall it profit a man, if he shall gain the whole world, and lose his own soul?* Tell the class the story of the woman who, when her house was burning down, rushed back to save her money and lost her life in the process. Describe how so many people work desperately hard to acquire possessions and pleasures, only to have the enjoyment of them snatched away by illness, old age and death.

Describe, for example, some of the world's rich and famous who live in fear of assassination. Their homes are sometimes so protected that they are like prisons. There are people so rich that they cannot go out without a bodyguard following their every step. What have they gained? Why, even poor families living in a flat or cottage have more freedom and pleasure! Apply this spiritually to all, rich and poor alike: what can we possibly gain in this world for which it is worth losing our souls – our opportunity to be forgiven, to know the Lord and to go to Heaven? Make some suggestions relevant to your class. Would they rather plan their lives for themselves without seeking the Lord's guidance and risk making terrible mistakes? Are they prepared to throw away their eternal future for a very few years of sinful excitement?

(6) 'What shall a man give in exchange for his soul?' This last question of the Lord provides the final reason for taking these matters very seriously. Point out to the children that some of the mistakes that we make in life, we can afford to pay for. If we break something we may be able to afford to have it repaired. If a man fails in business, he may be able to mortgage his home and satisfy his creditors. If children get into trouble they may find that a sincere apology helps. But if we offend the Lord, piling up a great number of sins, what can we pay to be forgiven? The richest man on earth cannot pay for the forgiveness of his soul.

Tell the class that the only Person Who can restore our souls is the Saviour Himself. That is why He was ready to put up with all the hatred of the religious leaders, and the suffering, and supremely with death on the cross – so that He would have the right to save the souls of all those people who would leave all and follow Him. That is why it is so important to belong to Him.

(7) 'Whosoever shall be ashamed of me . . .' *Whosoever therefore shall be ashamed of me and of my words . . . of him also shall the Son of man be ashamed, when he cometh in the glory of his Father.* As the Lord looked around at the crowds listening to Him, He knew that many would stop following Him at this point. If belonging to Him would involve suffering and hardship, then they would not want to know Him. With sorrow the Lord warned that if they were ashamed of Him now, then on the day when He returned in all His glory, He would have to be ashamed of them. Warn your class against thinking that they can ignore God and yet think that He will still welcome them to Heaven. These words tell us the opposite.

Encourage all those who sincerely want to know the Lord to surrender their lives and their hopes into His kind hands. Tell them that He will take over their lives now, and then on that great coming day He will recognise and welcome them. He will take their immortal souls into His safe keeping, ready to enjoy the wonders of eternity together with Him and all His people.

Gain – loss – dung. Remind the children that no person who has surrendered his or her life to Christ, and sincerely wanted to follow Him (including these disciples), has ever regretted that pivotal act of life. We learned in a previous lesson how the apostle Peter viewed his choice. Now the words of the apostle Paul confirm these words:– *What things were gain to me, those I counted loss for Christ. Yea doubtless, and I count all things but loss for the excellency of the knowledge of Christ Jesus my Lord: for whom I have suffered the loss of all things, and do count them but dung, that I may win Christ, and be found in him (Philippians 3.7-9).*

Close by telling the class of a shopkeeper who was anxious to win customers. He held a sale, lowered his prices and was overjoyed as the shop filled with customers and the till rang all day. Describe his horror when, weeks later, he realised that his gain was short-lived. He had lowered his prices much too far and, in reality, had made a terrible loss. Now he faced bankruptcy. Warn the children never to be fooled by the promises of this world into thinking eternal losses are great gain!

Visual Aid

On seven pieces of card print out the words of the Lord Jesus using the seven headings of the lesson. (Use contrasting colours to divide the words which refer to saving life from those which speak of losing it.) Place, or pin, these on a board or chart as you explain each phrase. Encourage the children to learn these by heart. They are important words.

The Currency of Heaven (96) 18:05:06

The Rich Young Ruler Is Devalued

Mark 10.13-27 Matt 19.16-30 Luke 18:18-30

Aim: To show that no earthly currency can buy membership of the kingdom of Heaven. Only the Saviour can purchase eternal life for us.

Teachers' Introduction

This brief incident is full of opportunities for us as Sunday School teachers. The rich young ruler pictures the aspirations of many young people today. The lesson which the Saviour had to teach him is therefore very applicable to our children. Yet unless the lesson is prepared with care, it may merely repeat the same arguments presented in the previous week's lesson. A number of illustrations with a common theme – currency – are suggested in these notes.

Lesson Outline

Describe this unusual occasion. It was not every day that a rich young man presented himself to the Lord with such good intentions. Help the class to picture the confident ruler. Most people were very polite and friendly to this rich young man, and so he was accustomed to being listened to with enthusiasm and respect. In today's world, if such a man wanted to join any club or society, he would simply write out a cheque or show his gold credit card, and no obstruction would be put in his way. All the leading townspeople wanted to be seen with him.

He seemed to think that it would be the same for religion. He asked the Lord what he must do in order to inherit eternal life.

Although he possessed much earthly security, he was anxious to insure his soul as well. Compared with many other rich young men he was reasonably well-behaved, so that when the Lord reminded him of some of the qualifications necessary to please God, he immediately claimed that he had kept them since he was a boy.

Although Jesus loved this young man, He would not have been impressed by his boasting. The trouble was that the young ruler knew nothing about God's standards, and he knew nothing about his own heart, or his weaknesses. He had some hard lessons to learn. Instead of receiving the ruler into His circle with honour, the Lord asked difficult questions, and laid down a standard calculated to send the proud young man sadly away.

(1) Another currency. The rich young ruler had to learn that earthly goods have no value in Heaven. Neither the ownership of a vast estate and mansion, nor the power of a ruler, nor the accomplishments of a scholar, have any 'buying power' to secure from God any spiritual favours, such as forgiveness. Use the illustration of a boy on a holiday abroad with his parents. He has a large sum of money (for a boy) in his pocket – but it is in English currency. One day he becomes detached from his parents and lost. To his dismay he finds that his money is useless. In cafés and at the station everyone laughs at his 'foreign money'. Some of the shop assistants think his ten-pound notes are only worth the equivalent of a few pence!

It was something like this for the rich young ruler when he discovered that the riches and power which impressed his fellow men, were worthless in the 'Bank of Heaven'. Ask your class if they are inclined to make the same mistake. Do they think that God will never turn away people who have done well here on earth? Many act as if this were the case. Will young people who do well at school and in sport, especially those who are popular and reasonably well-behaved, be turned away from Heaven? It is possible, as the rich young ruler found.

(2) The missing pounds. The wealthy young man had to learn that he had completely overlooked the things which really matter. Explain to the children that the first and most important commandments were not mentioned – those which tell us that we should give our love, worship and service to God. This was because it had never occurred to the young man that he was meant to put God first in his life. (The Saviour would test him on this point a few moments afterwards!)

The young ruler was like a person who had only heard of pence, and knew nothing of pounds! In ordinary life he would have considered such a person a fool, but in spiritual matters he was a fool himself. How easy it is for us all to think the same way. How proud we are of our few little good deeds when we should be ashamed of our enormous neglect of God. Even children know that a few duties done grudgingly can never replace real and heartfelt love and affection for their parents. How much less for God!

(3) A bad mistake. The ruler had to learn that he had badly miscalculated his own worth. He was very shrewd in normal life, and knew the value of his estate. He could no doubt estimate the number and cost of the workers he needed. In all probability he studied the price of grain and followed the stock prices at Jerusalem. He may have been sent away to school and university to learn the skills of leadership and commerce, yet when it came to eternal matters he seemed to think that an 'on-the-spot' assessment would do. What was the state of his soul? He set the exam, and gave himself top marks in a matter of moments.

How filled with contempt he would have been if anyone had dared to make such a fleeting and ignorant judgement on his farms! The Lord Jesus had to show him that he had left out the most important question in his exam-paper – one in which he would have totally failed. It turned out that he was entirely ignorant of the sinful state of his heart – particularly of his love of possessions. How easy it is to say we are good people if we decide for ourselves what *good* means. How different when we look at ourselves in the mirror of God's Word, and judge by *His* standards.

(4) The terrible truth. The rich young man had to learn what he was really like. The Lord Jesus did not argue with him. With one simple sentence the Saviour showed him the truth about himself. Jesus simply asked him to sell his riches, give them away to the poor and to follow Him (note that He did not ask for the money to be given to Him). In a moment the young man was shown where his heart really lay and what his true motives for living were. Suddenly his proud boastings came to an end, when the Saviour put him to the test. In an instant he discovered that beneath his thin veneer of goodness and respectability lay a mass of selfishness and greed – in a word – covetousness. His 'master' sin was revealed.

He had just boasted that he kept the laws – *Do not steal . . . Defraud not* (v 19), yet when the Lord asked him to share his riches with the poor, he was very unwilling to do so. The fact that he wanted to hoard and spoil himself with gifts provided by God, whilst others were hungry and desperately worried, made him little better than a common thief. Demonstrate this principle to the class in other matters. Show how his righteousness was quickly dismantled and he was declared a moral bankrupt.

(5) Only one hope. The Lord loved the young man for his eagerness to find eternal life, but had to teach him by a hard lesson that no one can have eternal life unless he first renounces all trust in his own achievements and 'worth', and puts *all* his trust in Him as the only Saviour. He told the young man to get rid of everything on earth which made him think he was valuable and worthy of Heaven, and to become dependent on Christ alone. By this command, the Lord exposed the young man's covetous heart, showed him how much he trusted in his own accomplishments, and showed him how trust in the Saviour is essential in order to be saved and to go to Heaven.

If the young man had followed Christ, he would soon have seen how He came to redeem sinners, to pay the price of His people's sins on Calvary, and to rescue them from ruin and hell. He would have seen Him give His life on the cross of Calvary to take the punishment of sin for people like himself. He would have seen that Christ provides eternal riches from His store of righteousness. No earthly riches or accomplishments of his own could have made the young man fit for Heaven. Do we renounce all foolish ideas that our 'goodness' is good enough for Christ? Have we realised that only by handing our lives to Christ and trusting in His death on Calvary, can we be forgiven?

(6) Jesus invites young children. We do not know if the ruler ever returned to Jesus to receive forgiveness and true riches. We know he went away sad and grieved because he was not willing to give up his great possessions and to give up his trust in his own good life and accomplishments. Perhaps this is one of the reasons why the Lord Jesus so gladly welcomed young children when their mothers brought them to Him. Children know they are poor, and that any possessions they may have are gifts from their parents and friends. How much easier it is for them to acknowledge their need of the righteousness and goodness which the Saviour freely gives to those who trust in Him. Urge your class to seek the Lord while they are young, to receive His grace and mercy before pride poisons their hearts against Him, and before possessions and worldly gain consume their emotions and energies.

Visual Aid

Draw an outline figure in card of the rich young ruler cheerfully approaching the Lord. As you explain his attitude place across the figure the words: 'RICH', 'YOUNG', 'GOOD', 'CLEVER', 'CONFIDENT'. Then reverse the figure and attach the words which describe him as he left the Saviour realising his failure in God's sight: 'POOR' (in God's sight), 'SELFISH', 'GREEDY', 'PROUD', 'SORROWFUL'.

The Cost of Our Salvation (97) 25:05:03

Counting the Cost

Mark 14 – 15; Hebrews 12.2

Aim: To impress upon the children the enormous cost to the Lord Jesus Christ of our salvation.

Teachers' Introduction

Teachers will have their own way of conveying to the class the depths of pain borne by the Saviour. We must avoid an emotional assault upon the sympathies of the children, especially the younger ones, who can be artificially stirred by vivid descriptions of suffering. We can describe the Lord being nailed to the cross for our sin without over-dramatic gasps of horror and sorrow, offending their sensitivities. It is good to emphasise the *deeper* sorrows which the Lord endured when He bore away, in His pure and holy being, the eternal punishment of the sins of His people. We should help children to see that the Saviour's spiritual anguish was infinitely greater and more important than His physical torture, though that was terrible.

Above all, in describing Calvary, we have to be like the Saviour Himself, Who saw these sufferings in perspective. He was willing to endure them because He knew they would please His Father, and accomplish Their desire – the salvation of His people. We remember that the Lord – *for the joy that was set before him endured the cross, despising the shame (Hebrews 12.2).*

Lesson Outline

Introduction. Explain to the class that many people in this world experience suffering, but very rarely do they do so willingly or intentionally. (Teachers of younger classes can use a simple illustration of a boy lying in hospital with a broken leg and a sore head. Had he realised the results he would never have ridden his bicycle in such a dangerous place!) However, in the Garden of Gethsemane we learn that the Lord Jesus Christ knew exactly what was going to happen to Him. And although He was horrified and *exceeding sorrowful*, He was willing to go through with it for our sakes.

The Lord saw His death on Calvary as a 'cup' full of bitter, terrible agony, which had to be drunk by Him in order that we might be saved. Ask the class if they have realised how much the Lord loved sinful men and women, boys and girls. What did the Lord see in that cup which would happen to Him in the space of a few days? He saw that in order to save us He would be:

(1) Betrayed by a 'friend' *(Mark 14.18, 43-45).* Jesus knew that Judas, one of His own disciples, would kiss Him as a sign to the enemy, so that He could be arrested at dead of night. Help the class to feel the pain that this act of treachery must have given the Saviour. Have the children ever been betrayed by someone they had supposed to be their friend? Disloyalty is always especially hard to bear.

(2) Deserted by His friends *(Mark 14.50).* Describe how, in the moment when the Lord was (humanly) most in need of support and friendship, all His disciples *forsook him, and fled.* Again describe this feelingfully so that the class appreciates how hard this must have been for the Lord. Throughout His ministry He had known great opposition, but had been comforted to know that this little band did not want to leave Him *(John 6.67-68).* Now they had gone, and He had to endure His greatest trials alone.

(3) Unjustly condemned *(Mark 14.57-64).* Discuss with the class the sense of injustice and fair play which even criminals have, especially when they are on trial! How indignant we all are if we are accused of a crime of which we are innocent. How much worse then for the perfect, sinless Son of God to be accused of blasphemy, and then of making Himself a king. And yet the Lord did not answer back.

(4) Deserted by the crowds *(Mark 15.13).* Describe the deep hurt borne by the Lord Jesus as the crowds, who only a week previously had welcomed Him into their city, were persuaded to scream out in hate, *Crucify him*! Those same people whom Jesus had tenderly pictured as *sheep having no shepherd*, and for whose eternal safety He was prepared to give Himself, now wanted to see His life torn from Him. The citizens of Jerusalem whom the Saviour had desired to gather together, *even as a hen gathereth her chickens under her wings (Matthew 23.37)*, now refused to recognise Him as anything but a fraud and criminal.

As the Son of God, the Lord Jesus knew full well that all this would happen, but as the Son of Man He deeply felt the disappointment. Perhaps the children have been similarly let down by those whose support they were counting on in some important matter. Give examples suitable for the age of your class.

(5) Degraded by the Romans *(Mark 14.65; 15.15-20).* One of the worst things the Lord must have seen in that cup was the terrible scorn and derision which would be poured out upon Him following His 'trials'. He was spat upon, and beaten while blindfolded. Even *the servants* [officers] *did strike him with the palms of their hands* (v 65). After His trial before Pilate He was scourged (explain to older classes that this included being beaten with leather thongs in which pieces of sharp metal were secured) and delivered over to the Roman soldiers to be crucified. These took Him into their headquarters where a division of Roman soldiers came to dress Him up in purple, and thrust a crown woven from thorns upon His head, mocking and taunting, *Hail, King of the Jews!* During this charade they beat His head with a reed, spat upon Him, and cynically taunted Him, kneeling and bowing to Him. What treatment for their Creator, the Lord of Glory! What hatred for the Friend of Sinners!

(6) Humiliated by the Jews *(Mark 15.11, 27-32).* Ask the class how they would feel if they were disgraced, and made to look silly, perhaps wrongly, in public. (Teachers could, for example, describe the embarrassment felt when a mother tells their friends all about one of their personal failings.) Show how much worse it was for the Lord to be rejected in favour of a proven criminal, Barabbas. And how distressing it must have been for the only sinless person to be nailed aloft between two common thieves, to die. And to intensify this deep humiliation, the Lord's enemies taunted Him, jeering at His teaching and miracles, as if He were a freak at a fairground. Try to take in the fact that all this was done to the Saviour – God Himself – the One Who created and Who sustains all things.

(7) Nailed to a cross *(Mark 15.25, 29, 37).* According to the age of your class (see 'Teachers' Introduction') describe how the Lord was nailed to the cross, lifted up to the view of the crowds, and left to die in the midday sun.

(8) Punished for our sin *(Mark 15.33-34).* Explain that all these terrible sufferings are not to be compared with this last one. Tell how the sun went dark. Enlarge on verse 34 and ask – Why did God forsake His own Son? Describe how at this moment all the guilt of God's people descended on the innocent Saviour. The very sins which revolted Him were drawn around Him like millions of rags of human guilt, and He suffered their full punishment. Ask the class to picture the revulsion the Lord must have felt as His pure body and soul were made to carry our vile sins. This could perhaps be compared with someone with an open wound being made to plunge it into a vat of boiling salt water.

Sin always means separation from God, and at that moment the Lord Jesus Christ felt (on our behalf) separation from His own Father, with Whom He had always been one *(John 10.30).* He bore the pain that His people would have had to bear in hell for ever. Yet that pain was concentrated into the space of a few hours.

Well might the sun in darkness hide,
And shut his glories in,
When Christ, the mighty Maker, died
For man the creature's sin.

The loss. Now bring the class back to the Garden of Gethsemane where the Lord saw into this great cup of sorrow ahead of Him. No wonder that He was *very heavy* and *exceeding sorrowful.* Describe how His human frame shrank from this great ordeal, and He prayed that, if it were possible, this cup should be removed from Him – yet in the same sentence He accepted it, saying, *nevertheless not what I will, but what thou wilt* (v 36). What life-giving words these are for us! For the Lord Jesus they immediately led to *death and shame,* whilst for us they opened the possibility of *life and health.*

The gain. Explain that it was indeed the eternal purpose of the Lord God to give His only begotten Son, that *whosoever believeth in him should not perish, but have everlasting life (John 3.16),* for *neither is there salvation in any other (Acts 4.12).* Had the Lord Jesus refused to drink this cup of sorrow no one could have been saved. Our world would have faced immediate judgement and Satan would have succeeded in his evil design to bring down to hell every member of the human race. How grateful and adoring we should feel towards the Saviour!

The joy set before Him. Return to the theme of gains and losses. We have seen the great cost of our redemption to the Saviour. In closing, teachers should turn to the great gain purchased by the Lord at Calvary. Refer to *Isaiah 53*. As a result of the anguish of His soul, the Lord Jesus would see His offspring – the many who have been saved through His death – and be satisfied. Refer to *Philippians 2.8-10* where we read that, because He was obedient to the death of the cross, His Father has – *highly exalted him, and given him a name which is above every name: that at the name of Jesus every knee should bow.* Finally picture the scene in Heaven which the Lord had in His mind as He took on this agony – the great host of people from our earth who will sing the praises of the Lamb *(Revelation 5.9-13)*, dressed in the spotless white robes which He obtained for them at Calvary *(Revelation 7.14)*.

Close by urging your class to ask themselves the question posed in Charles Wesley's hymn:

'All ye that pass by,
To Jesus draw nigh,
To you is it nothing that Jesus should die?'

How tragic if any child, having heard about the Saviour's love and determination in the Garden of Gethsemane, should turn heedless away! Instead they should answer with Isaac Watts:

Love so amazing, so divine,
Demands my soul, my life, my all.

Visual Aid

Draw an outline of a cup into which you can place cards bearing the eight lesson headings as the lesson proceeds. This will fix these points clearly in the children's minds.

Gaining from Loss (98) 01:06:03

Peter's Denial

Mark 14.26-31, 54, 66-72

Aim: To demonstrate, through this tragic incident, that proud self-confidence can lead us to ruin. To show that the Lord's lovingkindness is such that He can turn even our failures to our everlasting good.

Teachers' Introduction

Some of our class may have some knowledge of these events. How can we make the lesson interesting and hold their attention? If we follow our theme of gains and losses, then the pattern of application will become obvious. Teachers with classes who know most about this incident should make the applications continuously through the lesson, while for younger classes it will be best for the children to feel the pathos of the events before making application at the end.

Lesson Outline

Introduction. Make the children curious by suggesting that if they are not Christians they probably fall into one of two categories. Either they are afraid and shy of following the Lord, or they are too confident and self-reliant, thinking they can withstand the storms of life without God's help. Our lesson will have advice for both types. Teachers can caricature both kinds of unbelief and help the children see into which category they fall.

Setting the scene. Suggest that this is one of the saddest events in history. Then go on to describe how Jesus warned Peter and the other disciples that they would desert Him at the moment when He would be taken *(14.27)*. He explained that once He, the Shepherd, was arrested, they, like sheep, would run away.

Great loss – to Christ and Peter. So that the children will enter into the tragedy of this occasion, remind them that they have probably known great disappointment or loss at some time. Show them how much greater the grief and sorrow of the Lord must have been.

Peter deserted Jesus. First remind the class that Peter was probably the boldest disciple. It was he who had insisted that he would never desert Jesus. Even if the other disciples were to let the Master down, he never would – so he claimed. He would rather die than deny the Lord *(14.29-31)*. Jesus had named him Peter *(John 1.42)* – which meant, a stone – and Peter was confident he would live up to that name. If his faithfulness could not be counted on, then whose could? Would Jesus have to stand trial completely alone? Tragically we read of all the disciples (including Peter) that, when a crowd armed with swords and clubs and led by Judas surrounded the Lord, *they all forsook him, and fled (14.50)*. And later, when Peter's loyalty began to return, the best he could do was to follow *afar off (14.54)*, and that did not last long. So the Lord lost all the help, comfort and support of His closest supporters at the moment He needed it most.

Peter denied knowing Jesus. When challenged, Peter denied all knowledge of Jesus three times, in the most vehement terms *(14.66-71)*. Describe how his bravado melted as he took up a cowardly position amongst the high priest's servants, warming themselves by the fire and no doubt celebrating Christ's arrest. Explain that Peter not only refused to be identified with His Saviour but used curses to extricate himself from any suggested association. He was frightened and embarrassed at being associated with the Son of God – the Ruler of the universe! What a coward – to go to the lengths of swearing and cursing against his kindest Friend. How disloyal to say – *I know not this man of whom ye speak (14.71)*.

Peter wept bitterly. But Peter's denial of his Lord and Master not only cost Jesus great sorrow, it also cost Peter very dearly. At the moment the cock crowed for the second time Jesus looked at Peter *(Luke 22.61)*. Though Peter was a very tough character, he wept bitterly. When he considered the outright lies he had told, his cowardice and his failure to live up to his promises, he felt so deeply ashamed it almost broke his heart. We do not know how long it took Peter to overcome his tears, as he is not mentioned again in the Gospel narrative until resurrection morning. Probably it caused him constant grief, alleviated only by Jesus' words to him at the Sea of Tiberias *(John 21.15-17)*.

Great gain. Explain to the class that God's ways are higher than our ways, and His thoughts than our thoughts. He is able to work all things together for good to those that love God *(Romans 8.28)*, and even this sad incident was used by the Lord for Peter's benefit and ours. What good came of it?

(1) Learning to believe the Lord. Peter learned once and for all that he should never doubt Christ's word. Only hours before he denied the Lord, he had been told exactly what would happen. Instead of believing Jesus and trembling at the thought of what he might do, he dismissed the idea totally. He was full of self-confidence. But who was proved right? His bitter experience taught him that Jesus knew him better than he knew himself and that he should never again brush aside His words.

Can we learn from this too? Have we learned to respect the Lord? He has never lied, yet men and women are full of unbelief towards Him. Will He have to teach you to believe the Gospel through some tragic event, as He did Peter? Will you have to experience the depths of sin and failure before you believe what He says about the nature of your heart? Will some possession or person have to be taken from you before you treat Him seriously and make your treasure in Heaven?

(2) Discovering our weakness. Peter learned about his own terrible weakness. This robust fisherman, so full of brave promises and dogmatic assertions, found himself snivelling denials before a young girl. This seasoned disciple discovered that he could be gripped and overcome by mortal fear. Have we discovered our weaknesses, or do we imagine that we can take on the storms of life single-handed? Are we optimistic about our ability to handle the future? Are we at a loss to see why we need a

Counsellor and Guide through life? In later years Peter warned other Christians to be vigilant because their adversary, the devil – *as a roaring lion, walketh about, seeking whom he may devour (1 Peter 5.8)*. Do you hope to overcome the devil – who has defeated every other person in the world apart from Christ – without the Lord's help?

(3) Appreciating the Lord. How much more Peter must have loved the Lord after this disaster. If he was taught his own weakness, he was also taught what a wonderful Saviour he had. That Jesus, Who knew how Peter would fail Him, was prepared to go through such suffering to redeem him, was truly amazing. That the Lord was willing to forgive Peter and give him further service must have been more than Peter could have expected or comprehended.

Does the lesson move you too? Had you realised just how much the Lord was willing to bear for a sinner like you? While Peter was denying the Lord and disbelieving His word, He was already beginning to go through the pain and agony necessary for our redemption. Nor should we look with disgust at Peter, for we have sinned just as grievously, and we are probably even weaker.

(4) Experiencing true repentance. Peter learned more than ever before what real repentance means. Have you? Becoming a Christian does not mean lightly giving up one set of friends and pastimes for another. It means real sorrow and grief for our sin. He *wept bitterly*, as Luke tells us.

(5) Tasting forgiveness. Ask the class if they have ever had the sweet experience of making it up with a parent or friend with whom they have quarrelled. How much better to find peace with God. Imagine how Peter felt when Jesus looked at him, not with disgust, revulsion and rejection, but with kindness and forgiveness. Think of his relief and joy when he discovered that he would not have to suffer for his vile behaviour. He could sleep with a restored conscience knowing Christ Himself bore his *sins in his own body on the tree, that* [he], *being dead to sins, should live unto righteousness: by whose stripes* Peter had been healed *(1 Peter 2.24)*. If you have never done so before, ask the Lord to wash away your sin and give you a sense of forgiveness.

No excuses. We close by returning to our first question. Are you too cowardly, or too confident to follow the Lord? However cowardly, the Lord is willing to forgive us our failure just as He did Peter's. Peter later became one of the strongest leaders of the early churches, daring to do all kinds of things because the Lord gave him His special strength. He will also do great things for you. If, on the other hand, you are too proud and confident to feel any need of a Saviour, be warned by this event. If the apostle Peter could meet with shame and failure, how much more will you as your life unfolds? If Peter came to depend on the kindness and mercy of the Saviour, how much more should you.

Visual Aid

Provide two outline figures of a boy or girl (teachers can use the template shown on page 51 of *Lessons for Life 2*). On the first outline print the words, 'Afraid, Shy, Cowardly?' and on the second print, 'Too confident, Self-reliant?'. Use these as you ask the children into which category they fall (see Lesson Outline, Introduction).

On the reverse side of the first outline print, 'The Lord forgives and strengthens'. On the reverse side of the second print, 'Be warned!'. Use these as you apply the lessons of Peter's denial.

Profit or Loss? (99)
The Parable of the Sower

Mark 4.1-20

Aim: To help the children discern their true position before the Lord. To encourage them to see themselves in one of the four categories described by the Lord in this parable.

Teachers' Introduction

We have left this lesson until last because it draws together the points which have been highlighted in the current series and applies them to the individual. The more we look at this parable the more we see how perfectly it pictures the human heart in its response to God. If we help our children to search their motives and desires, then the parable will convey a great spiritual challenge, and there will be no risk of boredom even for children who are familiar with it. The following outline suggests how the parable can be applied to the young. This approach has been well-tried and receives rapt attention. It can easily be adjusted for older classes.

A visual aid, in picture or model form, of the field and its four types of 'soil' will make the lesson more memorable and also save precious time for the spiritual application. (The children could be encouraged to subsequently make their own drawings at home, complete with pictures of the four types of people Jesus described. It will help them think the matter through and could provide some interesting results!)

Lesson Outline

Introduction. Explain to the class that the Lord told His disciples a parable about the seed which a farmer sowed on his land. Some of it was profitable but some was a complete loss. Later He told the disciples that the different kinds of ground pictured four different reactions of people to God's Word. As we hear the parable we must ask – Which do I resemble?

Group 1 – The path. *When they have heard, Satan cometh immediately, and taketh away the word.* Describe briefly how the birds devoured this seed, which fell on a pathway well trodden down by passers-by. Explain that the seed represents the Word of God, or the Gospel. The soil of the path represents people who hear the Gospel, but who never take it in. It pictures some children who attend Sunday School or church and manage to listen to some of the lesson, but they do not attempt to concentrate properly, or to understand. They do not think seriously about the Saviour, and on their way home they forget everything. Satan finds no difficulty in snatching the Word from them. It is as easy for him as it is for birds to snatch up seed from a path.

This hardened pathway is the main public thoroughfare through the field. It is the way all the 'traffic' goes – a picture of the main, most popular lifestyle in our society. In other words, the soil of the hardened pathway also represents the person who follows the chief fashions and pleasures of this world – people who go with the crowd in everything. Such people are 'hard ground' as far as God's message is concerned.

Sadly, many young people have had the evolutionary, materialistic view stamped on their minds from earliest days. Because they accept these ideas (following the crowd) their hearts are hard, and they have no desire to consider their Creator or His claim on their lives. Point out that to disregard the Lord God and His offer of mercy is the worst kind of sin, and leads to condemnation at the end of life. For all whose hearts are like hardened ground, and who reject the seed of the Gospel, this present life ends only in tragedy and loss. (A minus sign or cross can be placed across this section of the visual aid to indicate a loss to the farmer – and to the Lord.)

Group 2 – The stony ground. *When they have heard the word, immediately receive it with gladness; and have no root . . . when affliction or persecution ariseth . . . they are offended.* Explain that there were some areas of any field in those days, particularly at the edge, where the ground had large stones or rocks just beneath the surface. Although the seed sprang up at first, it could not survive for long. The soil was thin, and the root could not go down far. This soil also dries out quickly in the sun, and the fragile seedlings would die.

This pictures children who get a little further than those in group 1. They listen much more carefully and find the lessons more interesting. They like the idea of being Christians, but they do not think deeply enough about it. They get the idea that turning to the Lord will make life easier for them. Jesus will be their Friend and they will have a place in Heaven. These children may belong to a church group where many of their friends are Christians, and this causes them to decide they want to be Christians too.

However, becoming a Christian is the most important thing

Make up 4 cards, fold them in half and draw the pictures of the grounds on one half, and the application as shown on the other. Explain the parable with the meaning folded behind and reveal it when ready.

VA 1 – Visual Aid for use with Lesson 99 – 'Profit or Loss?'

that can ever happen to anyone, and it is not a shallow, light-hearted matter. Young people who 'decide' lightly to be Christians resemble the seedlings which soon shrivelled and died. This is because they have believed *only in their heads* that Jesus is the Saviour, and have only superficially respected Him in order to get an immediate thrill, and to feel that they really 'belong' to their Christian group. They have never felt ashamed of their sins, or pleaded with Christ to forgive them and change them. They have never deeply realised that, in order for them to be saved, the Son of God had to give His life on Calvary's cross, and they have never experienced the wonder of true conversion.

They have therefore no depth, and the first strong temptation which comes along in their lives, shows they have no true appreciation of the Lord, and no lasting work of His Spirit in their hearts. The least little difficulty, the smallest sacrifice reveals they have no real love for Him. Soon they will be back at the disco, or whatever else tempts them away. Sunday School was good for learning interesting things about the Lord, and for some good activities, but when following the Lord means being different from others, or refusing to go along with something wrong, then they can quickly forget it.

What an opportunity this category gives us to stress the reality of genuine conversion. It is so much more than, say, joining a club. Those who follow Christ promise (with His help) to serve Him *to the end.* Explain that the farmer must have been disappointed that the seed which shot up so quickly and appeared to be doing so well, turned out to be a waste of his time and money. How sad, too, the Lord must be with children who want to be Christians only as long as it excites and benefits them. Are we in this category or group? (Another minus sign or cross can be added to the visual aid.)

Group 3 – The thorny ground. *They . . . hear the word, and the cares of this world, and the deceitfulness of riches, and the lusts of other things . . . choke the word.* Describe the soil which appears to be good and deep, but buried in it, unseen, are thousands of thorn and thistle roots and seeds, which will spring up with the good seed, and choke it. This pictures another outcome when people 'become Christians' without truly repenting and surrendering their lives wholeheartedly to the Lord (so never being genuinely converted or changed by the Lord). Such false Christians seem fine until something else comes along which they like better. After saying they have given their lives to Christ, they soon show that their minds and hearts are still chiefly concerned about worldly matters.

Some boys come to Sunday School and show real interest, even seeking to be Christians. But when a Sunday football team is started they discover what matters most to them. Some girls say they have given their lives to the Lord, but their anxiety to excel in exams, or (as they get older) about boys, takes priority over the Lord. Many adults went to church when they were young but as they grew older they preferred enjoying themselves in the world and working to fill their homes with possessions, and so on. Gradually all these worldly things squeezed out time for God, until their 'Christian' lives were choked out altogether. What will they say to God, the great Farmer, when He looks for fruit in their lives? They will have to be entered on His loss account. Are we in this group? (Enter another minus sign or cross on the visual aid.)

Group 4 – The good ground. *They . . . hear the word, and receive it, and bring forth fruit, some thirtyfold, some sixty, and some an hundred.* Describe the good ground in which the seed made good roots and grew to produce an excellent yield. The good soil pictures many children and adults who, on hearing God's Word, realise that seeking the Lord is the most important thing they could ever do. Young people in this group come to Sunday School because they have a deep desire to find how to know God, to be forgiven their sin and to be pleasing to Him. They genuinely, sincerely repent of their sin, trusting only in the Saviour Who died on Calvary to take the punishment of sin for those who come to Him. They experience the Holy Spirit's saving and converting work in their souls, and become completely changed in their understanding and their behaviour.

Such converts, however young, are not easily overpowered when difficulties arise, for the Lord has first place in their hearts and lives. They are not tempted by worldly attractions because they know the Lord and His blessings, which are far better than anything the world can offer. They are ready to suffer scorn for the Lord if necessary. Any hardship or persecution seems trivial in comparison with what He suffered for them. People begin to notice that they are different because they belong to the Lord. Like the rich grain gathered at harvest time which is used to produce flour and bread and other products, the Christian's life is one of great usefulness to God and other people.

A Christian never wastes the precious life given him by his Maker. Like the wholesome wheat plant which produces seed for future healthy crops, so a Christian brings others to the Lord. Only this category or group is profitable to the farmer and to the Lord. (Enter a plus sign or tick in this section of the visual aid.) Only such a 'convert' is a true Christian. Do you belong to this category? If not, face up to the emptiness and futility of your life and turn to the Saviour. Recognise that life was given to you by God and that you have frittered it away on yourself. Ask Him to forgive you for wasting precious years and ask Him to restore you, to put new life into your soul and make you fruitful in His service.

Visual Aid

See VA 1 on page 45. Enter a minus or plus sign as appropriate on each picture.

Revision (100)

Aim: To draw together and enforce the arguments of this series – that the advantages of the Gospel far outweigh any short-lived gains to be derived from a godless society. To urge the children once again to leave behind their old life and place themselves and their eternal souls in the hands of the Saviour Who demonstrated His great love for them on Calvary's cross.

Lesson Outline

Arrest the attention of the children by telling them some stories of people or children who act foolishly on impulse.

Eg: (a) people who rush out in a car without first planning their route with the help of a map, and who later find themselves retracing their journey after getting lost, and wasting much time, petrol and patience; (b) children who hand over their hard-saved money on the spur of the moment for something which catches their eye, only to realise a little later that they would have much preferred something else, if only they had stopped to think and look around first. Suggest that impetuous behaviour can be costly in the little affairs of life, but when it sweeps us into major decisions it is often disastrous. Point out that the Lord, by contrast, calls us to weigh these major issues of life very carefully. We are urged in Scripture to stop and think about the things which really matter.

Mention that unbelievers often scoff at Christians, accusing them of running away from real life and refusing to face up to its challenges. Tell the class that the lessons of this series show the exact opposite. Christians are those who think about the really important issues of life and death, whereas unbelievers run away from these matters. What is the purpose of life? Who made us? Is there a God? Where did sin come from? May we know God? The Bible is always urging men, women and children to reason and consider. It is unbelievers who never face up to what happens at death. They take a massive gamble, assuming that life ends at death, or, if not, that they will somehow get by in the day of judgement. Worldlings save for their pensions, make their wills, arrange for their funerals, but shrink from asking what will happen to the real 'them' (the soul) when death arrives! They scoff at God's commandments and rules, but blame the Lord for the suffering that is present in the world – not facing the fact that suffering is the result of sin and lawlessness.

Ask the children if they remember the gains and losses we have asked them to consider during this series. Head two columns on a board or sheet, 'GAIN' and 'LOSS' and ask questions along the following lines. (Alternatively, use the following headings as a means of *briefly* reminding the children of the key losses and gains of each lesson.)

(93) **LOSS** John the Baptist came to prepare people for the coming of the Lord. He warned them to repent. What does repentance mean? How did they show it? How do we show the Lord that we are truly sorry for our sin?

GAIN Soon the Lord Jesus appeared. Why was He baptised? How did He wash away our sin? Who does He send to change the hearts and lives of those who repent and believe in Him?

(94) **LOSS** What did the four fishermen leave behind *(Mark 10.28)*?

GAIN What did they gain? (Teachers could refer also to *1 Peter 1.4: An inheritance incorruptible, and undefiled, and that fadeth not away.*)

(95) **LOSS** Jesus said that those wishing to follow Him must deny themselves and take up their cross. What did He mean? Can children name people who, in trying to *gain the whole world*, have lost their souls?

GAIN What did the Lord promise to those who were willing to lose life for His sake and the Gospel's? How can a child respond to this promise?

(96) **LOSS** What did the Lord ask the rich young ruler to sell *(Mark 10.21-22)*? Why was he so grieved?

GAIN What did the Lord promise him if he was willing to sell all and follow Him (v 21)?

(97) **LOSS** In what ways was the Lord Jesus humbled and pained in the days and hours before He died (refer to lesson headings)?

GAIN How did God the Father exalt Him after His death on Calvary's cross *(Philippians 2.8-11)*?

(98) **LOSS** What did Peter do after the Lord's arrest which later caused him to weep *(Mark 14.66-72)*?

GAIN What did he subsequently learn about the loving-kindness of His Saviour *(John 21.15-17; 1 Peter 2.24)*?

(99) LOSS Describe the three areas of the field where the sower's seed produced no crop *(Mark 4.4-7).*

GAIN What kind of heart is to be compared to the good soil where the seed yielded a crop and produced thirty, sixty and a hundredfold *(Mark 4.8, 20)*?

Summarise the choice that you have put before the children during the course of these lessons, using the words of Moses: *I have set before you life and death* [gain and loss] . . . *therefore choose life . . . love the Lord thy God . . . cleave unto him: for he is thy life* [gain] *(Deuteronomy 30.19-20).*

Urge every child not to be fooled by the paper-thin promises of this deceitful world, but to look to God Whose promises are true and certain. Encourage each one to follow the apostle Paul's example who counted all his worldly achievements and ambitions as loss, and gained Christ: *The excellency of the knowledge of Christ Jesus my Lord (Philippians 3.7-8).*

LOSS Ask the children to consider some of the popular pursuits and habits which they would have to leave behind and repent of if they seriously wanted to find the Lord and know His blessings. Eg: the casual, careless attitude to God of young people today; the lying, deceitful ways so natural to the unsaved; the unclean talk and jokes heard so often on TV and shared in playground literature.

GAIN Describe the value of knowing and serving Christ in our day and age: the joy and peace of having sins forgiven; the power of a new spiritual life and a new character; the excitement of a mind which understands God's Word, and spiritual matters; the certainty and security of knowing that our future here and in eternity lies in God's kind hands; the benefits of having God's wisdom in making our decisions day by day; the experience of prayer being constantly answered; the happiness of belonging to a family of the Lord's people in our local church.

Series 13
1 Samuel – 2 Chronicles 9 *(except 1 Kings 12 – 2 Kings 25)*

GREAT DIFFERENCES:
Lessons from the Lives of David and Solomon

101 – How the Differences Come About

How early in life can a child be converted to God? How does this happen? In this lesson we learn from David's own lips about the boyhood experience which made such a great difference to his entire life. It could be the same for us.

102 – The Difference God Notices

Seven of Jesse's older sons are turned down by the Lord in favour of their younger brother. Why? What does God look for in us?

103 – Different Approaches to Battle

Saul recommends fighting Goliath with a sword and shield but David sees the battle quite differently. Life is a battle. How is it to be faced?

104 – The Difference in Friendship

Jonathan and David, potential rivals for the throne, become the best of friends. Their friendship also reminds us of the love which the 'Friend of Sinners' has for us.

105 – Christians Are Different

Saul is ruthlessly cruel in hunting down his imagined enemy. But when they meet in a cave, David shows him only kindness and loyalty. The difference in character between those who respect the Lord and those who deny His existence is seen here. Do we remember that God always watches us?

106 – The Difference Time Makes

What happens to the average worldling in middle life? Once the glamour of youth is past, what is there left to enjoy? But David finds the Lord blesses him more and more as life proceeds. Christian young people also may face the future knowing that the Lord will be with them and grant them great usefulness and fulfilment in life. Nor need they fear death.

107 – Different Attitudes to Sin

David relaxes his guard and Satan takes advantage of his laziness. One sin leads to another and soon he is guilty of grave misconduct – a warning for all. But this lesson also tells us how the Lord makes David face up to his sin. Would we, in a similar situation, refuse to accept responsibility for our behaviour and try to avoid God's condemnation of our sin?

108 – The Difference Repentance Makes

Psalm 51 provides us with the opportunity to 'listen in' as David humbly and earnestly asks the Lord to forgive his great sin. The words of his prayer have much to teach us about the way of true, heartfelt repentance and sorrow. We are shown God's lovingkindness towards those who ask His pardon.

109 – The Difference at the End

Absalom, David's rebellious son, treacherously leads the people of Israel to war against their own king, his father. Despite this, David is bitterly grieved to learn about his death. Neither does the Lord wish any of us to perish but rather to repent and be saved like David. Be warned by Absalom that, *the way of transgressors is hard (Proverbs 13.15).*

(These pictures feature in the Bible Learning Course sheets – see page 252.)

Write hymn verse here

Look upon me, O Lord, forgive,
Let a repenting sinner live;
By all Thy mercies large and free,
I come, dear Lord, to trust in Thee.
(*Psalm 51*, Isaac Watts)

Make eight cubes from stiff card using this template, or cover any box or block of a suitable size. Paste the drawings opposite on one face of each cube. Write the hymn verse suggested at the beginning of the lesson notes on another face. Write David's approximate age on a third face, then the lesson title on a fourth.

Build a tower of blocks as the series proceeds.

VA 2 – Visual Aid for use with lessons on '*Great Differences*'.

30-Crowned King

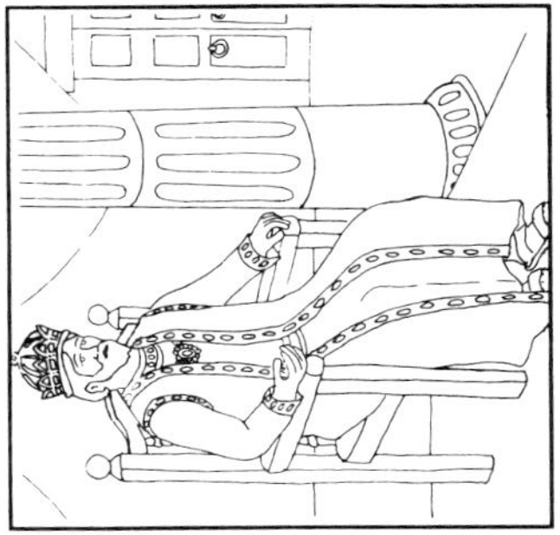

50-Fell into sin

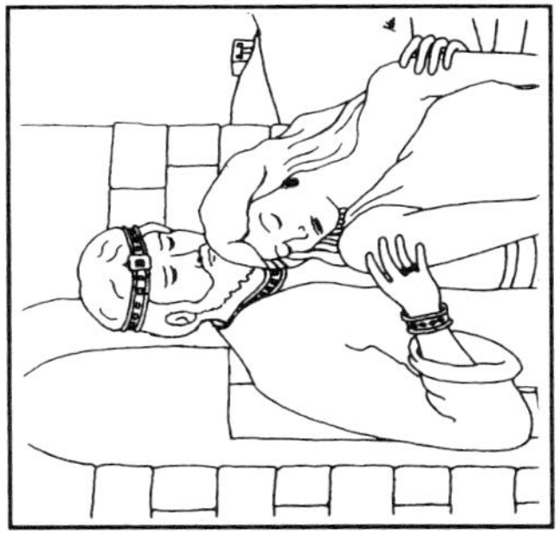

60-Saddened by Absalom

70-'Slept' and was buried

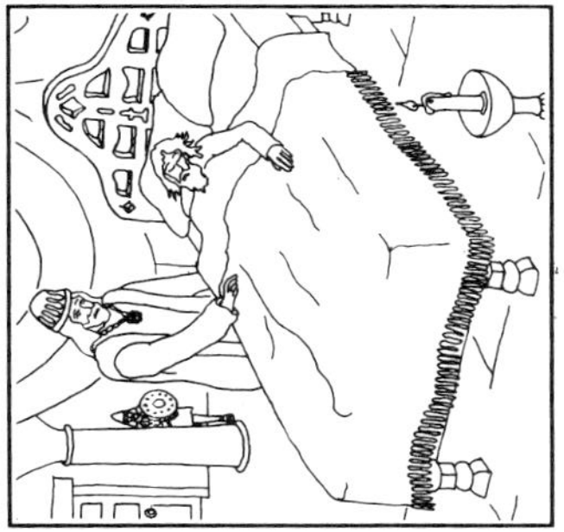

10- Converted

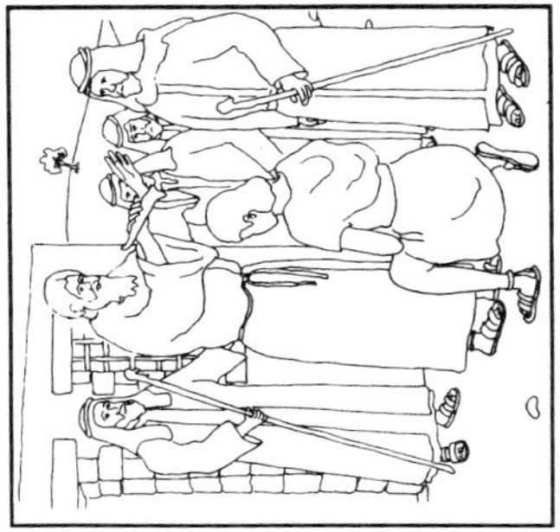

15- Anointed

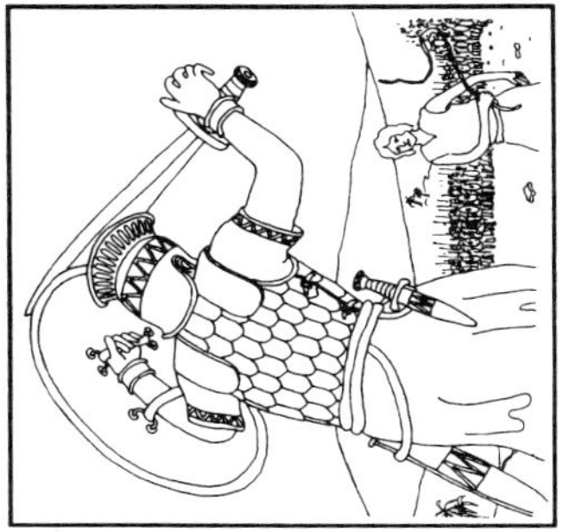

20-Fought Goliath

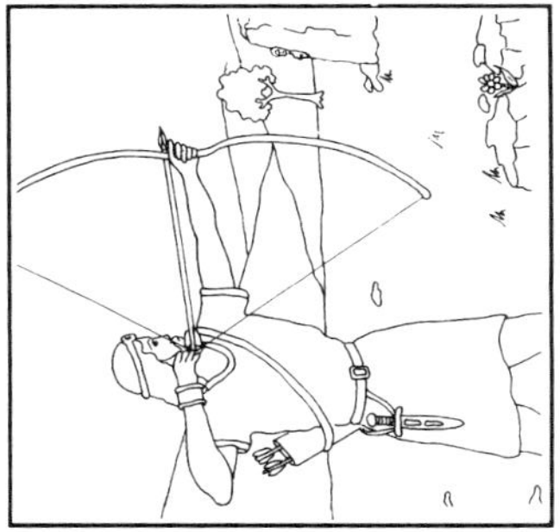

25-Loved by Jonathan
Hated by Saul

110 – Great David's Greater Son

A lesson to revise and test the children's knowledge and understanding of the main lessons drawn from the life of David. An opportunity also to show them how David foreshadows the life of his greater Son, the Lord Jesus Christ, our Saviour.

111 – Solomon – In all his Glory

As a young man Solomon is asked by the Lord, 'What shall I give thee?' Surprisingly he asks for an understanding heart rather than long life, riches or honour. But the Lord bestows all these things. What answer would we give to such a question?

112 – Solomon's Downfall and Rescue

Solomon allows his heart to be turned away from the Lord God and he learns from bitter experience that life away from God is empty and vain. Children and young people are strongly advised to take his warnings seriously.

Teachers' Introduction to the Series

It would be disappointing if we were to teach the life of David without introducing the children to his psalms. With this in mind each lesson is headed with a hymn verse rendered from one of David's psalms. These have been chosen because the words are simple enough for a child to grasp and the subject is related to the lesson. Leaders and teachers can encourage the children to learn these by heart and look at the psalms from which they are drawn. Some would be suitable for singing to a well-known tune.

Visual Aid

These hymn verses are also incorporated into the visual aid for the series (VA 2, pages 54-55). This provides a novel and graphic presentation of the course of David's life. (Teachers who find the three dimensional presentation too difficult or unsuited to their class's age-group can adapt the idea to make a flat chart featuring the same points.)

How the Differences Come About (101)
David's Conversion (The Psalms of David)

He took me from a fearful pit
And from the miry clay,
And on a rock He set my feet,
Establishing my way.
(*Psalm 40, Scottish Psalter,* 1650)

Aim: To show the children the chief 'stepping-stones' to conversion and the way in which the 'great difference' is brought about.

Teachers' Introduction

Before we can embark upon an excursion into the life of David we must show the children how he first became a true believer and child of God. If he had never turned to the Lord as a boy or youth nothing that we know of him subsequently would have happened. This boyhood experience altered his entire life.

At first glance, it may seem that there is no account in the Scriptures of David's conversion. All we learn from *1 Samuel* is that when Samuel visited his home to anoint him, the Lord had already described him as *a man after his own heart (1 Samuel 13.14).* We may, however, turn to the *Psalms* for help. And if we look particularly at those which breathe the air of David's shepherd days, we soon find those sentiments and thoughts which are common to all the Lord's people as they pass through the experience of conversion. David's reasoning, and his subsequent knowledge of the Lord's converting ways, are described very vividly in the *Psalms,* and should appeal to the children.

The success of this lesson will again depend on our determination to keep to the point. We have selected a number of verses which cover all the great 'ingredients' of Christian conversion – fear of the Lord, acknowledgement of sin, true repentance, trust in God alone for forgiveness, and the ensuing knowledge of God's love and purposes. If we simply explain the significance of these 'Gospel' verses we shall have a powerful lesson, with a very real opportunity to explain how a child can turn to the Lord.

Some teachers may be fearful of a lesson with no 'story' to join the points together. For this reason we suggest that teachers come prepared with a picture of a pleasant pastoral scene, depicting the hillsides outside Bethlehem where David minded his sheep (see VA 3, pages 60-61). In the course of the lesson, cards (on which the teacher has previously written the key verses used in this lesson) can be fixed on the picture. These cards can be distributed amongst the class at the beginning of the lesson. Children can be called upon to read them at the appropriate point.

Lesson Outline

Capture the children's interest by telling them that this new series is about one of the world's greatest kings. It will be of special interest to children to learn that David was converted while still a boy. How do we know this to be the case? Next week we will be learning how David when still a youth was anointed to be king of Israel. He was chosen by the Lord for this great honour and responsibility because the Lord said of him that he was already *a man after his own heart.* So we know that David belonged to the Lord even as a young person.

But how can someone so young become converted? Could a person in this class come to know God? Today we are going to read some of the great words which David later wrote down. They will help us to see what went through his mind as he turned to the Lord. They will show us how even a child can find out about God and then turn to Him.

We are going to imagine that we can look back and see David sitting on the hillside, watching his sheep. In the distance is the little town of Bethlehem. As an inquisitive boy, David explored the earth with its trees, plants and flowers, all teeming with life. Unlike a city child of today, he had firsthand experience of the miracle of life and birth, having assisted many a ewe in the lambing season, and having cared for her tiny offspring as they took their first shaky steps. He had watched the sky – vast and mysterious, yet working perfectly to order. The sun was never late up, nor a second too early. David did not have to say, 'If spring comes next year . . . ' or, 'If summer arrives . . . ' It always happened (and always will). Often he had sat on the hillside as evening drew on, spellbound by the magnificent painting drawn by the sunset across a vast sky. Later he saw the stars take up their places in perfect order under the huge dome of night, and he said:

(1) *Psalm 19.1 – The heavens declare the glory of God; and the firmament sheweth his handywork.* David as an experienced observer came to the conclusion that this immense universe, so minutely under control, could not have happened by accident or chance. He came to believe that it spoke loudly and clearly of the God Who made and designed it all.

(2) *Psalm 14.1* – he came to the conclusion that only a fool could say, *There is no God.*

(3) *Psalm 8.3-4* – having looked out at the sky, David looked back at himself and began to see himself in a new light. Instead of considering himself as all-important, he wrote: *When I consider thy heavens, the work of thy fingers, the moon and the stars, which thou hast ordained; what is man, that thou art mindful of him? and the son of man, that thou visitest him?* When he thought of God looking down on our world as we might look down at a continent from an aircraft, David began to realise how small and insignificant he must look – how unimportant he must seem to the Maker of all things.

(4) *Psalm 139.7-12* – yet as David looked closely at the things nearest to him, the tiny insects, the flowers and grasses, he realised that God was so great that He had designed and provided for the small as well as the large. Queens and presidents only know special people. They cannot remember or deal with every adult or child under their rule, but God is so great that He knows all. David realised that this meant that God knew all about him too. Insignificant as he might be, he could not escape from God, nor hide from Him. Therefore he said – *If I ascend up into heaven, thou art there: if I make my bed in hell, behold, thou art there . . . If I say, Surely the darkness shall cover me . . . the darkness hideth not from thee.*

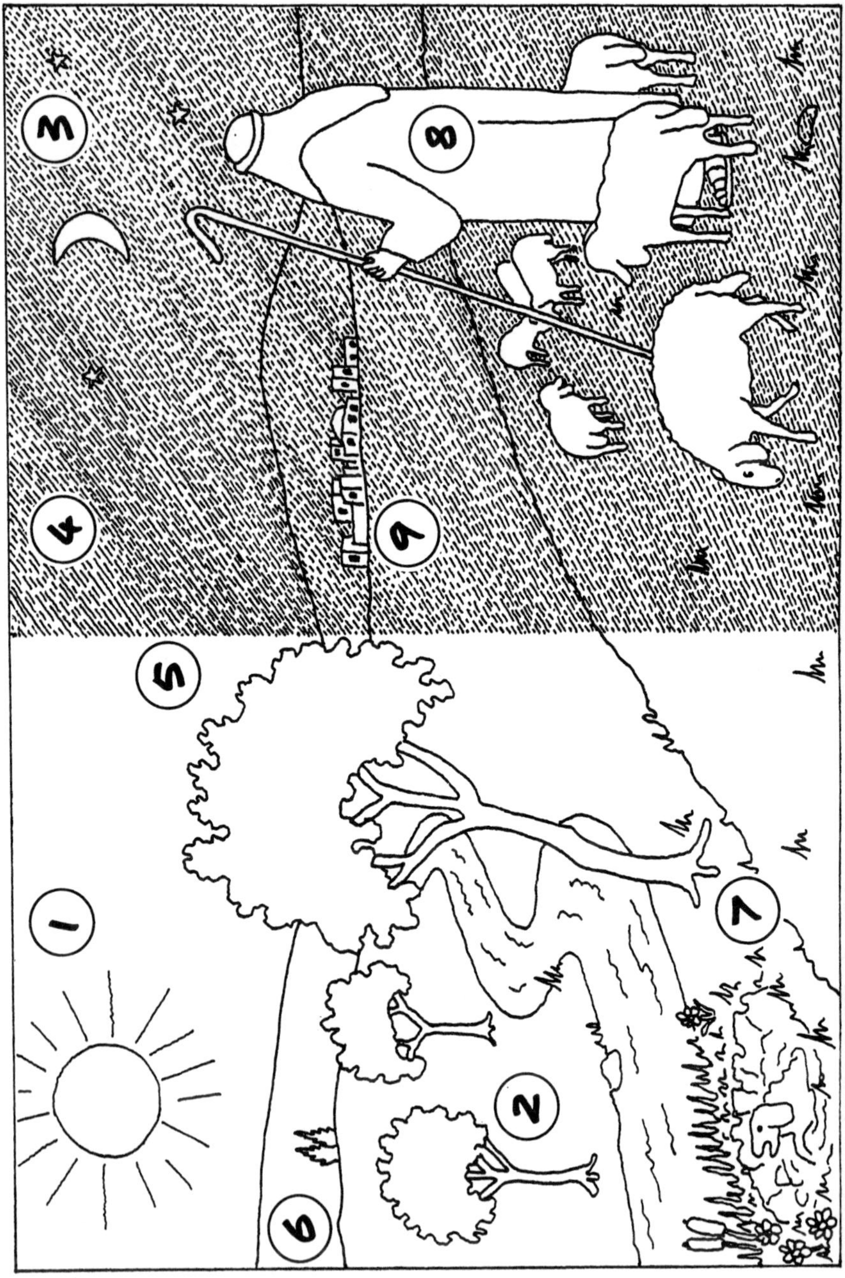

VA 3 – Visual Aid for use with Lesson 101 – 'How the Differences Come About'.

Copy out each numbered verse from the Psalms in the lesson. As you describe the steps of David's conversion, place each over its number in the picture.

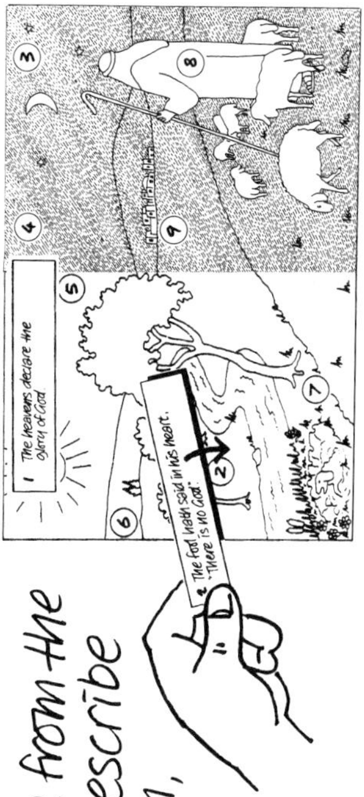

1 The heavens declare the glory of God.

2 The fool hath said in his heart, "There is no God."

3 When I consider thy heavens ... what is man, that thou art mindful of him?

4 The darkness hideth not from thee.

5 I acknowledged my sin unto thee... and thou forgavest the iniquity of my sin.

6 As far as the east is from the west, so far hath he removed our transgressions from us.

7 He brought me up also out of an horrible pit, out of the miry clay.

8 The Lord is my shepherd; I shall not want.

9 One thing have I desired of the Lord... that I may dwell in the house of the Lord all the days of my life.

So it was that David realised that God knew all about him, and that all his sin and failure was exposed to God's view. Every time he told a lie to his parents, every time he cheated his brothers, every time he played with unclean thoughts, the Lord knew all about it. He may have succeeded in hiding these sins from his family, but God saw everything. And if he should succeed in overcoming some of these wrongs, then the sins of pride and selfishness would take their place. Did that mean he was cast off from God for ever? Would he sink deeper and deeper into sin as life progressed, till he sank into hell? The next verse from the *Psalms* gives the answer.

(5) *Psalm 32.5* – in this verse David tells us how he came to be converted: *I acknowledged my sin unto thee, and mine iniquity have I not hid. I said, I will confess my transgressions unto the Lord; and thou forgavest the iniquity of my sin.*

(6) *Psalm 103.12* – as an inquisitive boy, David must often have gazed at the horizon, watching the sun as it appeared to travel from east to west. How far was it, how many thousands of miles, from one side of the earth to the other? Then he would think of his sins which were great, and put his trust in God Whose power and love were great enough to take them far away – *as far as the east is from the west, so far hath he removed our transgressions from us.*

(7) *Psalm 40.2* – David remembered something that he had often done for his sheep. Sometimes a sheep would wander off and slip into a pit lined with wet, sludgy clay. The poor animal would feel itself being sucked under as it bleated for help. David would rush to its rescue. Using his crook to extricate the animal, he would pull it out of the pit and set it firmly on a rock. As he pictured this in his mind's eye, he saw it as a perfect illustration of what God had done for him. *He brought me up also out of an horrible pit, out of the miry clay, and set my feet upon a rock, and established my goings.* Point out to the class that it was nearly always a dangerous and risky procedure for David to extricate a sheep that had fallen into such a pit. His own life might well be in danger as he struggled to pull the sticky creature out of the slimy clay. David recognised too that it would

not be easy, even for the Lord, to rescue him from the pit of sin. A price would have to be paid. He spoke of the Lord as his Redeemer *(Psalm 19.14)* – one who was prepared to pay a high price in order to buy the freedom of a friend or relative.

We now know, in greater detail than David, just how much the Lord Jesus was prepared to pay as He died on the cross of Calvary to rescue us from sin and to set us free. Yet even a thousand years before Christ came, David knew it was the Lord Who would save him – his Rock and his Redeemer. Rescued from the punishment of sin, he knew the Lord would give a new point and purpose to his life, so that he need no longer slip and slither into sin, but instead have his life grounded on a firm foundation – the saving power and the Word of the Shepherd Who would give His life for the sheep.

(8) *Psalm 23.1* – but this was not all, for from that time on the Lord became his constant Guide and Protector – *The Lord is my shepherd; I shall not want.* Just as David kept and provided for his sheep, so he knew that he belonged to the Lord Who would watch over him all his life. Could he ask for more? Soon David was to be promised an earthly throne with all the power and riches that were involved. But what was his dearest wish throughout life? The next verse tells us.

(9) *Psalm 27.4 – One thing have I desired of the Lord, that will I seek after; that I may dwell in the house of the Lord all the days of my life.* Tell the class how we shall shortly learn that the lonely shepherd-boy was to be moved from his quiet occupation and placed at the forefront of his nation. Seldom would his life be quiet or insignificant again. Soon the hopes and fears of Israel would be fixed on him. In the years to come he would become a very powerful king. Yet he would never give up this first wish and this great ambition – to spend his life, and his eternal future, in the worship and praise of God.

A pattern for us. These psalm extracts are the words and prayers of David, but every converted person experiences the same great change of attitude to God – repentance and new life with the Lord. All are moved to ask the same great questions that David asked. Have you? Have you ever realised that there is a God Who made the heavens and the earth? Do you know that although He is great and holy, He knows your every thought? Do you know that you can hide nothing from Him? Many people *subconsciously* know this, but they are unaware that God is also willing to forgive their sins. Have you ever asked for God's forgiveness? Have you ever been deeply sorry for your sin – like David? Only those who have, are forgiven. Has He lifted you from the miry clay of your sin? Do you know what it is to have the Lord for your Shepherd? Do you sense His nearness and daily protection? The last test of our lives is this: What is your greatest desire and ambition? If you are truly saved it will be simple. You will want above everything else to be with the Lord and His people not only in this life but for ever.

Though David lived about 3,000 years ago his advice to children, young people and everyone else still rings across the centuries: *O taste and see that the Lord is good: blessed is the man* [person] *that trusteth in him (Psalm 34.8).* Teachers can add their word of testimony to David's. They too have 'tasted and seen' (tested and tried) the Lord's goodness and kindness and found it to be all that David described. Remind your class that Christian conversion leads to the greatest difference that can ever come about in the life of a person, young or old. How wonderful if our class members were to be, like David, 'crowned with God's lovingkindness' in early days.

Visual Aid

VA 3 (see pages 60-61) provides the lesson with a helpful illustration, highlighting various points of David's testimony. (See note at end of the 'Teachers' Introduction'.)

The Difference God Notices (102)

David is Anointed King

The greatest joy my heart desires,
And for which all my soul aspires,
Is in God's house to spend my days,
My life devoted to His praise.
(*Psalm 27,* Anne Steele)

1 Samuel 13.13-14; 16.1-13; Acts 13.22-23

Aim: To emphasise that God sees and assesses us by the state of our hearts. Other considerations pale into insignificance.

Lesson Outline

Remind the class that David, converted as a child, was destined to become one of the world's greatest kings. Indeed there is a sense in which David was *the* greatest human king of all time, for the Lord God promised him that his kingdom would endure and be established *for ever (2 Samuel 7.16)*. In the weeks to come we shall learn that, although David died and was buried, yet his kingdom, unlike any other kingdom in this world, lives on for ever. In this lesson we shall concentrate on discovering how God chose David for this great honour. As we learn how the Lord selected David to be king, it will teach us how He judges us, and whether or not we can expect His favour. Suggest to the class that there may be those amongst them who have always assumed that they please God, live good lives and qualify for Heaven. This lesson will provide a 'soul-check' for all. Others may not even believe in God, imagining that they will enjoy a successful life without Him. This lesson will show them what they are throwing away.

A royal vacancy. Remind those children who were present for the lessons on King Saul that God had rejected Israel's first king after his proud and lawless behaviour. Samuel, their priest and former ruler, was told by the Lord not to mourn over Saul's rejection but to go and anoint a new and better king.

Selecting a king. Ask the children to imagine that they were given the unlikely task of interviewing a selected group (a 'short list') of young men considered suitable for the post of king or prime minister. What qualifications would they be looking for? To what kind of person would they award such an honoured position? What would they want to see in the CV of the best person? If the post of king seems too difficult an appointment for the children to make, help them consider some lesser role, eg: a bank manager, football manager, school captain or team leader. How would they fill the post? If given the opportunity when they are older, how would they themselves expect to qualify for a high-ranking position such as a ruler? Suggest some suitable virtues.

(1) Age. For responsible posts such as president and prime minister, grey hairs are usually a qualification, ie: 40 years or over! Certainly someone with experience is needed for a position involving power.

(2) Appearance. Remind the class that good looks and a smart appearance carry a lot of weight in a job interview. If we had the opportunity of selecting a king we should doubtless want a well built man with a pleasant manner and possibly a beautiful wife. In days gone by when kings led their armies out to battle, it was especially important to appoint a powerful, inspiring figure.

(3) Success. The last but perhaps most important item for which an examining board would be searching, would be some record of previous success and achievement. The candidate chosen for the job would have to prove that he had already succeeded in life, had a reputation for successful management and so on.

Qualifications overlooked. Surprise the class by telling them that when Samuel called upon the family of Jesse, a landowner in Bethlehem, he was told by God to turn down the seven most eligible members of the family and anoint instead their 'kid brother' as the future king. Describe the scene as Samuel was presented with Eliab, Jesse's eldest son, the tall, good-looking heir to the family wealth (which had been accumulated even before the time of Boaz, his great-grandfather), and a successful officer in King Saul's army *(1 Samuel 17.13)*. He seemed to Samuel to be the ideal age, have the ideal appearance, and have the ideal status, with wealth, position and achievement in his favour. He had been groomed for the headship of the family and estates, and Samuel had no doubt that this was the man God had sent him to anoint. Ask the children to imagine how bewildered and surprised Samuel was to learn that God had not chosen Eliab or his six younger brothers! Explain, as the Lord explained to Samuel, that He had made His judgement on a quite different set of criteria and had therefore come to a quite different conclusion. Samuel, like most of us, judged by what he could see – Eliab's attractive outward appearance – but the Lord looked inside at his heart – his desires, motivation, and inner character – and rejected him.

Looking inside. Show the children the wisdom of such an assessment. They would be the first to ridicule a person who paid an enormous sum of money for a high-status car, only to find that it had a severely damaged engine. Overawed by its appearance, the buyer did not bother to get an engineer to check its performance! The condition of the *heart* of any man, woman, boy or girl is just as important to the Lord as the state of an engine to a car's owner, for the heart drives a person, as an engine drives a car.

Trusting God's judgement. Samuel, had he trusted his own judgement, would have chosen a splendid-looking king, but such a man's selfishness and pride could have proved a disaster for Israel, just as Saul's had done. Instead, Samuel acted on the Lord's word and rejected not only Eliab, but Jesse's six other sons until no one was left to be considered. Samuel was puzzled and asked if Jesse had another son, perhaps one so young that he had been overlooked, a mere boy in the sight of his brothers. (Note that Jesse was *an old man* at the time Goliath challenged Israel, suggesting that David was a late arrival in the family.)

News of Samuel's arrival in Bethlehem had travelled fast around the little town, leading to a deputation of elders seeking an assurance from Samuel that he had arrived on a positive mission. David, however, had been completely left out of the excitement. Perhaps he had been told to get on with his work and not meddle in affairs too important for him. Or perhaps he had chosen to stay with the sheep and young lambs who needed his care, rather than abandon them for the sake of hearing the latest news.

Acting at once. Whichever was the case, Samuel refused to sit down or consider anything else until he had seen this young man. Then, as soon as David arrived, the Lord assured Samuel that this was the person of His choice. Though David was the youngest brother, the old priest took his horn of oil and anointed him in the presence of his family. The Lord confirmed the appointment by granting David a special awareness of His presence and power, by the Holy Spirit.

What made David different? (a) His heart. The Lord described David as – *a man after mine own heart, which shall fulfil all my will (Acts 13.22;* see *1 Samuel 13.14).* Perhaps the children are puzzled. What exactly does this mean? Remind older classes that we are all motivated by our hearts, or our affections. Love of ourselves, or love of things or pleasures, determines how we live. Help the younger classes to understand by producing two 'hearts', one cut from blue card, and marked – 'COLD, STIFF, HARD AND PROUD'. Explain that this describes the heart of the unbeliever (represented by the eldest brother of David). The unbeliever may be attractive in many ways but he is cold towards God, stubborn to His call, hard-hearted towards the Lord Jesus and His great love, and so proud that he sees no need of a Saviour.

Next produce a heart cut from a warm-red sheet of paper and marked – 'WARM, HUMBLE, GIVEN TO THE LORD'. Use this second heart to describe the believer (represented by David). Explain that as a child David did not resist and harden himself against the Lord. Instead he listened to the Lord Whose handiwork he saw all around him as he kept the sheep. He listened to and remembered God's written Word which was read at worship with his family. He experienced the wonder of conversion which we followed in our previous lesson. He grew to love the Lord with all his heart (God's first command to men and women), and so the Lord became increasingly real to David as the days passed.

(b) His aims. People might have thought that David lived a lonely life out on the hills with his sheep, but David was never alone. The Lord was with him, and David wanted to know and please Him more than anything else. Ask the class, 'What is your first desire? What is your greatest ambition?' Explain that because David's heart and desires were fixed on God, his whole life was affected. The anchor of his heart never shifted. We shall see in the weeks to come that soon his life was to become very stormy and tempestuous, but none of this changed David.

In *isolation*, he was not alone, but praised the Lord, as we see in his songs or psalms. In *danger*, he was not afraid, so that even wild animals, giants, or vicious enemies could not intimidate or scare him. The Lord was his Helper. In *sin*, he was not for long proud and unapproachable. Once his heart was touched by his guilt, he was ready to repent. In *power*, he did not become haughty, but remembered the weak and poor. In *success*, he praised the Lord and taught his own family and people to do likewise. And even in *death*, he desired to dwell with the Lord for ever.

It was because the Lord knew that David's heart was right that He appointed him to be king. In this way David became a picture or type of the Lord Jesus Christ of Whom the angel said – *the Lord God shall give unto him the throne of his father David . . . and of his kingdom there shall be no end (Luke 1.32-33).*

Conclude the lesson by asking your children to whom their hearts belong. Encourage those whose hearts already belong to the Lord. Remind them that Jesse and Samuel did not know that David was the Lord's – but the Lord did. Adults may be doubtful as to whether we are really converted and saved – but the Lord knows. Be open to His Word, and His directions day by day as David was, and He will direct your path. Urge those in the class who still have no personal knowledge of the Lord to come to Sunday School next week and learn how David was saved, delivered and protected by the Lord, his Shepherd, throughout life. Urge your class to pray the prayer of David: *Search me, O God, and know my heart: try me, and know my thoughts: and see if there be any wicked way in me, and lead me in the way everlasting (Psalm 139.23-24).*

Visual Aid

See suggestion under the heading, 'What made David different?'

Different Approaches to Battle (103)
Saul Fails – David Succeeds Against Goliath

Lord my God, do not forsake me,
Let me know that Thou art near;
Under Thy protection take me,
As my Saviour now appear.
(*Psalm 38, The Psalter,* 1912)

1 Samuel 17

Aim: To demonstrate that only those who put their trust in the Lord will know success against the powerful enemies which everyone encounters in the battle of life.

Teachers' Introduction

Some children may be familiar with this event, and imagine that it is not worth listening to. If we follow the usual approach which simply tells how a young shepherd-boy beat a great giant, we shall be playing into their hands. Furthermore, we shall not do justice to the biblical account. Teachers should read the narrative from *1 Samuel* with care, because the purpose of the chapter is to show that those who put their trust in carnal weapons (in this case, swords and shields) will eventually be humiliated, whereas those who put their trust in the Lord, though they may be inexperienced and lightly armed, will be victorious. In this lesson we will focus on the differences between Saul's *approach* to the battle and David's, rather than the more familiar David-versus-Goliath scene.

Lesson Outline

Remind the class that King Saul was an experienced warrior. Fighting was a way of life for him. Nowadays he would be a professional general, as well as king. He had gathered an army of hundreds of thousands, and gone out to battle.

Saul's confidence. Describe a battlefield of those days with thousands of soldiers assembled on either side of a valley, housed in tents and ready to engage in conflict as soon as their officers gave the word. Battle plans would be made in a pavilion arrayed with flags of war. Help the children imagine Saul and his men, dressed for battle in the valley of Elah – confident that they could defeat the army of the Philistines *(1 Samuel 17.1-3)*. The class may remember that King Saul, who by birth was a farmer's son, had been elevated to the position of Israel's first monarch by the Lord. But instead of maintaining a humble spirit in this honoured position, he had become proud, and set himself above the law of God. He had shown contempt for the Lord's servant Samuel and as a result the Lord had withdrawn His power from him.

The unbeliever's confidence. Liken Saul to present-day British unbelievers, who – like him – have benefited from a past environment which owed so much to godliness. Tell the class that those who scorn religion today, and have contempt for God's commandments, owe their freedoms and privileges in life to a Christian heritage. It is because Britain once had so many Christians that we still have lingering traditions of family values, social order, welfare provision, free education and many other benefits besides. Yet these unbelievers, like Saul, confidently imagine that their lives will be better without God and religion, and they scorn those who teach the moral values of God's Word. Saul arrogantly thought he would succeed without God.

Taken off guard! Describe the shock and horror of Saul's army when, to their surprise, the Philistines used a new strategy. Instead of their army advancing *en masse*, they put forward a representative or a 'champion' who challenged the Israelites to send out someone for a personal duel. Children know Goliath was a 'giant', but they may not have heard the exact, terrifying statistics given in the Bible account. Read verses 4-7 with updated measurements. *The Guinness Book of Records* documents men of 8'11", but Goliath was over 9'6"! His armour was huge and weighty. For 40 days he threw down his challenge. Read the spine-chilling words to the class (vv 8-10). For 40 days the people of Israel reacted with fear and dismay (v 11). Even

King Saul lost his bravado, realising he was no match for this giant. The man who had proudly disdained God's instructions was now reduced to fear – realising that, if he went forward, he would be humiliated and killed in the sight of both armies. Faced with this unequal match, he became a coward. Remind the class that Saul was not the only one to be taken by surprise. Life is full of dangers and unexpected difficulties for us all. That is why it is madness to discard God from our thinking.

A different reaction. As time went on there came to the battleground the young shepherd whose conversion to the Lord we followed in an earlier lesson. He was not considered strong enough or old enough even to be a soldier. He was just a young man on an errand from his home to his elder brothers. But he knew the Lord. When David heard Goliath's challenge to the Israelites his reaction was totally different. Instead of cowering away, he was stirred to anger. How dare Goliath speak so insultingly to the Lord's people! How dare he defy the armies of the living God! Someone must demonstrate that the Lord was with His people. Someone must prove that the Lord Who had promised to protect His people was alive, and was true and real. Before long, David volunteered his services to King Saul.

Describe David's reaction when Saul tried to belittle him, pointing out that he was a mere youth. David would not be intimidated. He knew the Lord and had experienced and proved His power to bless in other frightening circumstances. How had he escaped death from a marauding lion and bear when they had attacked his father's sheep? It was the Lord Who had saved him then (v 37), and it was the Lord Who would save him now. Remind the class that there are circumstances in life which no human, however clever, experienced or enlightened, can handle – as we notice all around us. Only those who know the power of the Lord can face the battles of life with the quiet confidence of David.

Different weapons. Compare the expensive, regal but clumsy suit of armour which Saul trusted and recommended, with the simple sling and stones which David chose to take into battle. What a demonstration of David's complete trust in the Lord! All children have had the experience of trying on adult clothes which have swamped them and made it almost impossible for them to move. David was by now a young man yet Saul's uniform was still oversized for him. Nevertheless, it was truly courageous of him to refuse the armour which might have offered some protection.

Help the children to picture the scene – the heavily armoured giant towering over the apparently unarmed lad. Goliath was insulted. Yet even when he roared at David and threatened to hand his carcass to the birds and beasts, cursing him in the names of his heathen gods, David remained calm and determined. Read his own words to the class – *Thou comest to me with a sword, and with a spear, and with a shield: but I come to thee in the name of the Lord of hosts, the God of the armies of Israel, whom thou hast defied. This day will the Lord deliver thee into mine hand; and I will smite thee, and take thine head from thee; and I will give the carcases of the host of the Philistines this day unto the fowls of the air, and to the wild beasts of the earth; that all the earth may know that there is a God in Israel* (vv 45-46). David wanted everyone present, including King Saul and the army of Israel, to know that no sword or spear would save him, but only the Lord Whose name and honour had been insulted by this Philistine.

A different result. Help the children to enter into the spirit of the occasion by telling how David, skilled and nimble, moved swiftly to attack. His weapon, though it appeared simple, was really superior. Compare it with a modern revolver. Aimed by a practised marksman, the stone flew silently and hit its target with deadly effect. Even before Goliath had aimed his oversized spear, he reeled and fell on his face to the ground. David used Goliath's own sword to complete his victory. David was vindicated; Goliath was killed; the Philistines fled, and Israel rejoiced.

Two kinds of weaponry for life. Show that a similar victory belongs to all the Lord's people. People who trust in God go into life with different equipment from that of unbelievers. Instead of trusting in drink, entertainment, selfish ambitions, possessions, etc, to see them through life, they put their trust in God's weapons – such as salvation, prayer, God's guidance and help, and their reading of God's Word. Others may be amused and scornful of them, but God's children have the Lord with them, and their lives are made powerful. Worldlings just have no idea how real and powerful the Christian life is.

Ask the children to consider what 'armaments' they will take up for the battle of life. Will they trust the equivalent of Saul's armour or David's weapons? Many children today are told that in order to succeed, all that matters is doing well at study, or at work, getting good jobs, or 'looking after themselves' and getting what they can. Some learn from an early age to lie and cheat, or to be very aggressive to get what they want. They believe this kind of attitude will enable them to get most pleasure and success out of life.

How pathetic and unarmed the young Christian appears by contrast! It is like comparing young David with King Saul a little earlier, when clad in his royal armour! But suggest to the children that they compare the same people some years later. The unbeliever may by then have met his 'Goliath'! Will his suit of unbelief and self-confidence have enabled him to conquer the strong and powerful enemies of life? Will he have conquered himself and his weaknesses? Will he be able to handle tragedies and death? Or will he have to run and hide? Will he have overcome the devil or will he still be insisting that the devil does not exist, while he does exactly as he is tempted? Will he by then have a ton of unforgiven sin to carry with him to the grave? Urge your class to place their lives under the blessing of the Lord, Who came down to earth to save and redeem all who believe in Him.

Two kinds of result. The last battle for everyone – or the last 'Goliath' – is the moment of death. Saul was terrified of Goliath, and the self-confident unbeliever in God becomes a coward at death. David, when he faced Goliath, was assured of the upholding hand of the Lord, and the believer in Christ faces death knowing it is the beginning of a great adventure. The Christian knows that although he is weak, the Lord is stronger than a hundred Goliaths, and He has promised never to leave or forsake him. How foolish to remain a worldling!

Suggest that young believers, who may feel very lonely and awkward as they take their stand for the Lord in daily life, *remember David.* Help them to recall the unkindness and accusations of his brothers, the contempt of Goliath, and the temptation he was under to accept help from Saul. Encourage them to remember that they are not alone in facing great threats and forces. They should think often of the Lord, and His almighty power as David did, and then they, too, will experience great victories in life, and at the end, victory over death.

The Difference in Friendship (104)
David and Jonathan

O guide my loyalties, that I
Shall love the friends of God,
And form no harmful, hurtful tie
With haters of the Word.
(Psalm 15, Evangelical Psalter)

1 Samuel 18.1-4; 19.1-10; 20; John 15.9-15

Aim: To use the friendship of David and Jonathan to illustrate what a difference it makes to know the Lord Jesus Christ, the Friend of Sinners.

Teachers' Introduction

It is not surprising that so many of our best hymns dwell on the friendship of the Lord Jesus. The discovery that the Lord of Glory, Creator of Heaven and earth, is willing to call His disciples *friends* should never cease to amaze us. We shall pick out several highlights in the friendship of David and Jonathan to show the real nature of friendship. In making the application, bear in mind that the children's concept of a Christian – gleaned from school assembly or from television services – will be very defective. Aim to show them that real Christians are different because they know the Lord as a personal Friend and Saviour. A simple word of testimony will greatly strengthen the lesson.

Lesson Outline

Ask the class what a real friend is like. Make some suggestions: (a) someone who really likes you; (b) someone who will help you, and not leave you when you are in trouble; (c) someone who likes to give you things; (d) someone who 'sticks up' for you when others criticise. Explain that the Lord Jesus was called (jeeringly) the 'Friend of Sinners'. To help understand what this means, we are going to learn about one of the greatest and best-known friendships of all time – that of David and Jonathan.

(1) An unlikely friendship. Describe the unusual nature of David and Jonathan's friendship. David had just killed Goliath and was speaking to King Saul. Jonathan, the king's son and heir, developed a great love for the young shepherd from the countryside. Soon they were prepared to make a 'vow' of friendship *(1 Samuel 18.3)*. Show the class that the Lord Jesus – King of Heaven – is willing to enter into a personal friendship with individual people. His friendship is so strong and so personal, it is as though the befriended one is the only person in the world needing to be saved, and He has been willing to pay any price to win that person's salvation and love. He knows our individual names, and counts the hairs of our head. There is much less to commend any of us to Him than there was to commend David to Jonathan. At least David was the hero of the day, but we are mere nobodies, and stubborn and rebellious. What a sin it would be to refuse such friendship!

(2) A costly friendship. It was Saul who vehemently pointed out to Jonathan that his friendship with David would cost him his throne *(1 Samuel 20.30-31)*, but such was Jonathan's friendship for David that he accepted this, knowing it to be the Lord's will *(20.13-14)*. Help the class to see what a great sacrifice this must have been for Jonathan. Think of what men will give for power and position! Yet Jonathan was prepared to protect

David and even help him gain the throne *(20.18-42)*. Briefly relate this incident, omitting aspects which do not illustrate the main point. Then explain how the Lord was willing to leave the courts of Heaven, and be considered a nobody, in order to make us children of God *(Philippians 2.7-8)*. There is no one else in the world who would do such a thing for us. Other leaders – whether religious or political – want our support, our money, our votes, but they give very little in return. Certainly they have no personal interest or contact. How can we ignore such an act of kindness from God's own Son?

(3) No greater friendship. In *1 Samuel 20.24-33* we see that Jonathan was even prepared to put his life at risk for David. From this incident, help the children to see what friendship really means. Explain that Jonathan loved David more than himself, and therefore he was prepared to say and do things that placed himself in great danger. Usually we only see this in families – perhaps when a mother instinctively risks her own life to save a child. There are few friendships as great as this *(John 15.13)*. How amazing then that the Lord Jesus should not only court our love, but be willing to make the final sacrifice – to give His life for us. How much we owe Him!

(4) A lasting friendship. We have seen how close the bond between David and Jonathan was. Jonathan died in battle and David was deeply grieved *(2 Samuel 1.17-26,* especially *26)*. Once Jonathan was dead, David might well have feared that his descendants would claim the throne, yet he kept his vow to Jonathan by bringing Mephibosheth to his palace and to his favour *(2 Samuel 9)*. Tell the class how close the relationship is between the Lord Jesus and His people. When I belong to Him, He walks with me, He guides me, He promises never to leave me nor forsake me. The day of judgement is a day to fear unless I know that God's Son will stand by me, and He will do just that.

David stood by his promise to Jonathan. Every friendship must be a two-way affair. We hear a great deal about Jesus' love for us, but do we know what it is to love Him? Are we willing to stand by Him – whatever the cost? Use the sentiments from

Newton's perfect hymn on this theme,

One there is, above all others,
Well deserves the name of Friend:
His is love beyond a brother's:
Costly, free, and knows no end;
They who once His kindness prove,
Find it everlasting love.

(5) A pattern friendship. Explain that it was when Jonathan saw David's great zeal and concern for the Lord's name and honour that he originally formed his deep attachment for the young shepherd-boy, an attachment which was to override all other ties. It was because David, and he alone, was prepared to take on Goliath, who daily derided the God of Israel, that Jonathan felt a close friendship with him. Their friendship cannot be explained in terms of a similarity of personality. It was their common love for the Lord which welded their friendship.

Explain that this is a mark or test of every true Christian. Real Christians are so affected by the love of the Lord Jesus, and so concerned for His glory, that their affection for believers of like mind overrules their loyalty to anyone else. The Lord insisted this must be so *(John 15.12; John 13.34-35; Matthew 10.34-37)*. He commanded His disciples to love one another. It is obvious when a young person has been converted, because he shows a genuine affection for the Sunday School, and the people he meets there. He prefers coming to the meetings to any other activity. He wants to linger behind, and it is clear that this is an important and special place.

Older classes may be interested to hear examples from history of the bonds which tied Bible-believing Christians together in days past. Tell them how Christians in the second chapter of *Acts* even sold their homes and property so that they could share their possessions with other believers who were in need. Early missionaries left their homelands to venture into unknown lands, suffered ill-health and often penury and death, as the cost of seeking out those who would be saved. (Teachers could describe incidents from the life of William Carey.) Once converted, the young believers braved the bitter persecution of their fellow-countrymen in order to share fellowship with those who had brought the Gospel message to them. Today, around the world, Christians from every kind of social and ethnic background have much more in common than any other 'grouping' of people.

Christians Are Different (105)
David Spares Saul Twice

Had not the Lord, my heart may cry,
Had not the Lord been on my side;
Had He not brought deliverance nigh,
Then must my helpless soul have died.
(*Psalm 124,* John Ryland)

1 Samuel 24; 26; see also Psalms 18, 57 and 142

Aim: To contrast the behaviour of Saul and David in this tense situation and show that this difference is typical of that between unbelievers and believers. What a difference knowing the Saviour makes!

Teachers' Introduction

One of the most tragic aspects of the worldling's life is the deterioration of his character. If life is kind to him and his 'luck' holds out, he may be blessed into old age with many physical benefits and advantages. But his character will show all the signs of hardening and rotting. The incident we have before us shows the grim picture of a man who had been forsaken by the Lord – the unbeliever. We see frustration and bitterness eating up Saul and causing his fits of mad temper. This lesson should make a real impression on the children if for no other reason than that it is so true to life. Aim to show them that the Bible sees people as they really are.

Explain that one reason why we are so anxious for them to be converted is that we want them to be spared this inevitable rotting of character which eventually leads to hell. Use the lesson to show that only God's power can save the character and make it calm, strong, deep and unselfish even in the most terrifying of circumstances. Show them how Christians can withstand the storms of life unruffled, because they have a Friend in Heaven, Who is ever present to lead and to guide.

The children will enjoy this drama and its outcome. We fear for David as he and his rough band of supporters hide from King Saul with his three thousand soldiers. The atmosphere must have become very tense as Saul decided to shelter in the selfsame cave as that in which David and his men were hidden. Would they be discovered and killed? The strangest part of the episode occurs when David stands by the slumbering Saul and refuses to take advantage of his superior position. The children will enjoy hearing of David's encounter with Saul the following morning when he produced evidence of the mercy he had shown when Saul was in his power.

But we must refuse the temptation to get so involved in these events that we omit to give them any practical relevance to our classes. Instead we can use them to demonstrate the *difference between a Christian and a worldling.* As we review the lengths to which Saul's frustration and hatred led him, we must show the children that humans become the weak slaves of their rotting characters. By contrast, we can describe David's calm trust in His Saviour despite the pressure he was under. Teachers are urged to read through *Psalms 18, 57* and *142* which were voiced by David in these very situations. They provide us with an insight into these events, and we should greatly value and use them.

Lesson Outline

David pursued by Saul. Set the scene for this episode by reminding the class that because of David's success and popularity, Saul's original love for him had turned to *jealousy* and *hatred.* On three occasions Saul had attempted to pin David to the wall with a javelin *(1 Samuel 18.11* and *19.10).* Then David had been cruelly persecuted and driven out of the kingdom. Show the children how Saul had become irrational and *selfish* in his behaviour because of his own lack of achievement and his jealousy of David. His *cruelty* knew no bounds.

Remind the class also that Saul had no reason to doubt

David's loyalty or to suspect any plot to overthrow him. It is true that he knew that Samuel had anointed David to be the future king, but David had always been willing to wait God's time and in the meantime he had been most supportive of Saul and his son Jonathan. The king of Israel had much to thank David for, especially his brave attacks on their enemy, the Philistines. Describe how the situation had gone from bad to worse. Saul had recently set out at the head of his army of three thousand armed men to hunt David down. David had only a small group of supporters and well-wishers. As David observed, it was like a king going out to battle against a flea! *(1 Samuel 26.20.)* Tell the class how, previously, Saul had been close to surrounding David and his men. David's life had only been spared when Saul had been called away to deal with his real enemy, the Philistines, who were making another raid on his territory *(1 Samuel 23.27-29)*.

David's opportunity for revenge. Now, as our lesson begins, Saul has returned to the wilderness of Engedi where David was living in rocky terrain, the home of wild goats. Try to create the atmosphere which prevailed. Picture David and some of his men sheltering in the deep recesses of a mountain cave. Then describe how Saul entered this very cave. Unaccustomed to the darkness, he must have been nearly blind compared with David, whose eyes were used to the darkness. No doubt the first reaction of David and his men, as they heard voices nearing the cave, was one of terror and alarm. But then, as the voices drifted away and only one or two soldiers actually moved into the cave, their feelings turned to those of excitement as they realised that the tall, powerful figure stepping into their cave was none other than King Saul. David knew the king well and would certainly have recognised his voice.

To kill or not to kill? Ask the class to imagine what thoughts would have raced into their minds if they had been with David at this moment. Would they not have drawn the same conclusion as David's men, that now the Lord had turned the tables and David should kill his vicious enemy? Describe how David silently approached Saul and cut off a piece of cloth from the edge of his robe. But that was all he did. Why did he refrain from ridding himself once and for all of his adversary?

The atheist's rules. Explain that if David had not been thinking as a man of God, he would have reasoned, 'Here is my great opportunity. Instead of being killed by Saul, I can kill him. I will win the esteem and admiration of my followers and then I will declare myself king. If I miss this opportunity, I may never gain the crown as God intended.'

Explain that this is the way an unbeliever in any day or age most usually reasons. He takes advantage of his circumstances. He sees where his advantage lies, and gets what he can, while he can. Even if a possible wrong is involved (eg: lying, cheating, stealing or, in this case, murder), he is not greatly troubled, thinking that he must protect his own interests or nobody else will. The atheist's 'ethic' is that it is legitimate to do whatever helps his cause unless it greatly harms another person. This thinking would have justified David in repaying Saul as he deserved, and pushing ahead with his own interests. Ask the class if this is the way they think. 'If a boy hits me, I will hit him back and I would have a perfect right to snatch any of his possessions at the same time. What does it have to do with anyone else? I will look after myself in the way I think best.'

The believer's rules. Then explain that believers see life quite differently. They believe in God Who is constantly watching over them, Who has laid down a set of rules and commandments which must direct their behaviour at all times. They also believe that God has planned out their lives and is well able to rule over the events of life and bring about their good without recourse to wrongdoing. It will never be necessary for them to cheat, or lie, or steal, however difficult or frightening the circumstances, or however great the short-term loss. The Christian's first rule is to fear the Lord, and to keep His commandments, trusting everything else into His wise hands.

David spares Saul. Now ask the class to see how this thinking guided David in his dilemma. Said David – *The Lord forbid* *that I should do this thing unto my master, the Lord's anointed (1 Samuel 24.6).* David's conscience even bothered him because he had cut Saul's clothing! He certainly refused to inflict any further harm on Saul and instead prayed earnestly to His God for protection and vindication. Some of his prayers from these episodes are recorded in the *Book of Psalms.* Use *Psalm 57* to show David's *calm* and *trust.* He knew that God could protect him from these 'lions' with their spears, arrows and sharp swords. Recount the events of the following morning and Saul's crocodile tears.

David spares Saul again. Pass on to the second incident of a similar nature *(1 Samuel 26)*, and describe the scene fully. Once again Saul's life rested in David's hands. The sleeping monarch, surrounded by an equally sleepy bodyguard, lay at David's feet, his spear beside him. David's henchman, Abishai, volunteered to wield the one fatal stroke – but once again David refused. He was certain that it would be wrong for him to kill him, as Saul had been appointed king by the Lord. He was also confident that God could remove his enemy in His own way and time, saying – *The Lord shall smite him; or his day shall come to die; or he shall descend into battle, and perish.*

Instead David took the spear and jug of water and removed himself to a safe distance. In the morning he was able to challenge Saul's men for their failure to protect their monarch. Briefly explain that on both these occasions Saul feigned sorrow and professed love and affection for David – but his change of heart was very short-lived, and David, knowing how quickly Saul's moods fluctuated, wisely ignored his offers of reconciliation.

What are your rules? Conclude the lesson by asking your class what rules their thinking. Do they act like David, or do they just assume that there is no God and they can do whatever suits them? For example, do they think stealing is harmless if the shop or person they steal from will not miss the article, or can afford the loss? Do they think that lies are permissible, especially to get out of difficult situations?

'I will do what I want.' Remind the class that such thinking has many drawbacks:–

(1) It is *unintelligent* – mindless. The Bible challenges us to *consider,* think, weigh matters; but often people, especially children, give no thought to how they behave or react to events. They either follow others, blindly, or do as their mood takes them.

(2) It is *arrogant.* It assumes that we have no rules, help or guidance. It tosses aside the wisdom of God's Word.

(3) It is *short-sighted.* If everyone behaved according to the same selfish rule, what kind of society would we all have to live in?

(4) It is *dangerous.* This attitude to life gambles on the hope that there is no God and no day of judgement.

Application. Ask the children who they would rather be like – Saul or David. Do they really want to reject the Lord? Inevitably they will know the failure of character and develop great bitterness to God. They will become even weaker as they grow older – bigger liars; more gripped by greed and selfishness. You must show how the 'older Saul' had become a cheap, shallow character at the mercy of his sinful nature. But David had, in youth, swallowed his pride, admitted his sinfulness and need of forgiveness and turned to the Lord, recognising that He alone could save and convert him. Urge your class to do the same. Then they will begin to experience His blessings and become more like Him. They will not find it hard to obey such a Master.

Once converted they will discover a great change of character. The Lord will even give them power to show kindness to their enemies as David did. As the years pass, instead of growing weak and giving in to every sinful suggestion, they will grow stronger still. Thousands of Christians have found this to be true. (Teachers can cite specific examples. Think of the character change of the apostle Paul.)

Visual Aid

Make or use a picture of Saul sleeping in the entrance of the cave of Engedi with his men. A figure of David – on a separate sheet – should be cut out from card. Place this on the background picture at the point in the lesson when David appears. Make cut-out words: 'jealous', 'full of hate', 'selfish' and 'cruel', and mount these over the picture of Saul as the lesson proceeds. Place the words 'calm', 'self-controlled', and 'strong' above the picture of David. These words can be referred to again as you describe the difference between the person who rejects the Lord and the one who is changed by the power of God.

The Difference Time Makes (106)

David – the King

Zion, where life anew is found
By people all the world around,
Here is the place of power and love,
Lifting our souls to God above.
(*Psalm 87,* Isaac Watts)

1 Samuel 31 – 2 Samuel 10; see also Psalm 89

Aim: To list the blessings which crowned David's life in middle years and to show that all believers experience God's overruling kindness and care over their lives, whereas the unbeliever's gains are shallow and short-lived.

Lesson Outline

Ask the class if they have ever thought what will happen to them later in life. Encourage them to plot the life of the average unbelieving person. Use pictures to show the pleasures of youth. Then ask – Why are people so anxious to stay young and to hide their age as the years go by? Make suggestions as to the course of the unbeliever's life. Middle age often brings the problems of unhappy marriage, children who disappoint, job dissatisfaction, family feuds, etc. Even worse, old age, for many, brings illness and loneliness and perhaps poverty. Ask the children how often they see this. What a miserable existence! And then – for everyone – there is death. It is only because men and women resist God's love that they have to experience such sorrow and frustration. Today we are going to see the difference it makes when a person becomes a Christian. Instead of life wasting away, it becomes fuller and fuller as we shall see in the life of David.

David's middle age. In the course of preparation teachers should read as many chapters as possible from *2 Samuel* and *1 Chronicles 11-29*. The meticulous lists of *Chronicles* provide, first, a mass of historical detail which increases our respect for the integrity of God's Word, and secondly, an insight into the vast government and management of David's kingdom (see, for example, *1 Chronicles 27.25-34*). As far as the lesson is concerned we can only give an overview and provide headings.

(1) He was anointed king of Judah and Israel. Without going into detail, tell the class that Saul and Jonathan died in battle. Lay the groundwork for a character study of David, by noting (briefly) that he in no way rejoiced at Saul's death, but he felt real grief, expressing it in a beautiful lament. Others expected him to celebrate the death of his bitter foe, but David viewed Saul's death rather as the Lord views the death of every unbeliever – *not willing that any should perish, but that all should come to repentance (2 Peter 3.9).* Nor did David rush with unseemly haste towards his coronation. Many politicians, after waiting for a long time in the 'wilderness', jump into office with great speed if a death opens the way, but David sought the Lord's guidance and took on his royal role only when the men of Judah anointed him king. Seven and a half years later the tribes of Israel also acknowledged him as their shepherd and king *(2 Samuel 5.1-5).*

Apply this point to the class by explaining that all true Christians believe that the events of their lives are overruled by the Lord. They may have to wait patiently at times, but His sovereign will certainly comes to pass. How different from the unbeliever whose future is dependent on his own wisdom and success at best, or on the whims of chance and fate. Urge the children to give priority to seeking the Lord, Who alone is trustworthy in the affairs of life.

(2) He established Jerusalem (Zion) as his capital *(2 Samuel 5).* Next describe how David drew together the tribes or families of Judah and Israel, who until recently had been engaged in civil war, and united them as one great nation. His first task was to conquer and fortify a city which would be their seat of government, justice and worship. Soon its walls were built and extended, the royal palace was located there (v 11) and the ark of the Lord *(2 Samuel 6.12)* carried with great celebrations to the place which David had prepared for it *(1 Chronicles 16.1-7)* – on or near the spot where their great patriarch Abraham had been assured that the Lord would provide a sacrifice in place of his son. The citizens of Jerusalem were indeed fortunate for the Lord protected them, and a good king ruled over them, administering *judgment and justice unto all his people (2 Samuel 8.15).* The Bible gives several instances of David's justice, respect and kindness to the type of people most sovereigns would overlook (eg: *2 Samuel 3.31-39; 6.19; 9*).

Tell the children that Jerusalem, or Zion, the city of David, has always stood as a picture of the heavenly Jerusalem – the spiritual city over which the Lord Jesus rules. He reigns in the hearts of all His people – those whose love He won as He gave His life for them on the cross of Calvary, those who qualify to be in His kingdom because their sins have been washed away by Him. Ask the class if they have their citizenship in the kingdom of Heaven. Have they ever acknowledged the Lord Jesus as their Saviour and their King? Do they enjoy the great benefits of living under His rule? Do they look forward to the day when they will see the heavenly Jerusalem, that beautiful city described in the last book of the Bible?

By contrast, the people who are citizens of this world only, are to be pitied. They live at the mercy of their fellow men and women. Hostilities of one kind or another are for ever welling up. Injustice and inequality can never be dealt with, for they have no king like Jesus. Anarchy and bloodshed are inevitable. They can only snatch at the passing excitements of the moment, for they have no eternal place of security, no protection from Satan's accusations, no heavenly home.

(3) He extended his kingdom. Using a map, tell the children how – *David went on, and grew great, and the Lord God of hosts was with him (2 Samuel 5.10).* It is estimated that his kingdom grew from approximately 6,000 to 60,000 square miles, stretching from the Euphrates River down to the borders of Egypt *(2 Samuel 8* and *1 Chronicles 18-20).* After prolonged and bitter military campaigns, the surrounding nations surrendered to David and his rule, making his kingdom rich and prosperous, everyone enjoying the benefit of his wise and just reign.

Compare David's great conquests with the conquests to be expected in the Christian life. All believers can win victories over their sins and failings as they daily battle against temptation and weakness. Gradually, with the Lord's help, they can look back on victories over pride, dishonesty, unkindness, etc, as they seek to please their Saviour day by day. Power will be given to them by the Lord to witness to family and friends so that some may be brought to the Saviour. Others will win respect for God and His ways as a result of the kindness and honesty seen in their lives. Secular teachers have often commented on the character difference they have observed even in very young children who come to know the Lord. The worldling, on the other hand, has little to gain after he or she has acquired money, comfort and position. On the day of judgement they will have no *personal, moral* or *spiritual* victories or achievements to present to the Lord.

(4) He received great promises from the Lord. Tell the children that whatever David's circumstances, whether he was in the thick of the battle, surrounded by enemies, or enjoying victory and success, he always expressed one great wish: *One thing have I desired of the Lord, that will I seek after; that I may dwell in the house of the Lord all the days of my life (Psalm 27.4).* We have already seen that he brought the ark of God to Jerusalem, and from *Chronicles* we learn how he made large and careful arrangements for the worship of the Lord there, providing for the priests and appointing their tasks. It was David's great desire to build a permanent home for the ark, a beautiful temple for the Lord, and, indeed, he planned it in detail and collected and stored all the rich materials necessary *(1 Chronicles 28).*

The Lord, however, declined his offer, for David was a man of war, and had shed blood *(1 Chronicles 28.3).* Instead He promised that David's son, Solomon, would have this great privilege. It was at this time that the Lord made a great and far-reaching covenant or promise to David which went beyond anything which could be fulfilled in an earthly son – *And thine house and thy kingdom shall be established for ever before thee: thy throne shall be established for ever (2 Samuel 7.16).* David was the first to acknowledge the great kindness of the Lord in granting this undeserved favour: *Who am I, O Lord God? and what is my house, that thou hast brought me hitherto?* His only answer was that the Lord had granted this honour for the sake of His word and His redeemed people, that the Lord's name might be magnified through them *(2 Samuel 7.19-29).*

Surprise the children by assuring them that God still bestows similar great and eternal promises on all His true people. All Christians acknowledge that they do not deserve to be saved or chosen by the Lord. They have sinned as much as everyone else and it is only the Lord Who has rescued and redeemed them, through Christ, Who gave His own life for them on the cross. So great is His love for those who believe and trust Him that He promises that no one shall ever be able to separate them from it *(Romans 8.35-39)* – neither life nor death, nor any power or created thing, present or to come.

Plead with your class to seek David's God Who can change their whole life and future. David's words to his son apply just as much to us: *If thou seek him, he will be found of thee; but if thou forsake him, he will cast thee off for ever (1 Chronicles 28.9).* Help them see the privilege and honour that the Lord extends to us – why, even the world's greatest rulers disintegrate into dust and ashes, leaving behind only monuments which will also disappear in time. Yet the humblest believer is assured of everlasting life, or as John Newton put it:–

Fading is the worldling's pleasure,
All his boasted pomp and show!
Solid joys and lasting treasure,
None but Zion's children know.

Visual Aids

(a) A bright visual aid will be particularly helpful in this lesson which has less narrative than usual. Make an attractive map which, to begin with, shows only Judah over which David first became king. Then add the names of the areas and countries which were added to his kingdom (eg: Israel, Philistia, Ammon, Moab, Syria, Edom, etc) as you go along, demonstrating the greatness of his conquests.

(b) Teachers could illustrate the first part of the lesson – the pointlessness of the unbeliever's life – by reusing VA 4, page 37, *Lessons for Life 2.*

(c) A large, brightly coloured crown on which the teacher can place a 'jewel' bearing the words of the four lesson headings will also provide a graphic and memorable addition to the lesson.

Different Attitudes to Sin (107)
David and Bathsheba

With shame I all my sin confess,
Sins against law and truth and grace;
And if my soul condemned should be,
That would be just and right for me.
(*Psalm 51,* Isaac Watts)

2 Samuel 11 – 12.15

Aim: To show that the person who is brought by God's Holy Spirit to acknowledge his sin and its loathsomeness, will also receive the message of pardon.

Teachers' Introduction

This and the next lesson deal with the events surrounding David's sin, Nathan's message and *Psalm 51,* but teachers can use their own discretion as to how they apportion the time. Teachers of older classes will probably want to deal with the facts together with Nathan's verdict in the first lesson, leaving the message of *Psalm 51* to the second lesson. Teachers of younger classes may wish to combine Nathan's tale and the psalm in the second lesson.

Lesson Outline

Remind the class that the Bible is a book with one single message from cover to cover. In its many pages God deals with the great problem of sin – how it entered in and spoilt our world right at the beginning of time, and how He made a way for it to be forgiven. Our lesson will describe how even the great King David fell into horrible sin, and how the Lord made him face up to it. Many people in David's position of power and authority would have brushed aside personal blame, excusing themselves and taking vindictive action against anyone who pointed a finger at them. David, however, accepted the Lord's rebuke, and admitted his guilt. The way in which he repented and asked for the Lord's forgiveness will have much to teach us, for we have all sinned and we all need to repent and find forgiveness from the Lord.

The beginning of David's sin. Describe the bright, spring day when David's army set out for a new season of conquest. One thing was different, for on this occasion it was General Joab who led the troops to battle. King David had decided to stay behind in Jerusalem. He had many affairs of state to attend to, and perhaps he felt he was entitled to some rest and relaxation. His men could bear the heat of battle but he would turn to other matters. Explain that this showed a sad change of attitude in David. Instead of being full of concern for the Lord and His cause, David had evidently grown complacent and proud. Perhaps it was the same with his personal battle against other sins. Instead of earnestly seeking the Lord's help daily to overcome them, perhaps he began to think that he was an experienced believer who had conquered most of his faults, and did not need to find much time to pray and study God's Word.

David's chain of sin. Teachers can then describe the events that followed, adapting the details to the age and background of the class, outlining the following points:–

(a) David was wasting time. He seems to have been 'spoiling' himself. He arose from his bed when evening came, we are told. It was still sufficiently light for him to see his neighbour from his garden roof. What was a king doing asleep in the afternoon whilst his officers and men were risking their lives in the battle of Rabbah?

(b) David looked where he shouldn't. It was during this period of idleness that his eye caught sight of the beautiful Bathsheba bathing herself. Instead of turning away, he gazed at her and began to want her.

(c) David committed adultery. He asked his servants who she was and discovered she was the wife of one of his bravest officers, Uriah the Hittite *(2 Samuel 23.39)*. That should have been the end of any desire he felt, but instead David sent for Bathsheba and committed the sin of adultery with her.

(d) David attempted a 'cover-up'. Almost all sins have to be covered up with lies and deceit, and this was no exception. Explain briefly that David attempted to free himself from blame by sending for Bathsheba's husband, but his plan of deception did not work, and so he formed a scheme which led him into even greater sin.

(e) David arranged for Uriah to be killed. Tell the class how Uriah returned to the battlefield carrying a letter arranging his own death! The letter addressed to Joab gave instructions for Uriah to be placed in the front line of the fiercest battle and left there, so that he would die. Joab followed his orders. Uriah and other brave men were killed; the news reached David; Bathsheba mourned for the set time and then moved into David's palace and became his wife, giving birth to a son.

A sad affair. Express your hope that the children will be surprised to hear that the previously godly David should have been involved in such a sinful episode. Make the following comments:–

(a) The Bible is an honest book. Unlike many histories and biographies which overlook the failures of their subjects, the Bible paints a true picture, telling all the facts, however bad.

(b) God uses such events in His Word to teach us how ugly sin is, and then to teach us how to escape from it – as we shall see.

(c) The difference between David, a true believer, and any

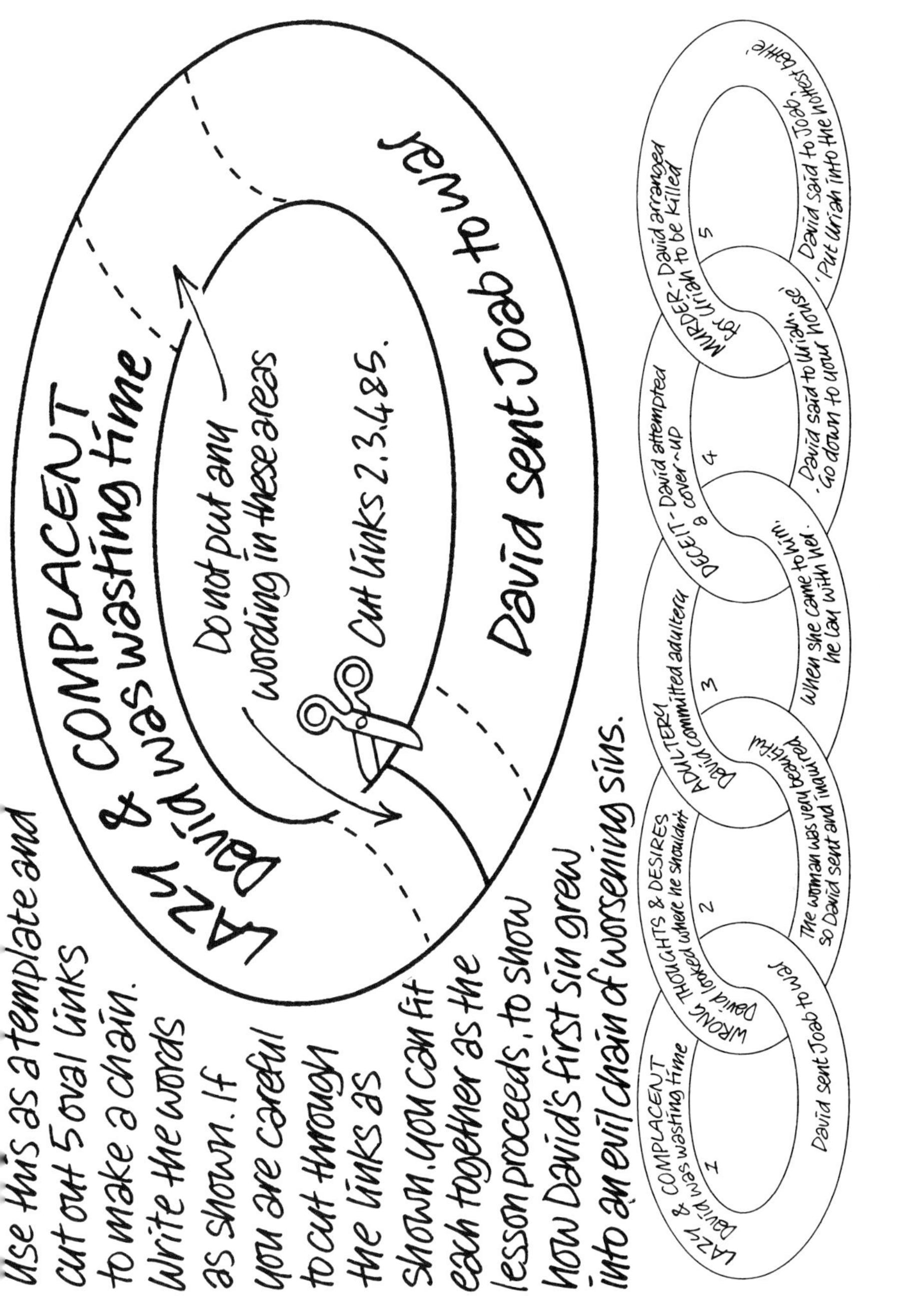

VA 4 – Visual Aid for use with Lesson 107 – 'Different Attitudes to Sin'.

unbeliever becomes clear, when we discover David's reaction to his sin at the time that the Lord confronted him with it.

(d) Sin is a very dangerous matter, because like a tiny spark it can start as something small and insignificant (in David's case laziness and complacency) but soon it flares up and burns as a fire over which we have little control, causing immense damage. One sin soon develops into a chain of sins (see VA 4 on page 93).

How important it is to come to Sunday School and learn the dangerous consequences of sin! How true to life the Bible is! Even more vital, we learn the way of forgiveness. What happened to David next can happen to us too:–

(1) David pretended nothing was wrong. It appears that David behaved as if his problem were solved. Uriah was dead. Bathsheba was his wife and he had a new son, but verses such as *Psalm 32.3-4* suggest that his conscience was not at ease. No doubt the children know the feeling! He probably tried to convince himself that he had done nothing too bad – after all it was quite accepted in those days that kings should please themselves. Life was cheap, and other monarchs did far worse things.

(2) The Lord convicted David. But David belonged to the Lord. However well he had hidden his sin from his fellow men, he could not hide it from God. The Lord also knew how proud and stubborn he would be, so in great wisdom and kindness the Lord sent the prophet Nathan to visit David with a story which would get under David's guard and hit its target with great skill (reminiscent of the tiny stone which toppled the giant Goliath), forcing David to see the ugliness of what he had done. The children will be fascinated by the heart-rending tale told by Nathan, and by its instant effect on David. Teachers will note its similarity with the parable of the Prodigal Son. The pathos of both stories demonstrates that the Lord's method, so often, is not to thunder law at the sinner, heightening hostilities, but rather to shame them into real contrition. As David condemned and pronounced punishment on the cruel rich man, Nathan boldly and firmly pointed his finger at the king and announced, *Thou art the man*!

If teachers describe the scene well, the children will be sitting on the edge of their chairs waiting in excitement to hear David's reaction to the charge, and to the judgement which followed. In any other Eastern court Nathan would have been silenced, arrested and most probably beheaded, but David was deeply affected by his words.

(3) David admitted his guilt. David listened shamefacedly. He had no answer to make, no excuse to give. All that Nathan had said was true, and more beside. It was the Lord Who had taken him from feeding sheep and made him king of Israel and Judah. It was the Lord Who had given him so much and was willing to give him even more. Yet it was the Lord Whom he had despised. He was indeed a callous murderer and an adulterer. The consequences would be terrible. David knew that he deserved to die and he confessed to Nathan, *I have sinned against the Lord.*

Point out at this stage that this is where we see the difference between the believer and unbeliever. Unbelievers, when faced with their sin, refuse to hear. God's Holy Spirit convicts them of sin and righteousness and judgement, but they will not listen. Even children whose consciences are still tender learn to bounce up after hearing God's warnings and judgements. Unbelievers convince themselves that there is no such thing as sin. They persuade themselves that they need self-assurance not self-condemnation. They blame their circumstances for shortcomings and react with anger to those who teach God's ways. David, by contrast, not only admitted fully and freely that he had sinned, but that he had sinned *against the Lord.* In our next lesson we shall learn how deeply he felt his sin, how unclean and guilty he felt, and how greatly he beseeched the Lord to forgive him and cleanse him.

(4) David was saved. Our lesson today ends with the Gospel message which Nathan was able to announce to David. There would be terrible consequences to such sin, but Nathan delivered words of great comfort, *The Lord also hath put away thy sin; thou shalt not die (2 Samuel 12.13).* Explain to the class that this is the Gospel message which God sends to everyone who acknowledges that they have sinned against Him, and that they deserve the sentence of death on their souls. He has found a way to take away sin. He has laid it upon His dear Son, the Lamb of God, Who took all our vile and ugly sins upon Himself and suffered the pain and punishment we deserve, so that we might be given eternal life instead of everlasting death and banishment.

Remind the class that although they may not have committed acts of murder and adultery like David, yet the heart-sins of hatred and uncleanness together with the ability to lie and deceive, which led to these sins, are everyday occurrences even in the lives of young children. They too need to grieve over sin, and admit it as David did. Then the Lord will show them the Saviour Who loved them and gave His life for them.

How do we know David was deeply sorry? The Holy Spirit allows us – as it were – to enter a time machine, and travel back three thousand years and tiptoe into David's bedroom so that we can overhear the prayer he prayed that night. Come next week and 'listen in' as we read *Psalm 51* together.

Visual Aid

VA 4 (see page 93) illustrates David's chain of sin.

The Difference Repentance Makes (108)

Look upon me, O Lord, forgive,
Let a repenting sinner live;
By all Thy mercies large and free,
I come, dear Lord, to trust in Thee.
(*Psalm 51,* Isaac Watts)

Psalm 51

Aim: To use this wonderful psalm of repentance to show the children how they also should approach the Lord for the forgiveness of their sins.

Teachers' Introduction

The children might on this occasion be encouraged to sit with their Bibles open, ready to identify the verses which answer the teacher's questions, so highlighting the Gospel argument. Certainly teachers should have the key words printed out. The lesson will present the Gospel very plainly and clearly, but teachers need to follow a well prepared presentation.

Lesson Outline

Remind the class of David's terrible sin of adultery with Bathsheba, how he attempted to deceive her husband, and finally arranged his death. Remind them also of how the Lord, through Nathan, made David feel the full horror of what he had done. Once David was made to admit his guilt his one great desire (unlike the reaction of so many people) was to find forgiveness. Ask the class if this is how they react to wrongdoing or sin. What would they do if they had lied, or behaved viciously towards someone else, or in the case of older classes, pored over a 'dirty' book or magazine? Would they pretend nothing was wrong, harden their consciences, and do exactly the same thing again without any hesitation? When sin really begins to hurt the conscience so that we want to be rid of it, how do we go about finding relief?

An example to copy. *Psalm 51* is a very private prayer which David prayed to the Lord. Although we live 3,000 years later, the Holy Spirit of God has included it in the Bible, and we are allowed to eavesdrop. Let us follow it carefully and it will show us many important things:–

(1) The character of sin. Did David simply kneel down and ask God to forgive him for committing his sins, and then jump up feeling much better about it all? That is what many people do. Some go to a priest, doctor or psychiatrist and get relief from their sin by talking about it. Some try to do some good deed to make up for the bad. All they really want is to ease their conscience, to feel free and happy again. Is this the right way? What did David do?

First, he recognised that he had sinned against his God and done this evil in His sight (v 4). Point out to the children that we so often think of sin as wrong things we do to other people (and this is true), but we must also remember that we sin against the Lord, our Maker. We have grieved and offended *Him*, and this makes our sin even more serious. We may apologise to our mother, make peace with our friends, throw away our 'dirty' magazines, but do we realise that God has seen and marked down our wrong?

Secondly, David admitted that he had always had an inclination for sin, even from when he was born (v 5). The Bible teaches that we are all born with sinful hearts. (How soon the youngest baby cries for its own way!) No one needs to teach us how to be proud, greedy, bad tempered, or selfish – these things soon surface even in the best-behaved of children, and the older we grow the more obvious they become.

Thirdly, David recognised that sin was deeply set in his heart (v 6), his innermost being, where God looked for noble things such as truth and wisdom. Many people today blame their failures and faults on their environment (their family and their circumstances), but David confessed that he did wrong because he himself was wrong in his heart. When we come to God we have to admit, like David, that our sin is in us and part of us, and we deliberately disobey God and want to go away from Him. We love sin much more than we love God. David spoke not only of his sin but of his transgressions, his iniquity and his evil (vv 1-4). He offered no defence – he accepted that God was justified in His accusations and blameless in His judgements (v 4).

One day we must all stand before God's judgement seat *(2 Corinthians 5.10)*, and we shall be speechless when He reveals our sins. How much better to face up to them now and find forgiveness through our Saviour, the Lord Jesus Christ.

(2) The effects of sin. There were three things David feared would result:–

(a) He feared God might cast him away from His presence, and that he would be rejected by God throughout his life and for all eternity (v 11).

(b) He feared that he would have no happiness or joy, particularly in walking with the Lord, because God would take away His Holy Spirit from him.

(c) He feared that God would not use him any more as His servant (v 13).

Did you realise that most of the unhappiness and frustration in this world is due to the effects of sin? Until we find forgiveness we shall always feel cut off from God, unblessed, dissatisfied and frustrated.

(3) The removal of sin. David knew his sin could not easily be remedied. He had stolen Uriah's wife and taken the life of this brave officer. How could these things be reversed? The sins of theft, adultery, deceit and murder were like a shocking, scarlet stain on the character of David. How could such glaring sins be removed? David did not pretend he could get rid of such terrible sin himself. Instead he pleaded with the Lord to come to his help. He used four words, with which most children will be familiar, each describing a different aspect of removing deeply-dyed stains. (Show the children a bright red blot on a clean, white handkerchief.) Follow the verses of the psalm as David prayed:–

(a) *BLOT OUT my transgressions* (v 1). Some stains can be covered (such as mistyped words, which could be covered over with an ink-blot in days gone by, or nowadays with a product like Tipp-Ex).

(b) *WASH ME THROUGHLY from mine iniquity* (v 2). If a stain is so bright that it cannot be covered over, then it may be washed out with soapy water.

(c) *CLEANSE ME from my sin* (v 2). If the object to be washed is actually manifesting signs of an organic infestation (in the minds of the children this would be associated with a mould or a foul smell), then a bleach or disinfectant has to be used.

(d) *PURGE ME with hyssop* (v 7). Explain that Jewish people used hyssop (a bushy plant which grew on walls) in the most extreme cases of staining – where people and their clothing had been contaminated by contact with leprosy, or by contact with a dead body. Before such a person could return to society, they had to be examined by a priest, and if he was satisfied, symbolically purged with hyssop and issued with a certificate of purification *(Leviticus 14.4, 6; Numbers 19.18; Hebrews 9.19).*

(e) Finally, David mentioned *sacrifices* (v 19). Point out that David knew that sin could not *really* be washed away by literal washing. This was just an illustration. His sin was far too serious to be removed that easily. He knew that a solemn sacrifice would be necessary in order to be forgiven. Tell the class that even almighty God cannot easily remove sin. Only by giving His own dear Son, the Lord Jesus Christ, to offer His own life on the cross of Calvary, could the Father forgive our sin. Nothing else in the universe can atone for sin. Only as the Saviour (the only pure and perfect person to live in our world) took upon Himself the punishment due to David (and all other sinners who would trust in Him) can sin be removed and forgiven. God could never just forget or brush away sin – it is too vile. He must punish it. And only Christ could take that punishment for us.

There was no other good enough
To pay the price of sin;
He only could unlock the gate
Of Heaven, and let us in.
(Cecil Frances Alexander)

David believed that the Lord was a God of lovingkindness and great compassion, and that He would wash away his vile (scarlet) sins, making them whiter than snow. (Remind children that a dirty, grimy city can be transformed to beauty in no time by a layer of dazzling, crisp, white snow.)

(4) The conditions for pardon. In closing make one last but vital point. Explain that David understood that the Lord would never forgive him if he intended committing the same sins over again. That would never be right. He must offer the Lord a broken and a *contrite* heart (v 17). The same is true for everyone who genuinely desires forgiveness. We cannot bribe God with sacrifices (as some of the Jews of David's time thought) or any other good work or religious act. Not even Sunday School or church attendance can earn God's forgiveness, especially if we use it as a cover-up for doing what we want the rest of the week.

We must be truly broken-hearted, ready to admit our

wrongdoing, and deeply sorry. The Lord will accept our prayer, forgive us and lead us to a place of favour and usefulness in His sight. Urge the children to go home and read this psalm through carefully. Better still, encourage them to use it as a pattern prayer, so that they too may be 'ransomed, healed, restored, forgiven' and made ready to praise 'the King of Heaven'.

Visual Aid

Use a replica of the chain of sin prepared for the previous lesson (VA 4, page 93). Print the following words: 'blot out', 'wash', 'cleanse', 'purge' and 'sacrifice' on the five links. As you teach section 3 (a), show the children the first link, then add the other links to the chain as you cover points (b) to (e).

The Difference at the End (109)
The Deaths of Absalom and David

Should every earthly friend depart,
Or should I lose my parents' [or children's] *heart,*
Then God on Whom my hopes depend,
Will still be Father, Guide and Friend.
(*Psalm 27,* Anne Steele)

2 Samuel 13-19 (especially 14.21-18.33); 1 Kings 2.10-12; 1 Chronicles 29.26-30; Psalm 3

Aim: To encourage the children to compare the end of an unbeliever (represented here by Absalom), with the end of a believer (represented here by David).

Teachers' Introduction

The rebellion of Absalom employs many chapters of the Bible, and it also includes many fascinating details. Our purpose, however, is evangelistic. We are concerned to select only those aspects which will, by the work of the Holy Spirit, jolt our children into serious consideration of eternal issues. We shall follow the technique of the prophet Nathan and use the pathos of these events (particularly a son using treachery against his father, and that son's tragic and unnecessary death) to stir the children's minds, and then – pointing the finger at them – show them how easily they could be in Absalom's position in relation to their *heavenly* Father.

Lesson Outline

Children are always curious about the subject of death and though young they have a curious ability to look at the subject objectively. Catch their attention by announcing that this lesson will contrast the death of an unbeliever with that of a believer. Remind them that this is a subject which many people avoid and are afraid to think about. Yet death is the one certainty of life.

(1) Absalom's privileges. Give a brief outline of Absalom's life. Begin by pointing out that Absalom had many advantages in life:–

(a) He was *born* a wealthy prince (unlike his father who knew many struggles and trials before he received a kingdom).

(b) He had an unusually fine physique. *In all Israel there was none to be so much praised as Absalom for his beauty: from the sole of his foot even to the crown of his head there was no blemish in him (2 Samuel 14.25).*

(c) He had a good and godly father to appreciate and imitate, and his father loved him very strongly.

(2) Absalom's cunning. Explain that Absalom, instead of appreciating and recognising what a fortunate young man he was, took advantage of his privileged position, behaving treacherously towards the father to whom he owed so much. Tell the class how David, full of affection for his son, forgave him a serious crime, foolishly and leniently allowed him to return to Jerusalem after a period of banishment, and embraced him almost as a hero *(2 Samuel 14.33).*

(3) Absalom's rebellion. Instead of being full of gratitude to his father, Absalom responded with snake-like behaviour. Describe how he sat at the city gates stealing the affection of David's subjects in a deceitful manner *(2 Samuel 15.1-6).* The children will be disgusted to hear how he used his great charm to turn the people against his own father. His aim was to steal his father's throne. (Perhaps the children have seen this kind of behaviour. Encourage them to respect the Bible for its true-to-life character studies.) Describe how Absalom's cunning conspiracy soon developed into civil war, and how he gathered his forces together in Hebron and prepared them to march to conquer Jerusalem.

Help the children imagine the pain which this treachery inflicted on David. What a cruel reward for his kindness! What a bitter blow to receive from his own son! David, anxious to avoid the destruction of Jerusalem in the battle which was imminent, left the city with his loyal supporters, all in tears *(2 Samuel 15.30)*. As always, he trusted himself into God's hands *(Psalm 3)*, leaving the ark of God in the capital with Zadok the priest and saying, *If I shall find favour in the eyes of the Lord, he will bring me again (2 Samuel 15.25)*.

(4) Absalom's brief success. Describe the scene as Absalom and his men marched unhindered into Jerusalem (a brief and hollow victory), and held a council of war. Though installed in the capital, Absalom recognised that he could not establish himself as king until his father was dead. Only then could he grasp the crown. A plan of battle was arranged, but was overruled by the Lord, *For the Lord had appointed to defeat the good counsel of Ahithophel* [Absalom's fellow conspirator], *to the intent that the Lord might bring evil upon Absalom (2 Samuel 17.14)*. The outcome was in the Lord's hands but Absalom did not know this, and he fondly imagined he would conquer. Imagining that his father's band of supporters were demoralised and exhausted, he no doubt gloated at his coming glory. Absalom had always held his father David's God and His laws in contempt, and no doubt he scoffed at his father's religious beliefs at this crucial moment.

(5) Absalom's tragic death. Whatever Absalom thought or dreamed, his end was near. Describe how, within days, he was found hanging from an oak tree, his long hair having been caught in its branches as he rode beneath. General Joab soon arrived and slew him, ignoring King David's instructions to spare his son. David was grief-stricken when the news reached him, for, despite Absalom's treachery, he still felt tremendous affection for his son.

Help the children to see the tragedy of this death – that such a favoured young prince should die in such circumstances. To think that he could have enjoyed such a worthwhile and happy life with the many opportunities open to him, but instead he steered himself to an humiliating end, with few who either pitied or admired him. Perhaps that is why his father *alone* mourned his death. David's words of grief ring across history, *O my son Absalom, my son, my son Absalom! would God I had died for thee, O Absalom, my son, my son! (2 Samuel 18.33.)*

The case of unbelievers. Suggest to the class that Absalom's rebellion and death is a picture of the rebellion and death of all unbelievers:–

(1) Their privileges. Remind the class that all God's creatures are granted by Him the privilege of life. The Lord is a very gracious God and full of lovingkindness. He is ready to give so many blessings and powers to the people He has made – just as David desired to honour Absalom.

(2) Their rebellion. Yet men and women will not have Him to rule over them, and their lives develop into a battle with their Maker. Often success seems to be within their grasp. They scoff at the Christian faith and imagine that they can run their lives and their world without God's help. They do whatever they want to do, and sin away their years, forgetting that their fate is in God's hands.

(3) Their death. How tragic when life draws to an end, and they must confront the very Lord Who *would* have been their Saviour, but Who must now be their Judge. How tragic that human beings, having been given such privileges by the Lord, should end their lives in a state of wilful rebellion against their Maker, ensuring that they must spend eternity in hell, banished from His love and favour. The Bible assures us that the Lord

God feels a pain, in some ways similar to that felt by David at Absalom's death, at the eternal loss of any sinner *(Ezekiel 18.31-32; 33.11; 2 Peter 3.9)*.

Urge the children to consider these things carefully. Warn them not to set themselves against the Lord and His requirements. Remind them, in case they think death is a long way off, that the path of rebellion against God is often taken in early years. Tell your class how much you pray that none of them will ever end their lives hopelessly.

David's end. By contrast tell the class how David returned by popular request to live out his days as king in Jerusalem. There were further trials and struggles, some brought about by his own foolishness and sin, but his destination was certain. *He died in a good old age, full of days, riches, and honour (1 Chronicles 29.28)* and *slept with his fathers, and was buried in the city of David (1 Kings 2.10)*, secure in the knowledge that the Lord would honour His promise and give him an everlasting kingdom. His early desire to *dwell in the house of the Lord for ever (Psalm 23.6)* was granted. He knew that at his death he would be shown the path of life and enter God's presence where he would enjoy fulness of joy at God's right hand, where there are pleasures for ever *(Psalm 16.10-11)*.

Remind the children that there are many differences in life between the believer and unbeliever, but the great and irreversible divide comes at death. What joy contrasted with what sorrow! Encourage them to seek the Lord early as David did, and have their eternal destination made secure for ever.

Great David's Greater Son (110)
Revision

Goodness and mercy all my life
Shall surely follow me;
And in God's house for evermore
My dwelling-place shall be.
(*Psalm 23, Scottish Psalter*, 1650)

Aim: To stir the memories of the children, to provide them with an overview of David's testimony as a typical believer, and to show how his life and reign illustrate the life and reign of the Saviour, his *greater Son.*

Teachers' Introduction

The attention of teachers is drawn to Peter's words on the Day of Pentecost – *David . . . is both dead and buried . . . being a prophet, and knowing that God had sworn with an oath to him, that of the fruit of his loins, according to the flesh, he would raise up Christ to sit on his throne; he seeing this before spake of the resurrection of Christ (Acts 2.29-31).* Teachers should also read *Psalm 72.*

Lesson Outline

Tell the children that the life of David is not only full of lessons for us as we follow *his* experiences, but there is also another way in which it teaches us. Although David was not a special person like the Lord Jesus Christ, the Son of God, yet God so organised the events of his life, that it provides a picture of Christ, Who would come to earth a thousand years after David. This kind of picture – a person in the Old Testament whose life is very like that of Christ – is called a *type.* God often pointed to David's life and said to the people – 'Look at David, I have arranged his reign to be a picture for you of what kind of king your coming Saviour will be' *(Isaiah 55.3-4; Jeremiah 30.9; Ezekiel 34.24; 37.24-25; Hosea 3.5).* We shall look at this picture of Christ in David's life, but remember that David was nothing like the Saviour in at least three major ways – he did not know all things, he did not have divine power, and he was not perfect.

(1) Anointed. Ask the children where David was born and grew up, and what he was doing when the prophet Samuel visited his family (at God's command, in order to anoint the future king). What reason did the Lord give for choosing David in preference to his older brothers? Then explain that just as David was anointed many years before he actually became king, so the Lord Jesus was appointed to be our Saviour even before the world was madc *(Ephesians 1.4).*

(2) The battle with Goliath. Ask why the armies of Israel under King Saul were so terrified of Goliath. Why was David, a young shepherd, not frightened? How did he answer Goliath's scornful taunts? How did he defeat the giant? Explain that the Lord Jesus Christ, at the outset of His ministry (work), was similarly confronted. The prince of hell, Satan, came to tempt Him in the wilderness. He defeated the evil one by resting on God's Word and promises.

(3) A period of humiliation. Ask who became jealous of David and attempted to kill him after his success over the Philistines. Ask the children to give examples of occasions when David nearly lost his life. Where did he hide with his men? Remind the class that the Saviour humbled Himself and also endured a period of scorn and hatred in His life on earth. King Herod attempted to kill Him before He was two years old. People scornfully called Him *the carpenter's son.* The religious leaders schemed His death early in His ministry, before He left Capernaum. At other times also they tried to have Him killed. But both David and the Lord Jesus were protected from their enemies by the sovereign and protective hand of God until it was God's time for David to be crowned, and for Jesus to be crucified for our sins, after which He was gloriously raised from the dead.

(4) King of Jerusalem by consent. Ask – When King Saul died, who asked David to be their king immediately? How many years later was it that the people of Israel also crowned him as their king? Which city did David establish as his capital soon after? What other names did the city have? Explain that the Lord Jesus has an unseen kingdom in the hearts of men and women, boys and girls who willingly and gladly accept His rule in their hearts and lives. These people, wherever and whenever they live, belong to the spiritual Zion or Jerusalem. They look forward to going one day to live in the heavenly Jerusalem. The Bible therefore uses the names Jerusalem and Zion in three senses to refer to:–

(a) The *earthly capital* of Israel first established by David and into which Jesus rode on a colt.

(b) The *people* who have been redeemed by the Lord Jesus and who gladly acknowledge Him as their King and Saviour – the citizens of Zion.

(c) The *heavenly city* which will be the everlasting home of all those saved and washed of their sins by the Lord Jesus.

Visual Aid

Use VA 2 (see pages 54-55). The 'building blocks' of David's life will be particularly useful as you revise the highlights of the series.

Solomon – In all his Glory (111)

1 Chronicles 28 – 2 Chronicles 9; see also 1 Kings 3-10 and Luke 11.31

Aim: To give a glimpse of Solomon's greatness, highlighting the main events and achievements of the chapters, and drawing the same *Gospel* lesson from them as the Saviour did.

Teachers' Introduction

The best view of Solomon's life brings together the accounts of *Kings, Chronicles, Proverbs* and *Ecclesiastes.* He inherited his father's great kingdom, made his humble request for wisdom in answer to the Lord's question, and became greater than all the kings of the earth in riches and wisdom *(2 Chronicles 9.22).* During this happy and spiritual period of his life, he built and dedicated the Temple, and was inspired to write most of the *Book of Proverbs* (which provides the subject matter of this lesson). Our next lesson will enter the trough of his later experience, when he fell from this great height of blessing into a mire of compromise and sin (through the influence of his many wives, who *turned away his heart after other gods*). The testimony of the *Book of Ecclesiastes* shows that at some time before the end of his life, Solomon was restored to spirituality. In his latter days he was inspired to reason with others, particularly the young, about the futility of worldliness, or life without the Lord. (It may be that many proverbs are from his later period also.)

Lesson Outline

Ask the children what answer they would give if they were asked by a very rich person to name any gift they wanted. What would they ask for? Suggest that you could make some good guesses. Supposing the person had the power to train you and promote you for a great sporting career, or offered to introduce you to any person you liked to name – what would you ask for? Remind the class that Solomon as a young man had inherited the large and prosperous kingdom which had been won and enlarged by his father through much toil and battle.

Tell them how the Lord appeared one night to Solomon saying, *Ask what I shall give thee.* Then tell how the young king, who could so easily have set his heart on riches, fame and a safe passage through life (in days when many princes met an early death on the battlefield, or as a result of fatal diseases which could not then be treated), made instead a surprising choice. He asked for wisdom and knowledge so that he might rule God's people wisely. Teachers should read God's reply from *2 Chronicles 1.11-12.*

Show the class how the Lord kept His promise to Solomon, highlighting examples which would be of particular interest to them, namely:–

His wisdom *(1 Kings 4.29-34).* Point the children to the *Book of Proverbs* and extract a few proverbs which, 3,000 years later, are still in everyday usage – 'A gentle answer turns away wrath' *(15.1)*; 'Pride goes before destruction' *(16.18)*; 'A good name is to be desired more than riches' *(22.1)*; 'Spare the rod and spoil the child' *(23.13).* Point out that psychologists and psychiatrists have ignored the *Book of Proverbs* to their own great disadvantage. Not only are Solomon's observations of human behaviour deep, profound and unchanging, they are also expressed in memorable sayings.

Even in his own day, people from East *and* West recognised Solomon's wisdom and great discernment. He wrote 3,000 proverbs! Teachers may like to refer briefly to the incident which records Solomon's wise and practical judgement in the case of the two women who both claimed to be mother of the same child. Solomon's method of establishing which of the two was the real mother gained him much respect at the time, and demonstrated his God-given wisdom in administering justice *(1 Kings 3.16-28).*

In addition to answering Solomon's request for wisdom beyond all that he could have anticipated or expected, the Lord gave him benefits for which he had not asked – riches, fame and honour, together with peace from his enemies, and a long life.

His riches *(2 Chronicles 1.14-17; 9.13-29).* His drinking vessels were of gold! He amassed the amazing total of 1,400 chariots and 12,000 horsemen. His palace, which took thirteen years to build, was panelled in cedar, and decorated with costly stones which had been shipped in from other countries *(1 Kings 7).* Ships from Tarshish returned every three years with cargoes of gold, silver, ivory, apes and peacocks. His throne was made of ivory, overlaid with gold, and it had six steps and a footstool attached to it, all decorated with carvings of lions *(2 Chronicles 9.17-19).* Stables, copper mines and evidence of prolific trading have come to light in recent years.

His honour and fame *(1 Kings 4.34; 10.13).* During his lifetime many other rulers from all parts were anxious to seek an audience with great King Solomon. The Queen of Sheba travelled hundreds of miles with a retinue of officers and servants to see the great man, and to hear his wisdom, and she was awed with all she saw and heard. During his life and after his death the fame of Solomon spread so that his wealth and wisdom has been admired by people of all nations. The Lord Jesus Himself referred to *Solomon in all his glory (Matthew 6.29).*

His long life. Tell the class how the Lord kept His promise to Solomon in this matter also. Before his death, David directed the anointing of Solomon and saw his son seated upon the throne of Israel, surrounded with majesty and with pledges of allegiance from his other sons *(1 Chronicles 29.22-27).* Solomon's right to govern was therefore never seriously disputed. Unlike his father, Solomon enjoyed *peace on all sides round about him* throughout his reign, which lasted forty years

Copy this drawing of the temple on to a large sheet of stiff card. Leave space on the right for flaps. Cut them individually so they can be folded forward as the lesson proceeds

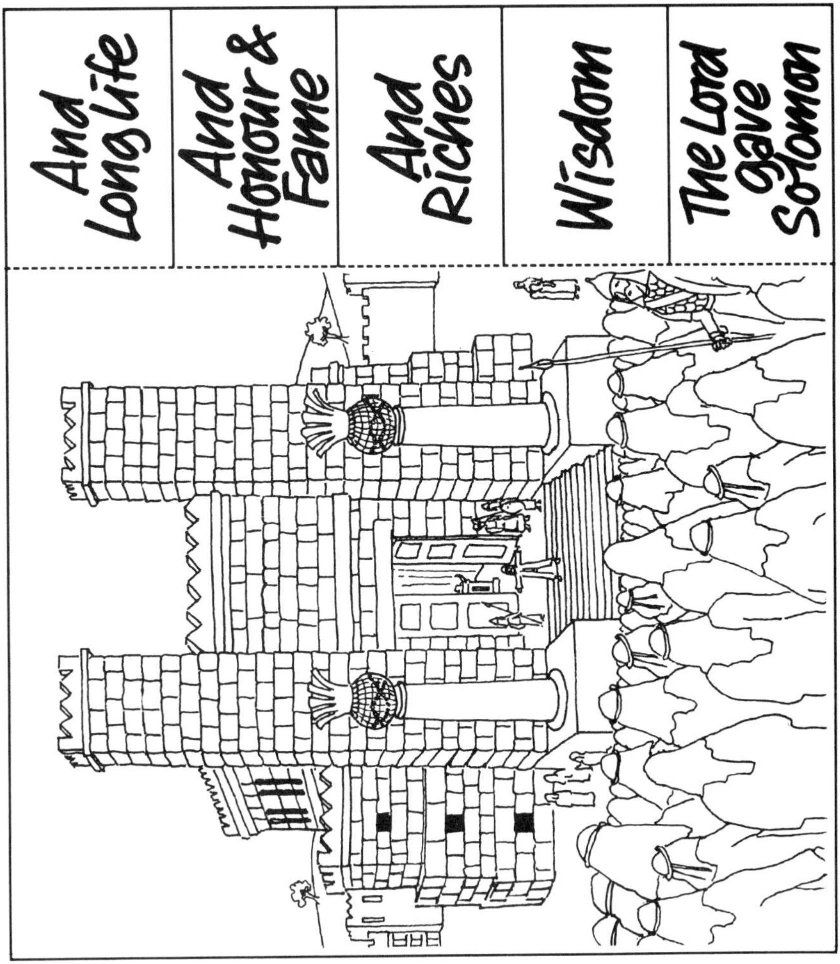

VA 5 – Visual Aid for use with Lesson 111 – 'Solomon – In all his Glory'.

(1 Kings 4.24-25). In addition, Solomon was able to build a great and beautiful dwelling-house for the Lord, in Jerusalem. (More details of this will be given in next week's lesson.)

A message for us from the Queen of Sheba *(1 Kings 10.1-13; Luke 11.31).* As the lesson draws to a close, stir the children's interest with a surprising warning issued by the Lord Jesus Christ. It is this: on the day of judgement they may be condemned by the Queen of Sheba! How might this come about, and why? What has the Queen of Sheba to do with a person of the late twentieth century? Can they solve this mystery?

Teach them the simple lesson taught by the Saviour. The Queen of Sheba came from the ends of the earth to hear King Solomon's wisdom. Yet in Sunday School we have an even greater privilege – we can hear the teachings of the King of kings! Do we regard the things we hear with the same respect? She travelled from a far country, through many dangers, loaded with priceless gifts, in order that she might obtain an audience with King Solomon. How carefully do we seek a real audience with our Lord Jesus Christ, Whom we may approach even though we have no gifts and treasures to bring, and no righteousness to earn His attention? How carefully do we follow the plan of salvation – something far greater than Solomon's buildings?

No excuse. 'Beware,' said the Lord Jesus, if we despise and ignore Him, we shall one day stand before the Lord God to answer for our attitude – and the Queen of Sheba will be a witness for the prosecution. We shall have no excuse for our insulting treatment of the Lord of Glory Who humbled Himself that He might become our Saviour. If she could travel so far to hear Solomon, a mere mortal, how much more ought we to listen to God's own Son.

Visual Aid

Use VA 5 (see page 111). Attached to a picture of Solomon's Temple, the words 'wisdom', 'riches', 'honour and fame', and 'long life' feature to highlight the chief points of the lesson. Unfold these as the lesson proceeds.

Solomon's Downfall and Rescue (112)

1 Kings 11

Aim: To demonstrate that the idols of this world 'turn away' our hearts from the Lord, and to present the advice given by Solomon at the end of his life, after he had experienced the bitter fruit of compromise.

Teachers' Introduction

Teachers should read for themselves Solomon's great prayer of dedication *(1 Kings 8.22-61)* and his exhortation to his subjects to devote themselves to the Lord, to walk in His statutes and to keep His commands (v 61). Read the Lord's promises and warnings to him at the beginning of chapter 9. Read also the *Book of Ecclesiastes.* If time is short, the first and last chapters are particularly relevant.

Lesson Outline

Open the lesson by telling the children how Solomon, while a young man, demonstrated his love for the Lord by building the magnificent Temple for which David his father had so richly provided *(1 Chronicles 22.1-5, 14-16)*. Solomon recognised that no building on earth could provide a dwelling-place for God Whom even heaven and the highest heaven could not contain *(1 Kings 8.27)*. Yet he believed that the Lord would hear the prayers of His people there, and forgive them in the many needful circumstances of life. Give some details of the riches dedicated to the Lord's house *(1 Kings 6)*, and remind older classes that the layout of the building taught the same spiritual lessons as the Tabernacle (Lesson 67, *Lessons for Life 2*). The Temple is always associated with the name of Solomon, and its glory reflected on him.

Solomon in later life. Remind the class of the many other magnificent blessings which God heaped upon Solomon. Consider how Solomon possessed the knowledge necessary to handle the vast riches and power which the Lord gave him – the wisdom of God had been penned by him. He knew how important it was to love and fear the Lord before all else *(Proverbs 1.7)*.

Turns away. Yet as the years passed Solomon became less satisfied with a godly life. He did not entirely desert the Lord but he began to divert some of his love to *many strange women.* At first he justified his marriage alliances as important political ties with neighbouring countries. But he shut his eyes to the subtle influence for evil each foreign wife would have. Soon temples to all kinds of foreign gods took their place in the city of Zion. Solomon may have imagined that these would not affect his love for the Lord, but slowly and subtly they *turned away his heart (1 Kings 11.2-4).*

From wisdom to folly. Solomon knew that he owed everything to the Lord. His large and wealthy kingdom had been painstakingly built up and left for him by his father David. It was the Lord Who made his name famous throughout the world. Yet as the years passed, Solomon began to forget this. He began to imagine that he could ignore and insult the Lord and that his kingdom would still hold together by his own wit and wisdom. He now lived for pleasure and the exercise of his great abilities in science, architecture, etc. He disobeyed his own proverbs and became dedicated to his own fulfilment. (The Lord Jesus later gave the warning, *Ye cannot serve God and mammon.*) There are none so foolish as those who imagine they please God when all the time their hearts are divided between Him and the world.

Compromise leads to hardness. Solomon had dispensed with God's way but it soon became evident that his own policies were disastrous. He became a heartless tyrant as he built up the number of his wives and mistresses, not caring for their feelings. Next, he lost the loyalty of his own people who had been terribly overtaxed to pay for his increasing extravagance (his lavish finery, his royal larder and luxuries from afar). Show the children that the person who tries to please the Lord *and* the world is in danger of forfeiting the blessing of both. As the world's pleasures turn sour on them, they then find it very hard and difficult to return to the Lord, though sometimes they may long to do so.

Hardness leads to destruction. Finally the Lord pronounced His sentence upon Solomon's pride, selfishness and idolatry. He decreed that his kingdom would soon be divided, and just a small section would remain for his descendants to rule over, and this would be preserved for David's sake, not his *(1 Kings 11.12).*

Ask the children if they are like Solomon. Point out that we all receive great blessings from God and depend on His goodness. Will we become proud like Solomon, as though we had created ourselves and owed nothing to God? Will we grow selfish and hard like him, caring nothing for the feelings of others? Will we forfeit a place in Heaven and have little on earth to show for it?

Destruction leads to remorse. Picture Solomon in old age as little better than the prodigal son as he sat feeding the pigs. Though still surrounded by the trappings of wealth, Solomon had a sick conscience. There was no joy in his soul. He had been granted opportunities beyond most people's dreams. He had been able to experiment with almost every pleasure, pastime and occupation known to mankind, yet his verdict was, *Vanity of vanities; all is vanity,* which means – everything is futile. None of these things had been able to make him happy or content. His wives, his riches and fame all left a bitter taste in his mouth, and were of no profit to him *(Ecclesiastes 2).* His architectural exploits, his landscaping ventures, his exploits into agriculture and 'antiques' were no more satisfying than his attempts to get pleasure from women, entertainment and other sources of 'fun'. Even his pursuit of wisdom and learning had turned sour on him, as he departed from the Lord.

Solomon writes to young people. However, Solomon came back to the Lord. Imagine him taking up his pen again, inspired by the Holy Spirit. This time he wrote sorrowfully of the sad and bitter lessons learned from his days of sin. As he reached the end of his writing, he appealed to young people – *Remember now thy Creator in the days of thy youth.* And – *Walk in the ways of thine heart, and in the sight of thine eyes: but know thou, that for all these things God will bring thee into judgment (Ecclesiastes 12.1; 11.9).*

The Lord rescues Solomon. We can, therefore, assume that the Lord, with great love and mercy, reached out to Solomon in his closing years and came to his rescue (as the father had come a great way to meet and embrace his prodigal son, *Luke 15*). Solomon no doubt returned to the Temple to pray to the Lord – 'I have sinned, I have done amiss, and have dealt wickedly' – words which he had used many years before at the dedication of the Temple *(2 Chronicles 6.37).*

Urge your class to take the priceless counsel of the wisest man in history second to the Lord Jesus Christ. They will never have the wealth, royal status or opportunities that Solomon had at his disposal, when he tried to get happiness from life *without God.* Next time they are tempted to experiment with godless living, urge them to remember Solomon and let his words ring in their ears. Remind them, too, that the lovingkindness of the Lord is so great that all who return to Him in heartfelt sorrow, trusting in Christ, can still be forgiven and washed from sin as Solomon was.

A greater Person than Solomon. Solomon has always been compared and contrasted with his great descendant, the Lord Jesus Christ. Here are two contrasts between Solomon, and his greater Son.

(a) Solomon, inspired by God, *said* many wise words, but he did not always keep them himself, as we have seen. But the Lord Jesus, though tempted in every way like us, never failed. He was without sin.

(b) Solomon enjoyed great wealth and honour, but sometimes at the expense of his subjects. The Lord Jesus, on the other hand, came to give even His life, so that we might benefit from Him.

Bring the lesson to a close by pointing the class to *Psalm 72* which speaks of the king's son and describes aspects of Solomon's reign, but it is clear that the Holy Spirit is speaking of a far greater King than Solomon – the Lord Jesus Christ. James Montgomery's famous hymn renders a portion of the psalm:–

Hail to the Lord's Anointed;
Great David's greater Son!
Hail, in the time appointed,
His reign on earth begun!
He comes to break oppression,
To set the captive free,
To take away transgression,
And rule in equity.

Visual Aid

Refer back to the visual aid prepared for the previous lesson (111).

Series 14
Acts (Part II)
EARLY REACTIONS TO THE APOSTLES' MESSAGE

113 – The Fickle Crowds

The people who cried *Hosanna* were persuaded to change their chant to *Crucify him* only a week later. Peter now challenges them to accept their guilt and seek God's forgiveness. Do we allow others to dictate our thinking about religion, or do we give real attention to the Bible's message?

114 – The Followers of Jesus

The disciples pass through a period of bewilderment, yet the Lord they love does not desert them. If we belong to Him, He will lead us all through life, and surprise us with the purpose or plan He has for our lives.

115 – The Religious Leaders

People who claim to be religious are the worst enemies of the early Christians. Sunday School children who harden their hearts against the Saviour are in danger of becoming His enemies too.

116 – A Searcher from Ethiopia

This man has travelled hundreds of miles to find the truth

about God. On his homeward journey he is still not satisfied until the Lord sends Philip to help him. Neither will we be truly content until we understand the Gospel message and know the Saviour.

117 – A Gentile Seeker

This man is good, prayerful and kind. But he still needs to hear the Gospel, and Peter is sent to preach it to him. Neither should we rest until we have experienced the Holy Spirit's converting work in our hearts.

118 – Revision

Who is the Holy Spirit? What does He do? How does He work? These lessons from the beginning of *Acts* supply the Lord's answer to these important questions.

Teachers' Introduction to the Series

This series of lessons turns our attention to the various reactions of men and women to God's message. Human nature has not changed down the centuries and we will see various types of children mirrored by the groups described in the opening chapters of *Acts*. We can help our class to identify with one or other of the people who either believed or who rejected the preaching of the apostles. Warnings or encouragements will be easy to apply.

This series will involve some setting of the scene – reaching back to the last days of the Gospel narratives. This will help the children to understand that the death and resurrection of the Saviour, far from being the end of the Christian message, marked the beginning of a whole new era. It will also provide an opportunity to teach four important topics, directly from their scriptural setting:–

(1) The true church. As we proceed it will hopefully become obvious to our classes that the early church was very different from any human organisation (and from religious denominations which so often parade as 'the church' of the present day). As teachers we must make a carefully thought-out attempt to redress the wrong ideas so common today. If we can describe, for example, the enthusiasm, the boldness, the power and the genuineness of the apostles, this will discredit the cold formality and hypocrisy which often claims the label of 'Christian' today, as well as the opposite extreme which reduces Christianity to the level of Gospel rock music.

(As teachers, we know how readily the Holy Spirit blessed the efforts of early Christians who gave their time, enthusiasm, possessions and even their lives to the grand objective of soul-winning. This series should be a great incentive to us to raise our own standards.)

(2) The Holy Spirit. Many children have a hazy and distorted idea of the Holy Spirit. When teachers reach the point where the Holy Spirit is described, a long theological explanation should be avoided. A natural and vivid description of the Spirit's work will emerge as this series is taught. We will be able to show that He is not the vague and ghostly presence some children imagine, but a Person of the Godhead, working in great power in the hearts of people.

Today, children will see misguided people who think that the Holy Spirit only works when people give up reverent, thoughtful worship, to become super-informal, 'clap-happy' and even rather wild – hurling their hands into the air, and so on. Such people imagine that the Holy Spirit is more likely to bless them if they worship like primitive pagans, working themselves into mild frenzies! But this is not true. The early Christians were not in the least like that, and the Holy Spirit's power was with them as they took up the awesome task of preaching the Gospel to a hostile world. They faced bitter persecution and angry threats, and the Holy Spirit strengthened them. He gave many of them the ability to speak 'in tongues', but not like those which people speak in today in some churches. The early disciples were given the power to speak *real* languages, and as a result many stubborn, doubting Jews were convinced that Jesus of Nazareth was indeed their Messiah and Saviour.

The first lesson demonstrates the power of the Holy Spirit in bringing about the conversion of thousands of previously antagonistic Jews. Both the first and second lessons show His willingness to bestow unusual gifts and miraculous powers to establish that God was revealing His New Testament Word through the men who had been with the Lord from the earliest days of His work, and who had been taught and trained by Him for this unique task.

The second lesson also underlines the very personal help and comfort which the Spirit gave to those men who were standing up to so much opposition and hostility. His presence enabled them to rejoice and step forward boldly. In the third lesson we see what happens to those who resist the work of the Holy Spirit in their hearts and lives. In the fourth and fifth lessons we cover the necessity of the work of the Holy Spirit before individuals are brought to find the Lord. We also see the way the Spirit superintends or arranges events – directing Peter to visit Cornelius, and then directing Philip to the Ethiopian nobleman. Such events enable us to speak of His wonderful overruling of the Christian's life.

(3) Baptism. Another subject which plays a prominent part in the history of the early church is that of baptism. Some children will think of it as a rite which somehow saves babies from hell. Again, we will not want to indulge in lengthy discourses, but we can describe it as naturally as Luke does in this account. When people had repented of their sin and experienced conversion, they were baptised as a sign to all that their sins had been washed away and that their new life in Christ had begun *(Acts 2.38-41; 8.36-38)*. It was a witness of their death to their old life, and their experience of a new life. It was a public act of obedience, and a pledge to the Lord that they would follow Him. Frequently, in those days, it led to the Jewish community persecuting them, and their own family casting them out.

(4) The Trinity. This brief excursion into *Acts* enables us to introduce children to the doctrine of the Trinity in the most natural and scriptural manner. As we look at these great events we see the role of each member of the Godhead in the salvation of men and women. VA 7 (see page 151) will help teachers to explain the doctrine simply but clearly.

The Fickle Crowds (113)

Many Repent on the Day of Pentecost

Acts 2

Aim: To show the children that they cannot afford to drift along with the crowd when it comes to responding to the claims of the Lord Jesus Christ. Either they must recognise their need to know the Lord, and seek His forgiveness, or on the day of judgement they will stand guilty before Him. Then there will be no more hiding.

Teachers' Introduction

Down the centuries of time there have been many objections to the Christian message, but far and away the greatest number of unbelievers have been people who were just careless and indifferent. On the Day of Pentecost, Peter confronted such a crowd. The contradictory cries of *Hosanna* and *Crucify him* had sounded from their lips in the space of a single week. Peter had to shake these people into seeing the desperate spiritual position which they were in.

In dealing with this subject we shall omit a detailed study of the Day of Pentecost. The preaching which so impressed the unbelieving crowds will be our chief concern. Modern children, though sophisticated in many ways, fall behind previous generations in learning to take up responsibility. With comparative security and much media advertising and peer pressure, they tend to follow thoughtlessly the crowd and the fashion. This lesson should be particularly applicable to their situation.

Lesson Outline

Begin by making the series relevant to the children by pointing out that, from the earliest days of the Gospel being preached, the reaction of people to God's message can be divided into several clear categories. As we learn about each of the main categories we shall ask the question – Which do you fit into? Today, we begin with the response of the crowds who heard the first Gospel message preached by an apostle.

(1) They had cried, 'Hosanna!' Ask the children to remember the occasion when a crowd of people had gathered on the road to Jerusalem, laying palm branches on the road and calling *Hosanna* to Jesus as He rode on a donkey up to the city *(Matthew 21.9)*. Discuss the excitement of being in a crowd (say at a football match). Then describe how a crowd can so easily be swayed.

(2) They had cried, 'Crucify him!' In the same careless way the crowd obeyed the voices of the religious leaders a few days later, crying *Crucify him*. They had seen the miracles of Jesus and heard His teaching, but all rational thought was thrown to the wind in the heat of the moment. It seemed almost fun to be forcing their will on the lordly Pilate. But just as a drunkard wakes up the morning after to discover the damage he has done in his drunken rage, so these crowds soon had to face up to their actions. The drunkard is brought in a sober state to the magistrates' court to face charges of damage to property, fighting and injury of others. In the cold light of day, he realises what he has done. The crowds in Jerusalem a few months later had to be confronted with their terrible action.

Should we just do what the crowd does, without giving any thought to the important things of life, such as our relationship with God? Are we in danger of following the crowd which takes the wide road leading to destruction? Do we trust all that we see and hear on the television, and copy what other children do, without asking whether it is right or wrong?

(3) They listened to Peter. Describe how another crowd gathered on the morning of Pentecost. Many visitors were in Jerusalem for this special Jewish feast-day. But on this day the crowd witnessed an unprecedented spectacle – a number of fishermen and other ordinary people from the north, standing and speaking with great persuasiveness, emphasising points with their hands in a very earnest way. More amazing still, people in the crowd who were visiting Jerusalem from many different countries (as far apart as Egypt, Italy and Persia) could hear these uneducated men speaking fluently in *their* languages, a remarkable miracle. Those determined to be cynical could

Use this question mark as a template and cut five out of stiff card. Write 'Are you like...' on the top. Prepare ten smaller cards with the wording as shown, and as the series proceeds place the appropriate cards on to the question mark.

The drawings opposite are the 'dots' at the base of the question mark.

2 The Followers of Jesus	Devoted Doubting Assured
3 The Religious Leaders	Hateful Stubborn Guilty
4 The Ethiopian	Reading Bible Asking Converted
5 Cornelius	Earnest Obedient Saved

VA 6 – Visual Aid for use with lessons on 'Early Reactions to the Apostles' Message'.

1

2

3

4

5

For use with 'question mark' visual aids opposite.

(These pictures feature in the Bible Learning Course sheets – see page 252.)

only murmur that they must be drunk, but the majority were so shaken by this extraordinary phenomenon that they were ready to listen and learn.

Before long, Peter called the crowd to order, and silence descended as everyone listened for his explanation of these strange events. He reminded them of Jesus of Nazareth and His recent crucifixion. Describe how many must have felt as they remembered the spectacle of Jesus dying like a criminal on the cross as a result of their jeers and demands. They remembered the fear which had beset them as darkness descended for several hours over the city of Jerusalem before His body was taken down and buried. Then rumours had circulated that some had seen Jesus risen from the dead. Now they listened to Peter, as they had never listened to anyone before. Do we listen to this message?

(4) They were pierced to the heart. Explain how Peter powerfully confronted them with their wickedness and wilful ignorance. They should have known from the miracles and teaching of the Lord that He was truly God's Messiah, promised to their nation for hundreds of years by prophets whose writings they had learned from childhood. Imagine the fear and shame of the crowd as Peter showed them that this very Saviour had been handed over to Pilate and crucified – by their demands! If they still had any doubt at all that Jesus Christ was the Son of God, God had rebuked it by raising Him from the dead. This Jesus was now seated at the right hand of God, and it was He Who had sent His Holy Spirit to enable the disciples to preach and speak in languages they had never learned. *Therefore,* said Peter to the crowd, *let all the house of Israel know assuredly, that God hath made that same Jesus, whom ye have crucified, both Lord and Christ (Acts 2.36).*

Help the class to appreciate how these people felt. Like people waking from a strange dream to face the reality of day, the truth now hit them. They had acted like thoughtless fools on the spur of the moment, but now they had to face the facts. They had wickedly crucified the Messiah sent by God, the One so long awaited by their nation.

Most children have experienced remorse, longing and wishing they had not got involved in behaviour which later they recognised to be wrong and inexcusable. Help your class to associate this with the feelings of the crowd on the morning of Pentecost. Perhaps they feel relieved that they were not in that crowd. But in a way they are just the same. How often children go along with what everyone else is doing, without thinking! How easy it is to say one week that we believe in God, and the next week to join the team going off to play football on Sundays! God holds us accountable for all we do, and especially for our attitude to the Saviour.

(5) They asked, 'What shall we do?' As Peter's words sank into the minds of the crowd their consciences were pricked and they cried out, *Men and brethren, what shall we do?*, and he urged them to repent. They had to drop all excuses and fully admit that they were fickle and guilty of great sin. Their only hope lay in seeking forgiveness from the Saviour they had so spitefully treated. If they were in earnest they would obey His command. They must leave behind their old, thoughtless way of going on, and seek a new life which God would give to them. For many this would mean real trouble from the enemies of the Lord. They would have to nail their colours firmly to the mast and join the ridiculed band of believers, who loved the Lord Jesus Christ. Many would be cut off from their families, others arrested and imprisoned. But they would know the Lord and His forgiveness and peace.

What should we do? Explain to your class that becoming a Christian today is just as great a turn-about. We too must repent of our sin. We have to realise that it was our sins which made it necessary for God's Holy One to be humiliated and crucified. When He was hung on the cross, all the sins of His people were placed upon Him, and He bore the punishment for each one. We have to be deeply sorry for all the pain and agony that the Saviour bore for us. We know what it is to be grateful to a friend who gives us a comparatively small gift. Have we ever been overwhelmed at the thought that the King of Heaven should willingly suffer for our sins in order that we, poor sinners, might be saved and given a place in Heaven?

It goes without saying that if we really understand this, there will be nothing that we would not do for the Lord. He has bought our salvation, and now we belong to Him. We shall no longer be ashamed to be numbered amongst His children and to stand boldly for Him wherever we may be – at home, or at school. A shop which passes into new hands often displays the sign, 'Under new management'. Similarly when we belong to the Lord, we cannot keep it a secret.

(6) They experienced God's converting power. Many of the crowd at Pentecost must have wondered how they would manage to take such a bold step. They trembled to think what lay ahead. But Peter gave them this assurance, that just as he had turned from being a cowardly denier of the Lord to being a brave preacher because of the new attitude given him by the Holy Spirit, so they would also be given the strength and courage to stand. It is God's promised gift to all His people.

Are there children here who believe what we tell them, but they are afraid to turn to the Lord? Peter said that day, that the promise was not only for people assembled there, but for their children *afar off.* In other words, God's promise is for all ages. If the Lord calls, He also enables. If He pricks our hearts, He also has the power to make us into His children and make it possible for us to serve Him to the end of life's journey.

Close the lesson on a note of encouragement, by telling how the Holy Spirit worked powerfully in the hearts of about 3,000 that day. Bravely they made a public and open profession of their repentance and faith in the Saviour (as they were baptised). Their doubts and fears were replaced by a great sense of privilege at being included with the Lord's people. Gladly they met together to praise God, read His Word and pray. They even sold their unnecessary possessions and shared the proceeds with those in need, a step which children will particularly recognise as a very practical demonstration of their change of heart. Assure your class that God's Holy Spirit still loves to convert men and women, boys and girls and bring them into the kingdom of God's dear Son. Express your desire that members of your class will soon be added to the number.

Visual Aid

Use VA 6 (see pages 124-125) throughout the series.

The Followers of Jesus (114)

Assured and Empowered

Acts 3 – 4.23; 5.12-32

Aim: To help children appreciate the importance and influence of the Day of Pentecost, and to give particular encouragement to young believers.

Teachers' Introduction

The Lord Jesus Christ when referring to young children said, *Of such is the kingdom of God.* Many adults describe how they enjoyed a walk with the Saviour in childhood, followed by a period of doubting and even backsliding before – in or after teenage – they made a fuller commitment to the Lord. Childhood faith is often challenged as young people develop into the world of more advanced science and education, or into teenage. To such we can give real encouragement and support through the course of this lesson. We can show that the disciples who served the Lord in the early Galilean days, and who were prepared to leave their families and jobs in order to follow Him, later experienced a period of doubt and disappointment at the time of His arrest and crucifixion. They were ready to go back to their fishing businesses. But when the Lord appeared to them as their risen Saviour, answering all their queries and problems, they were assured and devoted to Him once again. We can therefore assure our children that if their relationship to the Lord is genuine, even though they may come up against some bewildering situations, the same Lord will watch over them, intervene in their lives and help them.

Lesson Outline

Remind the class that last week we heard about thousands of

indifferent, easily swayed people who had been guilty of handing their Messiah to Pilate to be crucified, but the Holy Spirit moved in their hearts and brought them to conversion on the Day of Pentecost. This lesson moves on to a new category of people. It tells us about the men who had followed the Lord from the early days of His ministry on earth. Suggest there may be children in the class who have known about the Saviour from a very early age. This lesson will be especially interesting for them.

(1) They left all to follow Jesus. Ask the class if they can remember how the early disciples came to follow Jesus. Remind them of the day when Peter, Andrew, James and John left their fishing boats to follow the Lord. Briefly refer to the days that followed – the crowds, the miracles and the teaching.

(2) They knew days of fear and doubt. Describe the fear that gradually descended on the disciples as Jesus went on to Jerusalem, and the opposition gathered. The Lord had warned them that He must suffer and die, but their mistaken idea that He should reign as an earthly king made it difficult for them to accept these disclosures. Once they arrived in Jerusalem the hostility and hatred of the religious authorities was clear and, for them, frightening. Their fear culminated on the evening of Jesus' arrest. In panic they disappeared from the scene and even Peter denied all knowledge of his Master.

Help the children to enter into the spirit of dismay and bitter disappointment as they saw Jesus dying in apparent helplessness on a Roman cross. A conflict raged within them as they remembered His greatness, power, knowledge and holiness, all of which had convinced them that He was the Messiah. But now they saw Him in a weak and helpless state, dying in agony. What had gone wrong?

(3) They experienced days of joy and anticipation. Next, imagine their surprise followed by joy when they were met by the risen Saviour after His resurrection. Tell how once again Christ patiently explained to them that He had come in order to die and bear away sin *(Luke 24.44-48)*. Describe how He commissioned them with a seemingly impossible task, to preach this Gospel to the whole world. They must have wondered how they, eleven poor, ill-educated, working men, with great opposition arrayed against them, could even begin such a mission. Only Jesus' promise of heavenly power – in the form of the Holy Spirit – made it possible for them to contemplate this enormous task (v 49).

(4) They were filled with the Holy Spirit. Last week we learned how the disciples were filled with the Holy Spirit Who made so much difference to them. We heard how they faced the crowds gathered in Jerusalem without fear, and Peter boldly told them that they had crucified their Lord and Messiah. They discovered that God's Spirit authenticated their words by giving them the power to speak the Gospel in the languages of the many people gathered, just as He had promised many years before through the prophet Joel. Remind the class of the many languages in which their message was heard.

(5) They did miracles in the name of the Lord Jesus. Explain that even more amazing events were to follow. Describe the spontaneous way in which the lame man was healed *(Acts 3.1-11)*, followed by Peter's denial that he himself worked this miracle (v 12). Give his explanation for these events and describe his Gospel call to those who came to investigate (vv 13-26). Read these verses to your class, or summarise them.

(6) They were bitterly opposed. Tell the class of the fury of the religious leaders who, thinking Jesus was dead and finished, learned that His disciples were preaching that He had come back from the dead, and were performing miracles just as He had done. Regardless of the anger of the leaders, Peter became even bolder and accused these people (who only weeks before had terrified him) of being responsible for crucifying God's Son *(Acts 4.1-12)*. On the release of Peter and John, instead of toning down their campaign, the disciples prayed for more boldness to speak God's Word (v 29). Once again God answered their prayer. They felt the very house shake as the

Holy Spirit came again to give them the courage for which they had asked.

God continued to authenticate their preaching by enabling them to do wonders and signs which were reminiscent of those of the Lord Jesus. It was hard for anyone to doubt that they were indeed God's spokesmen. The Jewish crowds who were used to paying great respect to the priests and other religious rulers, now saw clearly that God had appointed these apostles and their followers in *their* place, and that the Church of Jesus Christ (not the Jewish 'church') was now being blessed with the presence of the Lord.

(7) They were put in prison, and released. If there is time, describe how they were thrown into prison, and how on the second occasion this happened they were wonderfully released by an angel *(Acts 5.17-23).* As the court met the following morning, they were found, not behind locked doors, but out in the open, preaching the Gospel again! (v 25.)

(8) Their message went into all the world. Perhaps Peter remembered how Jesus had promised him years before that not even the gates of hell could prevail against His kingdom. Explain to your class that in these lessons we can cover only the beginning of these exciting days, but since then the Gospel has been preached throughout the world. What seemed impossible to the disciples was possible with God. Assure the children that God's blessings are not confined to the early disciples. The same God is willing to convert and use us today. How can this happen? Suggest the following steps:–

Steps for us to follow. (a) Obey the call of the Lord, and like the early disciples, leave all to follow Him. This means leaving your old ways and sins and selfish ideas. True conversion will mean that you see Him as the only One Who can save you, and that it is a great privilege to belong to Him.

(b) Never be thrown into doubt or despair when things do not turn out as you want or expect. The devil will try to put many doubts and fears into your mind. All seemed lost to the disciples as Jesus died on the cross but in fact the greatest battle of all time was being won. Learn to trust the Saviour.

(c) Learn from the experience of the disciples that if you are truly converted, then you are a soldier in the Lord's army, with a new purpose in life. He will shape you for a special task, just as He did these disciples. Like a young soldier, prepare yourself for the battle of life. Read your Bible and allow the Lord to speak to you from it day by day. Learn to trust and obey your Saviour. Expect Him to do things through you. Be willing to suffer for Him like the early Christians, then you will know the same supporting power which they enjoyed.

The Religious Leaders (115)

Continuing Hostility for the Early Church

Acts 5.17 – 8.4

Aim: To demonstrate the stubborn pride of the hard hearts of the religious leaders in the face of God's wonders occurring around them. To warn the children against similar hardness.

Teachers' Introduction

We shall see in this lesson that the category of people who showed bitter hostility to the early church were *religious* people. This is not what our children might expect. Yet the martyr Stephen in his dying sermon said that it was often the case *(Acts 7.52)*. He accused the Jewish leaders of being stiff-necked, proud, stubborn, and of resisting the Holy Ghost. This is where the lesson becomes particularly relevant to our classes. As Sunday School attenders they may well be classed as 'religious'. They, like the Jewish leaders of those days, are in great danger of hardening their hearts to the message!

As a by-product of this lesson, it will help some of the older children to understand that religious leaders have frequently been suspect. They should therefore not be surprised if the leaders of present-day religion seem to deny and disgrace the message and character of the Gospel as we see it in the Bible.

Lesson Outline

We have heard how thousands of people were converted.

Down the centuries of time, millions have been added to their number. But there have always been those who have refused the Saviour. We ourselves know so many friends and relatives who want nothing to do with Christianity. Why is this? What will become of them? Is it possible that children in our class could turn against the Saviour and in later years be numbered among His enemies? How did people at the time of Christ grow to be His bitter enemies, and remain so? Let us trace their unbelief as it developed and hardened, so that we can learn from their mistakes.

(1) They hardened their hearts. Remind the class how the religious leaders had hated the Lord Jesus. They had witnessed the great miracles which He did and heard His amazing teaching, but because He did not belong to their 'club' and did not respect and admire them, their proud, stubborn hearts developed a hate and detestation for Him. Too often He had exposed their hypocrisy and fraudulent ways *(Luke 19.45-46)*. For years they had been anxious to get rid of Him *(Luke 6.11)*.

(2) They were determined to destroy Jesus. Failing to discredit Him in the eyes of the people, they schemed His murder, but without success *(Mark 3.6)*. It was not until He came to Jerusalem that their plans really began to take shape. Having paid Judas to lead them by dead of night to his Teacher, they were able to arrest Jesus away from the public gaze. Before long, they gained the Roman governor's consent and crucified Him outside the walls of Jerusalem. Their relief was great.

(3) They buried Him. They thought that He would never again draw the crowds away from them or humiliate them in the eyes of the people. His dead body was removed to a garden tomb where a heavy stone concealed the entrance. And just to be certain, they persuaded Pilate to set a guard of soldiers around the tomb. Jesus was dead and buried. Now they could sleep in peace.

(4) They refused to believe He had risen. Imagine the shock for these men when the news began to spread that Jesus had risen from the dead. His body had disappeared. However, they bribed the guard to say that the body had been stolen *(Matthew 28.11-15)*. An uncomfortable number of Jesus' followers claimed to have seen Him risen from the dead – up to five hundred. But the leaders hoped this would be only a temporary setback for them. Soon this 'madness' would pass over, they thought! They imagined it would be easy to intimidate these uneducated fishermen from Galilee, who had been terrified whilst Jesus was on trial. But this was not to be.

On the day that the Jews flocked to Jerusalem for the religious feast of Pentecost (when the leaders thought they would get back their authority once and for all), the crowds witnessed the powerful preaching and miraculous languages of the disciples. The cowardly disciples of Jesus had suddenly undergone a transformation of character. Instead of keeping a low profile, they appeared in public and addressed the crowds with extreme boldness, accusing them of having crucified God's Son, their Messiah, and urging them to repent. Thousands were affected. Events were proving daily that the leaders had judged wrongly.

(5) They remained unmoved. It might even have been hoped that all these events would have persuaded the priests and other leaders that they were wrong, and that Jesus was indeed the Saviour, the promised Messiah. Though it might break their hearts and for ever damage their pride, they would have been far better off seeking forgiveness of their sins as Peter showed them *(Acts 5.31)* rather than find themselves fighting against God (v 39). But, instead of believing, they hardened their hearts even more, and before long began to persecute the early Christians.

Ask the children if they could imagine themselves following in the steps of these men. Warn them that outright hostility to Jesus always begins in a small way. It begins when we show indifference to the call of the Saviour. We hear the invitation of the Lord, and we begin to see our need of forgiveness, but we delay. As the weeks go by the message affects us less and less and we begin to justify our apathy. Gradually we will leave off church-going. Years later, we may come to despise all that we once heard, and then openly reject the message of Christ. We may turn out to be hurting the Lord's people as the priests did. Teachers may like to quote some examples.

(6) Their opposition grew. Briefly review how the persecution increased:–

(a) *Acts 4.1-18.* Following the healing of the lame man by Peter and John the whole Jewish council met and instructed the disciples to stop their teaching and preaching.

(b) *Acts 5.17-18, 40.* They imprisoned the apostles, beat them and forbade them to speak in the name of Jesus.

(c) *Acts 7.54-58.* They were enraged by Stephen because he told them that they were no better than their ancestors who had fought against God's prophets. They cast him out of the city and stoned him to death.

(d) *Acts 8.1, 3.* They began a large-scale persecution of Christians so that many had to leave Jerusalem. Any Christians caught were arrested and committed to prison.

(7) They faced God's judgement. Ask the class if all this put an end to the work of God. Did it prevent the Gospel spreading? Did it frighten others so that no more were converted? Of course not! In fact it meant that the Gospel was taken to many more areas and Christians became even bolder – if time, *Acts 5.27-32* may be read. It was the priests and scribes who were frustrated! Eventually they died, to be judged by God. They went to hell in the full and dreadful knowledge that they had not only helped to crucify the Messiah, but had refused all His gracious offers of forgiveness. They had also insulted the Holy Spirit Who worked such miracles before their very eyes, in order to remove any reasonable doubts.

An example of God's mercy – even to a bitter enemy. Suppose we can see that our behaviour has often been like that of the priests and scribes. Is there any hope left? Can God forgive those who have fought against Him, His message and His people? Maybe we have attended Sunday School for many years and turned a deaf ear to the things we have heard. Has God any patience for us still? We know by now that the worst sin is to refuse His love. How then could He forgive those who have committed this sin week after week?

We begin to realise the greatness of God's love and mercy only when we realise that He will forgive and convert us even when we have opposed Him. Without going into details, tell the class that He did this to the chief persecutor of those days – Saul, who watched as Stephen was stoned to death. He later described himself as the 'chief of sinners' and yet God's grace was so mighty that Saul became the greatest Gospel messenger ever. So if children imagine that their case is hopeless, let them take courage and seek the Lord's forgiveness. A life lived resisting the Lord God is a life doomed to failure. Who can stand against God Who made Heaven and earth and sea? Even if the kings and rulers of the earth were gathered together against the Lord and against His Christ, they would have no success *(Acts 4.24-28)*.

Visual Aid

A piece of soft, fresh bread, contrasted with a hard, stale slice will vividly portray the process of hardening which can take place in the heart.

A Searcher from Ethiopia (116)

The Ethiopian Chancellor

Acts 8.26-39

Aim: To show from this remarkable account, that all true Christians were formerly far off from God, and have been brought near by the blood of Christ *(Ephesians 2.13)*. To challenge the class by asking if they have experienced such a conversion in their own lives.

Teachers' Introduction

This lesson should greatly encourage us. It describes the way by which a *seeker* came to the Saviour, and one from outside the Jewish world. As Sunday School teachers we have the privilege of explaining the Gospel message to many children who come from unbelieving homes yet who, under the Holy Spirit, become anxious to know Christ. We pray that the Lord will enable us to take up Philip's role to them.

Lesson Outline

Introduction. In recent weeks we have learned about three groups of people and examined their reactions to the message of the Gospel. Today we are going to hear of the conversion of a wealthy, powerful nobleman who was a *seeker.* (Is this the category we are in?) *Acts 8* tells us how a distinguished visitor from Ethiopia came to seek the Lord.

Far off. This man was converted from *far off* in many senses. Teachers may like to represent these in diagrammatic form:–

(a) The barrier of geography. Explain that this man had come to Jerusalem from Ethiopia, south of Egypt. (Check your Bible atlas for biblical Ethiopia, which was much further north than the Ethiopia of today.) So far we have been learning about people who lived in or near Jerusalem. Later the Gospel was preached in Asia, Greece and Rome, but this is a record of a conversion from Africa, to the south. This nobleman may have been one of the first black Christians.

(b) The barrier of history. The only historical tie between God's people and the Ethiopians went back to the days of the Queen of Sheba who visited King Solomon, but that was almost a thousand years before the time our lesson begins.

(c) The barrier of race and culture. The Gospel first spread amongst the peoples of the Mediterranean, but the man we shall hear about today was an African, whose national religion was a belief in thousands of spirits which lived in everything – animals, trees and people. Though the Ethiopian was a nobleman, he must have felt very nervous about entering the totally strange world of the Israelites.

(d) The barrier of wealth and power. The early church was mainly composed of ordinary, poor people. Those who had property and possessions had sold them and shared their goods with those in need *(Acts 2.45)*. They lived simply so that all their resources could be spent on spreading the Gospel message. But the subject of our lesson today is a man who managed the treasures of an entire country as chancellor to its ruler (a great queen).

A model for us all. Point out that we are all far off from God before conversion. Everyone needs to find their way back to the one true God Who made each one of us, and Who will one day be our Judge. Stress that the way back to Him never varies. The way of salvation is exactly the same whichever country we live in, whichever period of history we live in and whatever our ethnic origin. The way in which this wealthy African of the first century was converted is of great help to us. The way back to God from the dark paths of sin started for him at Calvary's cross, and so it must be for us all. Apply these points to the class in a practical way.

(1) He faced the facts. Explain that the nobleman must have become dissatisfied with the life he was living. Fame, influence and riches no longer satisfied his soul, and he became tired of his 'view' of life. He ceased to believe in his national gods and came to respect the superior teaching of the Old Testament Scriptures, that there is one God Who made Heaven and earth, a holy, just God, Who oversees the events of this world.

God's power and creation are still plain for all to see. Children today need to abandon the 'pagan' ideas of modern society and come to respect the superior explanation of life given in God's Word. Teachers can explain to older classes that the New Age teachings which are gaining ground (teaching that God is everywhere and that we are all part of Him) are exactly like ancient animistic religions – and proud of the fact. They should not be fooled into thinking these are new ideas.

(2) He set off on a great search. The nobleman of Ethiopia began a great search for the Lord, taking a long and dangerous journey to Israel. Though he had the convenience of a chariot, and attendants, yet his mission to Jerusalem meant leaving behind the comfort and security of the Ethiopian palace. Politicians of every day and age risk the danger of *coups* and back-stabbings during a period of absence. No doubt this was a possibility which the nobleman had to consider as he set out from Queen Candace's court. Ask the class if they are willing to put their present lives 'in danger' as they set out to seek the Lord. Such a quest will put at risk their selfish plans, and their sins!

(3) He studied the Bible. The nobleman went to find help. He travelled to Jerusalem where he knew the Jews worshipped the true God. He read their Scriptures diligently. He began to understand that God is a God of lovingkindness Who will not overlook sin but Who provides a way of forgiveness for all who look to Him. He was prepared humbly to ask for help and advice from Philip confessing that, left to himself, he could not understand the Bible.

We too must be prepared to seek help. The most brilliant mind has to recognise that he (or she) must become like a little child, humble and willing to learn, before he can see the kingdom of Heaven. Do you listen to your Sunday School teacher? The Lord Jesus promised spiritual treasures and understanding for those who listen humbly. If the mighty chancellor from Ethiopia was prepared to humble himself, why shouldn't we?

(4) He was found by the Lord. Describe the way in which the Lord crowned the Ethiopian's efforts. The prodigal son was met by his father while he was *yet a great way off.* The Lord calls us to return to Him but we can depend on Him to come and meet us. The nobleman would never have been converted had the Lord not sent Philip to help him.

Explain the strange setting for Philip's sermon in a luxurious chariot (the Rolls Royce of those days!) parked on the main highway which crossed the Gaza desert. The passage of the Bible which the nobleman was puzzling over was the key to understanding the way of salvation. He believed in God, but how could he know God? He had come from afar, but how could he be made close to God? He had been to Jerusalem but he did not hear anything from the priests which would change his life and bring him to God. He had the Word of God before him, but he did not understand it. Remind the class that they should never be satisfied until they have found the Lord and received His forgiveness for themselves. Attending Sunday School and reading the Bible are to be encouraged. They may put us on the right pathway, but they are not the same as knowing conversion to God for ourselves.

(5) He learned the way of forgiveness. Imagine the Ethiopian's delight as Philip drew up to the chariot and offered help. Immediately the eminent statesman invited the stranger to mount the chariot and guide him into an understanding of the scripture he was reading. Show your class the verses from *Isaiah* which were puzzling the Ethiopian. Simply and earnestly Philip unlocked the mysteries of the Bible.

(a) *He was led as a sheep to the slaughter (Acts 8.32;* see also *Isaiah 53.7).* He explained that Isaiah was speaking about the Lord Jesus, Who had come willingly to suffer and die, not for His own sins (for He was the perfect Son of God) but for our sins.

(b) *All we like sheep have gone astray.* Philip would have pointed the Ethiopian nobleman to the previous verse – *All we like sheep have gone astray; we have turned every one to his own way (Isaiah 53.6).* He must realise, however great and rich, that this included him. He must completely identify himself with this verse, admitting his own foolish and sinful ways to the Lord. As prime minister, responsible for the 'exchequer' of his country, he knew full well that when mistakes and errors are made, someone has to foot the bill.

(c) *He was wounded for our transgressions (Isaiah 53.5).* The nobleman soon recognised that his sin could not just be ignored and forgotten. Someone must bear its cost. Philip went on to explain that God had laid on His own dear Son, the Lord Jesus, the sins of all who seek His forgiveness. The Ethiopian was amazed and deeply touched that the Saviour had borne the pain and penalty of sin in this way. Philip told the nobleman much more about the Saviour – how the Old Testament had often prophesied His coming, and how recent events in Jerusalem had fulfilled all these predictions. Christ's death had fitted this prophecy from *Isaiah* exactly. He had been tried before the Roman governor, Pilate, and sentenced to a painful and humiliating crucifixion. Philip and his fellow believers were certain beyond all doubt that Jesus of Nazareth was indeed the promised One. His life matched every detail of these words. Philip had good news for the Ethiopian for the prophet Isaiah had promised that this coming One would extend God's kingdom throughout the world to the *ends of the earth (Isaiah 45.22)*. If only he would look to Christ he too could be saved.

(6) He believed and was converted. At last the chancellor's search was over. Now he could see it all. He believed in the Saviour with all his heart, and even before Philip asked for his response, he proclaimed his wholehearted trust. He wanted immediately to identify himself with the Lord's people. He knew and felt that the Lord had heard his prayer of repentance. He knew that peace had come into his soul. God had touched and changed his life.

(7) He was baptised. Help the children to picture in their minds the chancellor laying aside his robes of office and humbly stepping down with Philip into a nearby pool to be baptised, his retinue of staff watching. Soon Philip was *caught away.* The Ethiopian was not to see him again, but he went on his way rejoicing, knowing that he had found the Lord Who would remain with him for ever.

A final plea. All the lessons in this series show us how important it is to be converted. Have you ever really sought the Lord? Will you return home today without wanting to find Him? Copy the Ethiopian nobleman. Search earnestly and sincerely repent of your sins. Put away your pride and ask God to convert your life, and when you feel sure He has heard you, let your family and closest friends know that Christ is now your Saviour and Lord. Give yourself to the Saviour now and for ever, and if you mean these prayers fully and sincerely, you will experience for certain His answer.

A Gentile Seeker (117)
Cornelius – the Roman Centurion

Acts 10

Aim: To give special help to children who may be seeking the Lord but who cannot be sure that they have found Him, and to show how the Gospel was to be preached to people of all nations – not just Jews.

Teachers' Introduction

At the close of this series where we have noticed various categories of response to the Gospel, we note another earnest seeker, like the Ethiopian nobleman. The conversion experience of the young C. H. Spurgeon provides us with a parallel of both the nobleman and the Roman centurion. Like these, Spurgeon was a God-fearer. He could not rest until he knew the Lord for himself, and had received an assurance that his sins were forgiven. If we bear his experience in mind it may help us to use this lesson effectively.

Lesson Outline

Suggest from the outset that Cornelius could be compared in some important respects with certain children who attend Sunday School regularly. On the surface it may not seem that boys and girls in the twentieth century would have much in common with a Roman army officer of the first century, but just as he had come to believe and respect the God of the Bible, so there may be children in the class who take very seriously the things they hear at Sunday School.

Explain that this lesson teaches us, however, that fearing the Lord and even repenting of sin, is not the same as being certainly saved. Encourage young seekers to listen carefully and never to rest content until they have experienced for themselves the new birth.

(1) He feared God. Describe this Roman army officer, successful and wealthy, resplendent in his uniform, and possessing considerable authority. Explain that he had a real concern to please the one true God, having already turned away from believing in numerous Roman gods and goddesses. He was convinced that the God of the Bible, worshipped by the Jewish people in whose country he had been posted, was the only God.

(2) He was in earnest. Point out that Cornelius not only believed what he read in the Bible and prayed regularly, he also gave many gifts of money to the local, needy Jewish people. He was not a hypocrite, or one just seeking popularity. He was genuinely concerned to help them. The children will appreciate that this is a good test of genuineness, especially in a society, like our own, which is so grabbing and greedy. Ask if they too are willing to show their desire for God by their conduct, by turning away from selfish ways and showing kindness and concern to others in their daily living.

(3) He realised this was not enough. When, to his surprise, an angel appeared to Cornelius in a vision, he was ready to obey the heavenly instruction, and send for Peter. His obedience demonstrated that he was ready to hear and learn more about the way to God. He still needed to know that his sins were forgiven and that he was accepted by the Lord.

(4) He was humble. Help the class to appreciate what an extraordinary event is described here – a rich and powerful senior Roman officer called together his friends and family to take advice from a working class Jew, an ex-fisherman who had received no great education. Cornelius not only welcomed Peter to his villa, but *fell down at his feet, and worshipped him (Acts 10.25)*. Peter had to help him up, assuring the Roman that he, too, was just a man. Soon he was ushered into a large room where he found many people gathered to hear him. Remind the class that however clever and successful people may be in secular life, they must be ready to humble themselves before God, if they are to receive His gift of life and salvation. Are we also ready to acknowledge that, whereas we may be confident and successful at school, we have no hope of finding God unless we depend wholly on His Word to show us the way to Heaven?

Describe two other unusual aspects of this occasion. On the one hand, it was surprising that Peter should find himself preaching to a ruling Roman officer and his associates. On the other hand, at a religious level, it was unheard of for Jews to have dealings with Gentiles. Without going into the details of his vision explain Peter's surprise that he should be sent to preach to a Gentile (a non-Jew). Nothing short of a vision from God could persuade him that this was the right thing to do. Explain very briefly that because Peter had been brought up as a Jew, he shared the false idea of the Jews that God would not bless or save Gentiles. Peter and most early Christians, to that day, still had not grasped that the Lord Jesus had come to save men and women of all nations, as the Bible had promised. The events of this lesson teach us not only the wonder of conversion, but they show us how God convinced Peter and other Jewish Christians that Gentiles could also be saved.

(5) He listened to Peter's message. Peter explained that the Lord had overruled his Jewish error which had made him unwilling to visit Gentiles, and had shown him that God welcomes people of all nationalities who fear Him. Peter was embarrassed to be worshipped by the centurion, but glad to preach the Gospel to such a receptive audience. He told them:–

(a) Jesus of Nazareth (of Whom the centurion must have heard) had been sent by God and had been attested as God's appointed Messiah by His power and miracles. (Peter had seen Him raise the dead, walk on the sea, control the waves, feed a crowd of five thousand with a boy's lunch and heal numerous sick people.)

(b) He had been crucified to bear the punishment of sins for all who seek Him. Three days later God had raised Him from the dead. To this there had been many witnesses, including Peter himself.

(c) God had appointed Him to be Judge of the living and the dead.

(d) All who believe in Him would have their sins forgiven and be brought to know God. They would inherit everlasting life.

The Holy Spirit's work. It was as Peter preached the Lord Jesus Christ and His death for sinners on the cross that the Holy Spirit opened the spiritual eyes of the centurion and his friends. The centurion already feared God; now he saw his Saviour and he trusted his soul to Him. He saw for the first time that however sorry he might have been for his sins, and however hard he had tried to put his life right, yet he could only be saved because of what the Lord Jesus had done for him at Calvary. This knowledge made all the difference. Before he was *seeking* for God, now he had *found* Him.

It is the same for us all. We must all show God that we are in earnest by confessing our sins and leaving them behind, but we shall never be saved until we put our entire trust in Christ Who died to take our punishment. Without Him we could never reach God and we shall never know peace in our hearts and souls.

A special blessing. Finally, describe how on this unusual occasion other remarkable blessings were given. Something occurred which had not taken place since the Day of Pentecost again *(Acts 11.15)* – these new (Gentile) Christians began to speak in foreign languages just as Peter and the other apostles had done years before. This surprised Peter, but soon it convinced him that the Lord intended to save many Gentiles. If they, too, had received this miraculous gift of the Holy Spirit, and *repentance unto life (Acts 11.18)*, then God was saying that Jewish Christians should receive these Gentiles as fellow members of the church.

A point of interest for older classes. Teachers of older classes can tell how before very long many Gentiles believed. As the apostles went out into the world their message was received with joy by Asians, Europeans and Africans. Often it was their Jewish contemporaries who were reluctant to listen – even hostile. (We saw this in Series 4 on *Acts, Lessons for Life 1.*) Since those days the Gospel has spread throughout the world so that there are those in every land and nation who believe in the Lord Jesus Christ, the vast majority until now being Gentiles, though always a small number of Jews are included.

Emphasise the point, of importance to young people today, that the whole earth is the Lord's and *all* that dwell in it *(Psalm 24.1)*. The Christian Gospel calls all people everywhere to repent and turn to God *(Acts 17.30)*. Those who do so find themselves joined together in Christ Jesus, whatever their race or creed. Their loyalty and affinity is to other believers and, like these apostles, persecution and hostility most often comes from unbelievers of their own race. In other words, Christianity does not belong to any particular nation or race, but to *all*. The British missionaries of the eighteenth and nineteenth centuries faced great opposition from their own fellow-countrymen (eg: the British government outlawed the missionary William Carey in India, and later the European opium traders opposed Hudson Taylor in China, and British rum traders held back the work of the missionaries in Nigeria).

Finally, ask the class if they have experienced for themselves the work of God's Spirit in their lives. He no longer gives the gift of speaking foreign languages (a special token granted to help the Jews of those early days of the church to make big readjustments in their ways and thinking) but He still points the hearts and minds of people to the Saviour, and He still proves that people are converted by giving them new hearts and new characters.

Visual Aid

This simple visual aid aims to help children who may be confused by the terms *Jew, Gentile* and *Christian*. Draw two circles. Divide the first in half with a vertical line. In the left half print the word 'Jews', in the right print 'Gentiles'. Divide the second circle into four segments, and print one of the following words in each. Top left: 'Jews'; lower left: 'Jewish Christians'; top right: 'Gentiles'; lower right: 'Gentile Christians'.

Use the first circle to illustrate that before the coming of Christ the world could be divided into two groups – Jews and Gentiles. Use the second circle to show that after Christ's coming there were the four groups shown on the circle. However, the most important division was now between Christians – either converted Jews or Gentiles (shade this half in one colour), and non-Christians – Jews or Gentiles (shade this half in another colour).

Revision (118)

Aim: To revise this short series from *Acts* and, where appropriate, to allow these events to teach the children some facts about the Holy Spirit.

Teachers' Introduction

All revision lessons vary from teacher to teacher. Some teachers, using VA 6 (see pages 124-125), may wish simply to recount the highlights of these lessons and challenge the children by asking which person or group they most closely resemble, eg:

(1) The fickle crowds – are there children who could be labelled thoughtless and gullible? Are they easily swayed by the enemies of God, like the crowds who shouted *Crucify him*? Or are they ready to listen to the Gospel, like those same crowds when they listened to Peter? Are they prepared to admit their guilt, and ask what they should do – like the three thousand on the Day of Pentecost?

(2) The followers of Jesus – are there earnest children who have attended Sunday School for many years but are now encountering many doubts? Remind them of the great events which reassured those disciples – the resurrection of Christ, the coming of the Holy Spirit, the conversion of many thousands, the apostles' amazing ability to speak in languages they had never learned.

(3) The religious leaders – are there children who attend Sunday School in a proud frame of mind, thinking how good they are? Is it possible they could become enemies of God like the chief priests and scribes who imprisoned and threatened Peter and the other apostles?

(4) The searcher from Ethiopia – are there children who read the Bible, attend Sunday School but who do not yet understand that the only way to be forgiven is to believe in the Lord Jesus, Who came to bear the punishment of their sin? Urge them to be persistent like the important visitor from Ethiopia.

Soon the Lord will send them help (as He sent Philip), and they too will want to let others know that they have found the Lord.

(5) Another Gentile seeker – what was unusual about the Roman centurion? Why did he send for Peter? (He feared God, and was humble and open to the Truth.)

Another approach. Other teachers (especially those with older classes) may wish to teach a simple lesson on the person and work of the Holy Spirit – drawn from this series. Children and young people are often puzzled about this subject.

A member of the Trinity. Remind the children that the one almighty God has three parts – not really very difficult for us to believe when we consider how everything around us has various parts which make up a unified whole.

The children will already know of God the Father, and God the Son – the Lord Jesus Christ. Explain the wonderful third person of the Godhead, the Holy Spirit (use VA 7, page 151). Tell how God the Holy Spirit was present and active in the creation *(Genesis 1.2).* He spoke through the Old Testament prophets *(1 Peter 1.10-12).* He came upon the virgin Mary, enabling her to give birth to the Son of God *(Luke 1.35).* He raised the Lord Jesus from the dead *(Romans 8.11).*

His unseen power. Like the wind, He is unseen to human eyes *(John 3.8),* and unrecognised by unbelieving hearts, but His work for and through believers is glorious and powerful. Remind the children that the Lord Jesus had previously told His disciples that He was soon to leave them and return to His Father in Heaven. He had promised to send them His Spirit, Who would help them in His absence. The disciples had been commanded by Christ to take the good news of forgiveness into all the world – a task far beyond their capability unless they received *power from on high (Luke 24.49).* Ask the children where the disciples were told to wait for the coming of the Holy Spirit. Then sketch some aspects of His great work from previous lessons:–

(1) Truth – *He will guide you into all truth (John 16.13).* Help the children to appreciate that one of the disciples' greatest needs was to be guided into God's Truth and inspired to write the New Testament. The message which they were to preach and to write was to be the Lord God's message to the whole world – the only way of salvation. How important it was that it should be *God's* Word, not their own! (Compare it with a life-or-death prescription written by a doctor.)

As Peter faced the crowds on the Day of Pentecost, thousands of Jews were assembled from many parts of the world. What message was he to preach to them? He realised that this first sermon should be God's message and not his own invention. The Holy Spirit, Who had come in power earlier that day, inspired him and the other apostles to declare God's perfect and infallible Gospel to the waiting crowds. The Holy Spirit's gift, enabling Jews from far and wide to hear them speak miraculously in their own languages, assured these visitors that their message was from God.

Soon Peter and the other apostles were to write the books of the New Testament, God's Word, the textbook of Christian belief for all time. (If time permits, show a list of New Testament books so that the children can identify those written by the disciples they know. Explain which apostles wrote the others.) Before the apostle John died, the Bible would be complete and finished. How could the apostles be trusted with matters of such importance? The answer is that the Holy Spirit – the third person of the Godhead – came Himself and guided them into all Truth, as the Saviour had promised. It was the Spirit Who taught them and brought to their remembrance all that the Lord Jesus had said to them *(John 14.26; 16.13)*. However, He was invisible, because He came to glorify the Lord Jesus, not Himself *(John 16.14)*.

Point out to the class that because it was the Holy Spirit's work to guide those who wrote down the Bible, it must be infallible. We need never look elsewhere for Truth. How grateful we should be for this unchanging Book of God. Remind the children that people change their views. Even some church leaders have been corrupted and cannot be trusted. How wonderful that the Truth of God was written down once and for all, and its

Draw up a card as shown, cut two slots to fold the pictures up, concealing them. Write the words on the reverse of flaps. Unfold as you proceed.

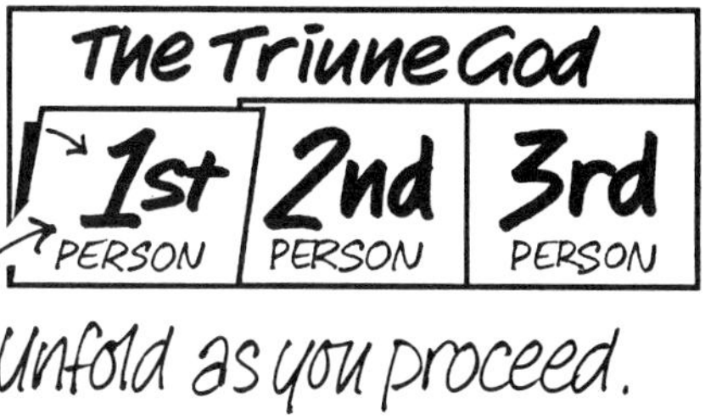

Top: VA 8 – For use with Lesson 121. Bottom: VA 7 – For use with Lesson 118.

truthfulness and content were guaranteed and sealed by the Holy Spirit. When we want to know about the great matters of life and death, and how to find and know God, we can turn to its pages and be shown the right way. Urge the children to always stay with a Sunday School or church which has, as its only rule and guide, God's holy Word.

(2) Witnesses – *After that the Holy Ghost is come upon you: and ye shall be witnesses unto me (Acts 1.8).* Another promise which the Lord Jesus made about the Holy Spirit was that He would enable the disciples to be His witnesses 'both in Jerusalem, and in all Judea and Samaria, and even to the remotest parts of the earth'. Ask the class to recall from these lessons how such a seemingly impossible promise came true.

(a) The crowds from many countries heard Peter and the other disciples on the Day of Pentecost *(Acts 2.9-11).*

(b) As the persecution set in, Christians were scattered throughout Judea and Samaria *(Acts 8.1)*, and further afield as the days went by.

(c) Distinguished and influential people from as far away as Rome and Ethiopia (to name the two we have learned about in this series) were converted and returned to their own lands with the good news.

Remind the class of how cowardly and frightened Peter and the other disciples had been. Only a few weeks before Pentecost Peter had denied all knowledge of Jesus to a girl in the high priest's courtyard. Then help them to contrast this cowardice with his new courage. How bravely he addressed the crowds! How fearlessly he pointed out their treachery towards their Messiah! How firmly he appealed to them to repent and be baptised for the forgiveness of their sin! How brave he was to tell the Jewish council that he would rather obey God than man, when threatened with imprisonment and even death! What could account for this?

Explain to the class that the apostles knew the answer, for when they were in particular danger and under the greatest threat, they prayed for the Holy Spirit's help to enable them to go on speaking His Word with all boldness *(Acts 4.29)*, and the result was that the place in which they prayed was shaken and they were filled with the Holy Spirit. They knew it was He Who gave them this great boldness.

Ask young believers in your class if *they* witness bravely to friends and family about the Saviour. Perhaps they are frightened as Peter was. Perhaps they are embarrassed to explain how much the Lord Jesus means to them. Remind them that if they ask the Lord's help, they too will receive the mighty help of the Holy Spirit Who will give them courage and ability.

(3) Convict – *He will reprove . . . of sin, and of righteousness, and of judgment (John 16.8).* The last point of this revision lesson centres on this promise of the Lord Jesus, that it would be the Holy Spirit's special work to convert sinners. Remind the class of the remarkable examples of this power as recorded in the early chapters of *Acts.* Mention the hostile crowds who were melted down by Peter's words. They acknowledged their guilt in nailing God's Christ to the cross. Luke describes how they were *pricked in their heart,* crying out, *Men and brethren, what shall we do?* Then he reports that three thousand repented and were baptised. The change that came about in their lives was dramatic, as we learned. From then on they loved to be at prayer-meetings and Bible studies led by the apostles. Rich Christians sold their possessions and shared the proceeds with those less well off. Luke uses four terms to describe their state – gladness, sincerity, praising, and added to.

Remind the class that this is still the work of the Holy Spirit and has been ever since. He alone converts sinful people like us, and brings us to know God. He alone makes us see how guilty and sinful we are. He teaches us that it was our sins that nailed the Lord Jesus to the cross. He pierces our hearts and pricks our consciences so that we desire to be forgiven and reconciled to God. He makes us willing to believe and obey God's Word. Before long, those around begin to notice a great difference in us as He breaks down our selfishness and makes us kind and thoughtful to others. Whenever children gather eagerly and regularly to hear the lessons of the Bible and to pray earnestly, then we watch to see the Holy Spirit at work in their hearts.

Encourage the children to welcome the Holy Spirit as the Helper promised by the Lord Jesus. Ask them – Has the Holy Spirit converted you? If not, remember His power to do so. Never despair, thinking that such a child as you could never become a Christian. Nothing is impossible with Him. Show the class how they can pray for His gracious help:–

Holy Spirit, from on high,
Bend on us a pitying eye; . . .
Make us know that Christ alone
Can for human guilt atone.

May we daily grow in grace,
And pursue the heavenly race,
Trained in wisdom, led by love,
Till we reach our home above.

(William Hiley Bathurst)

Series 15
1 and 2 Kings – Elijah and Elisha
SIN AND ITS CURE

119 – Sin – Rejecting God

Ahab the son of Omri did evil in the sight of the Lord above all that were before him. What a terrible epitaph! How did all this begin? Where did it lead? Whilst exercising judgement against Ahab, God shows great kindness and care to those who love Him – and He never changes.

120 – Sin – Playing with Other 'Gods'

On a mountain top the prophet challenges the people of Israel to make up their minds whom they will serve – either Baal or the Lord. He suggests a simple trial so that they can put both gods to the test. Before nightfall the people are convinced, *the Lord, he is the God.* We too must choose between the Lord and the gods of this world. We cannot serve both.

121 – Sin – Wounding the Conscience

Before Elijah has said a word, Ahab knows he has come to cause him trouble! His conscience tells him that God knows the murderous methods used by his wife to satisfy his lust for his neighbour's vineyard. Children, especially, should listen to conscience.

122 – Sin – Suffering a Fatal Disease

A great man urgently searches for a cure for his leprosy, and though the cure involves a humiliating bathe, he is persuaded to take it. The result? He returns home completely healed. Where must we go to have our sins washed away? Where can we find a cure for the fatal disease of sin?

123 – Sin – Meeting Death

The Bible describes us all as *dead in . . . sins.* Is there any hope? This lesson, which describes how the Lord's servant brought a dead boy back to life, shows that there is.

124 – Sin – Going to War with God

An inexplicable intelligence works against the king of Syria. His army is defeated by one man. Instead of facing imprisonment the conquered army enjoys a feast and the result is peace! Finding peace with God is our greatest need.

125 – Sin – Refusing to Believe God's Promises

People literally starving to death are promised food at give-away prices within a day. Too good to be true? Some doubt Elisha's promise but it comes to pass. Do God's promises to forgive us, guide us through life and take us to Heaven, sound too good to believe? How tragic if we were to miss God's blessings because we questioned His power to keep His promises.

126 – Revision

During this series we have learned how sin, like a monster, rears its many heads. Can you remember its chief characteristics? Better still, have you learned the way back to God so clearly illustrated in these lessons?

Teachers' Introduction to the Series

Many children today do not see their need of a Saviour because they have no real sense of sin. Reared and educated in an atheistic society, where no moral absolutes are acknowledged, they are trained to think of sin as an outdated, petty concept associated with religious hypocrites. The new code of conduct says that whatever makes me happy is *right*, whereas any pain inflicted on me, animals, or others, is *wrong*. God's *moral* standards are often ignored. As Sunday School teachers we need wisdom in addressing this problem and in preparing young children for the avalanche of propaganda ahead of them. The Word of God provides an approach which far exceeds our best schemes, approaching the subject in a way children will respect, and which will set them questioning the ideas of this godless age.

As we see Elijah and Elisha confronting the leaders of their age, all notion that sin is petty will be banished. Inward heart-sins will be exposed and condemned as well as the outward sins they lead to. Rejection of God will be shown to be the root sin, which gives rise to all the suffering and pain to be seen in this world. Those who reject the notion and danger of sin will be seen as gullible, foolish and escapist. Our object throughout will be to follow the principle of *Romans 5.20* – where sin abounds, grace abounds all the more. Having shown the children how real, ugly and dangerous sin is, and how much it dwells in each one of us, we shall be able to move to our real objective of pointing them to the Saviour.

Visual Aids

Teachers are encouraged to make and use the visual aid suggested in Lesson 126, throughout the series as well as for the revision lesson when it will be particularly helpful. A map which identifies the chief places and events of the series is also suggested in VA 9 (see page 159).

Sin – Rejecting God (119)
Elijah Confronts Ahab

1 Kings 16.29 – 17.16

Aim: To show that sin is no trivial matter, to warn against its consequences and to recommend the Lord's kindness and forgiveness to all who repent.

Lesson Outline

Introduction. Remind the class that we live in an evil world. Describe how people boast that the extreme immorality of our present society is something quite new. Prior to the 1960s, most people were ashamed of extreme immorality, and acknowledged that such a way of behaving was sinful. But the human race has always been inclined to rebel against God's standards, ever since the Fall of Adam and Eve. Tell of Ahab, who had the great privilege of reigning over Israel – the people who had been protected by God from the days of Abraham, and given the promised land.

A new queen. Ahab was king over this special people, yet he thought nothing of it, and as if to show his contempt for the past, he married a woman who in those days represented the *opposite* of the culture and standards of God's people. By bringing Jezebel, an idolater, with her god and her priests into his palace, Ahab was throwing away everything of value. Jezebel lost no time in trying to pervert the nation of Israel.

A new 'god'. Soon, at every street corner or market square, images and shrines to Baal were erected, followed by 'services' in which evil was flaunted. Dr Pfeiffer tells us, 'The popularity of Baal was doubtless due to his association with fertility in the varied aspects, human, animal and vegetation. The Baal cult was conducted by priests who conducted licentious rites in fields or high places. Wine, oil, first-fruits and the firstlings of flocks were brought to the priests. Dances and ritualistic meals formed part of the ceremony.'

Help the class to see how ridiculous it is for people today to regard themselves as sophisticated, looking back with contempt at generations who worshipped gods of wood, when in fact our present-day newspapers and advertising hoardings bear the closest possible resemblance to the false religions of the past. When modern society rewrites God's rules, and says that *wrong* is *right*, it is doing exactly what those evil religions did.

New ways. Describe how the people of Israel, who not many years before had gone to Jerusalem in a spirit of awe and reverence to worship God in the Temple built by Solomon, now threw all dignity to the wind to dance round the altars bearing hideous statues of Baal. Samaria in 860 BC had much in common with life in the 1990s.

The Israelites did not want to deny completely the God Whom their families had worshipped for centuries, but they

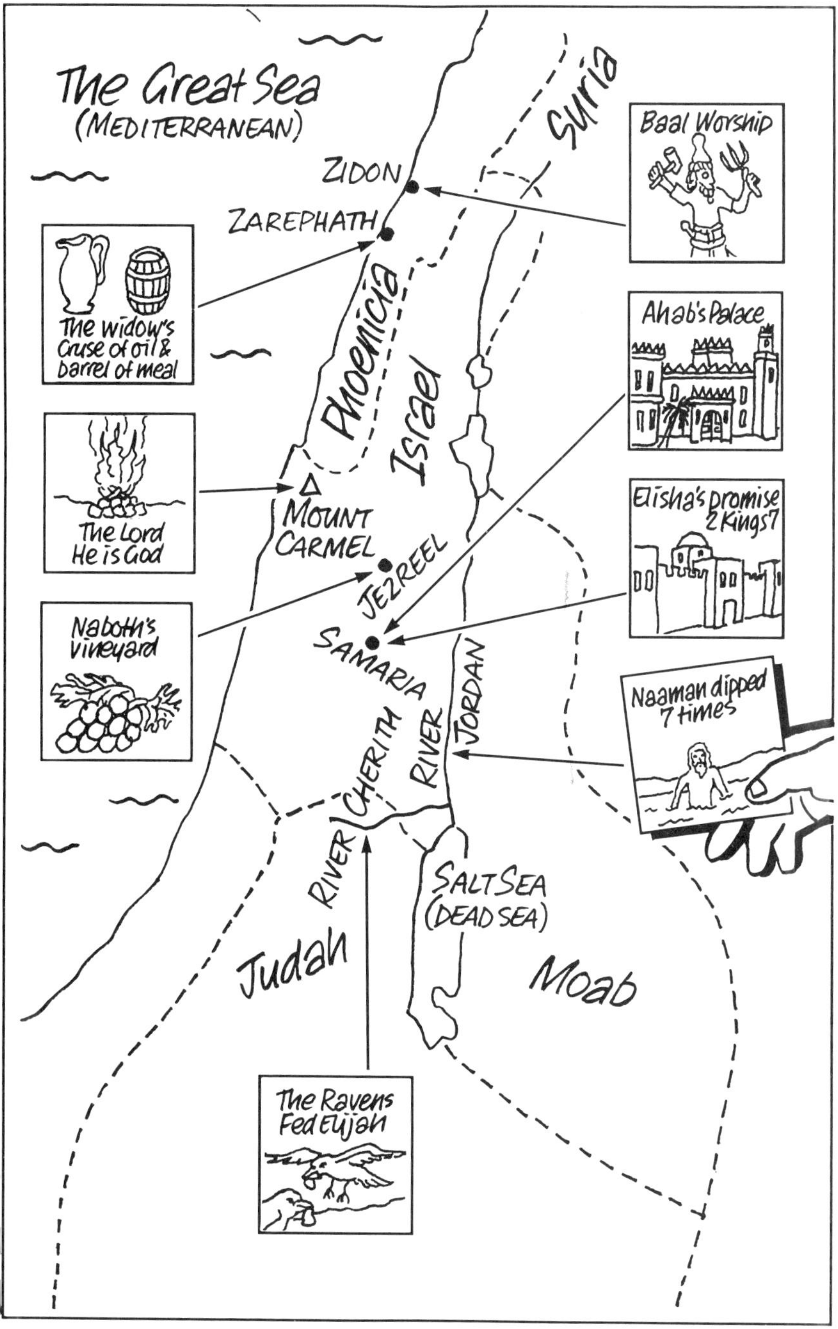

VA 9 – Visual Aid for use with lessons on 'Sin and its Cure'.

enjoyed the new 'freedom' and excitement which was available at the Baal shrines. Sometimes they would pay lip-service to the Lord, but they preferred the new god, for with this new religion there were no commandments, and all the immoral behaviour which had been condemned before was now an approved part of religion! Ahab did not care. He did not mind which god people worshipped, and he himself enjoyed all the sinful pleasures which Baal allowed, even though he knew they were forbidden by the true God.

The 'new gods' of today. A false god is anything we serve or depend on in place of the true God. Ask the children whom they love and serve. Explain that there are still many gods which steal our hearts away from the Lord. Let them make suggestions. Worldly gods promise fun and pleasure. They give the impression that the Lord restricts us, and that to follow Him is too hard and difficult. Children dream of things they want to have; things they can enjoy and boast about. Soon they are encouraged to throw constraint to the wind and enter into the life of the pub and the disco, and to succumb to the beat of evocative music. How easy it is to be carried away by these new things and to forget the God of the Bible, Who alone cares for souls. (Explain to young people that setting the words of Scripture, or the praise of God, to modern, carnal music is a compromise reminiscent of Ahab's attempt to mix the worship of the Lord God, Who is holy, with the worship of Baal.)

God sends a messenger. No one appeared to be worried by the state of affairs in Israel. Even the Lord's priests remained silent. But God had seen all. It grieved Him to see His special people sold over in this fashion, and He determined to warn His people that it would lead to disaster. He chose a man as His messenger, a man at that time unrecognised by the authorities. His name was Elijah.

Elijah's message. Describe how this prophet, fired by a zeal for God's honour and name, bravely and courageously addressed Ahab – *As the Lord God of Israel liveth . . . there shall not be dew nor rain these years, but according to my word (1 Kings 17.1).*

He delivered a brief but catastrophic message! No doubt Ahab shrugged it off at first, but soon he was to learn that he could not ignore God's prophet. The drought began to take its toll. Soon the lack of rain devastated the crops, and famine set in.

God's message to us. Many people today think they can ignore God, and sin to their heart's content without any adverse effects. Even children (brainwashed by television programmes which present a sinful lifestyle as good) do not care whether they please God or not. It just does not seem to matter. Other things seem much more important. But sooner or later we all discover that if we turn away from God and live for sin and self we shall reap bitter consequences.

The results of sin are to be felt on earth – discuss different ways in which they occur – and death (leading to a lost eternity) is the ultimate punishment. God warns all men and women of this. He has sent prophets like Elijah. He has sent His own Son, and today we have the Bible to alert us to our danger. We must not ignore our sin. We cannot stray away from the Lord without getting into trouble, sorrow and sadness. Give some up-to-date examples. We cannot serve sin without losing God's most precious gifts to us. How amazing it is that people will sin away their lives and forfeit all the help of God, and Heaven as well. Are we so foolish as to think that sin is a trivial matter?

God's kindness and care for Elijah. Help the children to see that Elijah was one man against the whole establishment. Ranged against him were Ahab and the princes with their royal riches, Jezebel with her cunning and hate, and all their other followers. Even so, God's servant was better provided for. God promises to supply all His people's needs, if only they will serve and obey Him *(Matthew 6.33)*. He never disappoints or breaks His word. Describe how He sent Elijah, (a) to Cherith where water and meat were available; and (b) to Zarephath.

God's saving kindness to us. Use this second tender incident to illustrate the way in which the Lord is able and willing to bless all those who have come to an end of themselves. Describe the poor widow as she made her way to the city gates to collect a few pieces of firewood to cook her last meal. Picture her sad state of mind as she came to terms with the fact that she was doomed. She had no money left, nor anyone to whom she could turn. She longed to help her boy survive but she had no means. Death seemed inevitable.

Describe how the Lord sent Elijah a hundred miles northward, for He had chosen this poor woman to demonstrate His lovingkindness to them both. Tell how she agreed to fetch the prophet a drink. But when he asked for bread also, she could only admit her terrible condition. Elijah solemnly assured her that as she went to do as he asked, she would discover her needs would be met – and so they were. Tell how her barrel of meal and cruse of oil were replenished by the Lord until the time that He sent rain, and she and her household were saved from famine. This is a magnificent picture of being saved through faith in Christ. We acknowledge to Him all our failure and weakness, and we do just as He tells us – which is to put our faith in His work on Calvary and His power to give us new life.

The picture in a nutshell.

The widow faced disaster. *So do we (spiritually).*

She had no one to help. *No one on earth can save us.*

She could do nothing to save herself and her boy. *Nor can we; we have no righteousness.*

She obeyed God's messenger precisely. *So must we – we must go to Calvary alone.*

She had never seen such a thing happen, but trusted. *So must we trust for new life.*

She was overjoyed to receive the blessing. *We too will be overjoyed and certain once God has saved us and changed us.*

Visual Aid

VA 9 (see page 159) provides a map of Israel at this period with pictures for the key places (eg: a raven at the brook Cherith, a palace at Samaria and a barrel and cruse of oil at Zarephath). Use this map throughout the series.

Sin – Playing with Other 'Gods' (120)
Elijah Challenges the People at Carmel

1 Kings 18

Aim: To describe the events on Mount Carmel so vividly that the children will see the obvious parallels between Elijah's situation and ours. To enable children to see through the harmful gods of today, and return to the living God.

Teachers' Introduction

This lesson must be a favourite with all Sunday School teachers. It is not so well-known as some of the other similarly exciting events recorded in the Bible, yet it is full of the drama, suspense, humour and victory that make it so rewarding to tell. Our aim will be to relate it in such a way that the children begin to see how foolish it is to imagine that they can be Christians and at the same time give their hearts to the carnal gods of today's world.

Lesson Outline

God's warning bites home. Ask the class why God had withdrawn His gift of rain from Israel. Remind them of the way in which Ahab had allowed Jezebel to bring in Baal worship with all its evil and degradation, and how the people had largely forsaken the Lord in favour of this. No doubt Ahab shrugged his shoulders and looked amused when Elijah first announced the coming drought, just as children often pretend not to care when they get into trouble.

Tell them how Ahab's contempt for the prophet and his warning began to change as he and his people began to feel the effects of the drought. Our lesson begins with the pathetic spectacle of King Ahab scouring the countryside for water to provide drink for what remained of his royal stables. Will the Lord have to bring some disaster or great hardship into our lives before we begin to take Him seriously? Very often this has been the case with hardened sinners.

Ahab's guilty conscience. After more than two years of drought the Lord sent Elijah to meet Ahab. Show the children that the king's reaction to Elijah is typical of any sinner's first encounter with God's servants – *Art thou he that troubleth Israel?* (v 17.) Immediately Ahab took the offensive and showered Elijah with abuse. People are the same today! As soon as we mention God to them they bitterly blame Him for allowing wars and suffering, instead of recognising His kindness and provisions and their obligations to Him.

Elijah had to remind Ahab that it was he, and not the Lord, who was ultimately responsible for the trouble which had come upon the land (v 18), and we as Sunday School teachers have to do the same. Explain briefly that the wars and suffering and evils of our present world have come about because men, women and governments deliberately and wilfully rebel against God's wise and just commands, refusing all His help and guidance. Our own griefs and sorrows (even those of children) are often the result of selfish, wrong behaviour.

Elijah's command. Ahab was a desperate man and had no alternative but to put Elijah's requirements into operation (v 20). He was in no position to argue with him! Describe the enormous gathering at Mount Carmel as the people of Israel assembled and were joined by the 450 prophets of Baal, plus 400 prophets of his female counterpart, Asherah. In its desperation the nation was prepared to give a hearing to the Lord's servant.

Elijah's challenge – one God or the other. Tell how Elijah came quickly to the point. His message could not have been more simple, nor more challenging – *How long halt ye between two opinions? if the Lord be God, follow him: but if Baal, then follow him.* Suggest to your class that this is all we ask them to do. We do not ask them to follow a mere theory or religious point of view. Instead we urge them to search for and prove the true and living God Who made the universe and everything in it, including us. If, however, there is no true God, no God as He has revealed Himself in the Bible, then they are free to believe and act as they like.

Older classes may already have come across the multi-faith teaching which says, 'Let us respect all the religions and philosophies of the world *[including atheism]*. One is probably as good as another.' This is just the same as the people of Israel were saying. Today, therefore, we must issue the same challenge as Elijah, pointing out the impossibility of this foolish viewpoint. Either the Lord is God and His Word the Bible is to be believed and obeyed, or else another religion is true and we should worship *its* god. Or perhaps there is no god at all, in which case we can all do as we please. However, it is ridiculous to say that we can believe all these things at the same time!

Elijah's proposal. Since the people remained sullenly silent, unwilling to commit themselves either to the Lord or to Baal, Elijah proposed a test which would demonstrate beyond all doubt which of the two deities was the living God.

(1) Testing Baal. Describe how Elijah gave the prophets of Baal the maximum opportunity to establish their god's credibility, and *they* had the advantage in every way. They had 450 plus a further 400 prophets, whereas Elijah was a lone voice. They were capable of making *far more noise* in their effort to arouse their god to action. They were not required to *douse their altar*, sacrifice and surrounding trench three times with barrels of water as Elijah did when his time came. They had *the support of the king and his queen*, who were bitterly opposed to Elijah and wanted revenge for all the trouble which he had brought upon their land. They also had *the support of the crowds.* They were allowed *a whole day* – from morning to evening to call upon their god.

No answer! Describe the drama of the occasion and the mounting excitement as the Baal prophets desperately called upon their god to act, to no avail. The children will enjoy Elijah's suggestion that they should shout louder, mocking that Baal was out, or busy, or sleeping and must be awakened! But no amount of screaming, or threatening or self-inflicted injuries could bring Baal to life. The fact was that such gods as Baal were not true gods at all. They were carved out of wood and stone, and they were deaf, dumb and blind. They were an insult to the intelligence of the many people who chose to worship them.

(2) Testing our gods. Recommend to the children that they put the gods of evolution, living for self, possessions, sinful pleasures, and so on, to the test. Do they enable us to live better lives? Do they help when we are in trouble and difficulty? Do they make it easier for us to die? Or do they drain us of time and money, and become useless in any hour of great trouble and need? What about the gods of alcohol and fun advertised daily on the television as the recipe for happiness and the givers of manliness or womanliness, etc? Do they work? Or do they destroy? Do they give real pleasure, or simply cover up the pain of sin-sick souls?

Is our society any better for having rejected God and His laws? Are we surrounded by happy, free people since the advent of the gods of permissiveness? Do people enjoy lasting and satisfying relationships, now that young people are encouraged to experiment with sexual relations from an early age? Have violence and fraud died out since the advent of secular, universal education? Ask thought-provoking questions suited to the age of your children.

No help! Suggest that, despite the noise and proud boastings of our atheistic society, the new gods have nothing to boast about, and many horrific crimes to answer for. By teaching children that they are nothing more than highly developed apes, a society has been produced in which people behave like animals (but without even the laws of the animal kingdom). Families are frequently broken up, little children suffer, and crime grows as never before. Not only are people frequently unhappy and afraid, but in their heart of hearts they know that they must one day face God's judgement on their sin.

(3) Testing the Lord. Contrast all the frenzied, but fruitless, activity of the Baal prophets with Elijah's authoritative call, *Come near unto me.* His situation reminds us of the hymn lines:

> *When other helpers fail, and comforts flee,*
> *Help of the helpless, O abide with me.*

The people of Israel had been flirting with Baal, and enjoying the immorality which this religion encouraged, but now they were in trouble. Their animals were dying, their crops were devastated, and their only hope was to turn back to the God Who had been their help in ages past, the God Whom they had betrayed and forsaken. List Elijah's movements, the building of the altar, the laying of the wood and ox pieces and the drenching of the whole with water. Most of all, try to convey to the class the earnestness of his prayer. Help the children imagine how he felt, because so much was at stake. He was anxious, not for his own reputation, but for the glory of God, and the religion of Abraham, Isaac and Jacob which the people had cast aside. He was anxious for the souls of the vast crowd gathered before him – people who had been duped and taken advantage of by the self-seeking prophets of Baal. We can picture him, almost with tears in his eyes, pleading with the Lord in the words of verse 37: *Hear me, O Lord, hear me, that this people may know that thou art the Lord God, and that thou hast turned their heart back again.*

The Lord acts. Elijah was granted a powerful, immediate answer. Verse 38 describes the Lord's response. Silently, but powerfully, the fire fell and consumed all. Point out that it always has been and always will be the case that when God's Spirit moves and works in the hearts of men and women, boys and girls, they are overwhelmed by a sense of awe and respect. *The people . . . fell on their faces: and they said, The Lord, he is the God; the Lord, he is the God.* Noise and confusion belong to those who follow a god of their own imagination, whereas reverence and a quiet and certain assurance is the mark of those who acknowledge the God of Heaven.

The conclusion. Baal is no god. The people realised that Baal worship must no longer co-exist with the worship of the true God. (At that moment they were prepared to hand over the men, who had done so much harm and damage, to Elijah for their just punishment.) Point out that this is the response of all truly converted Christians. They no longer want anything to do with all those habits which have done so much harm to their souls and the souls of their friends. Those who claim to be Christians, yet continue in show business or other compromising positions, simply have not learned anything from Elijah or his God. Even little children can sense that to love the Lord means turning from those things which lead people away from Him. They too must be ready to change the music they listen to, the books they read, the company they keep. How much more so should this be the case for teenagers and adults!

The Lord, he is the God. Close the lesson on the blessings which God immediately bestowed on His repentant people. Within hours Ahab was told that he could safely eat and drink the last items from his royal larder. Rain was on its way. The drought was over. Tell the class of the blessings to be experienced by all who return to the Lord and repent of their sins. Mention the wonderful provision of forgiveness already purchased by the Lord Jesus for His people at Calvary, and the joy of being received back by their heavenly Father. Comment on the great change of conversion, and the powerful help of the Holy Spirit to face the trials of this earthly life. Refer also to the friendship of fellow Christians.

Sin – Wounding the Conscience (121)
Naboth's Vineyard

1 Kings 21; see also 22.34-38; 2 Kings 9.30-37 and Psalm 103.8-18

Aim: Many people today think they can get away with anything, just as Ahab and Jezebel did. This lesson demonstrates that God sees all sin, and that we all need forgiveness.

Teachers' Introduction

Very often the problem in Sunday School teaching today, is that of convincing the children that sin is inexcusable, ugly and harmful. Our permissive society does not recognise the concept of sin, and certainly does not blame *sin* for the suffering and misery which ruins so many lives. This lesson will help us to show the children the *deceitfulness* of sin.

Ahab was persuaded that he could have Naboth's vineyard for nothing, but in fact the *price was high.* Elijah pronounced, *thou hast sold thyself*! Sin is still the same. Like many modern advertisements it parades its attractions without mentioning the selling price. The sting comes in the tail. Sin makes us work very hard before announcing the wages – *death (Romans 6.23).* In an age where many children are reaping the bitter fruit of sin sown by their parents, we shall find a surprising willingness on their part to agree with the great principles of the Bible. Help them discover how honest and true to life the Bible is. It faces us with our sin but it also shows us the way of forgiveness.

Lesson Outline

Describe how the spoilt and lazy Ahab took a fancy to his neighbour's vineyard. Show the children how unnecessary it was for him to pursue this whim, considering that he was a king with vast lands and estates, and, anyway, matters of far greater importance should have been occupying his mind. Use the illustration of a spoilt child who must have a particular toy, or he pouts and frets. Read how Ahab behaved in much the same way *(1 Kings 21.4).* Greed is not only selfish, it is usually utterly unreasonable also.

Two opposite attitudes. (a) 'My kingdom for me.' In explaining why Naboth was not prepared to sell or exchange the vineyard we can show the class Ahab's arrogant attitude to the kingship. He regarded his kingdom as his personal possession to do with as he pleased. He did not recognise any obligation to past or future generations as we saw in our first lesson. Here we see the attitude of our present society perfectly mirrored – and probably our personal attitude. Our present society throws away the benefits of the past generations, leaving very little for future generations. This is most true of *moral* teaching and principles of unselfishness. The destruction of *the family* is one of *the* most selfish acts of vandalism of our present society.

Show the children that as individuals they may have a similar attitude. Do they treat life as if it were their own property? Do they grasp at every benefit available, and lose all sense of obligation to God? Ask the class when they last genuinely thanked God for all His kindness to them, and if they realise that they should use their gifts for Him. We choose to ignore our Benefactor, to insult Him, and to deliberately live in a way which grieves Him. And we imagine we shall 'get away with it'.

(b) A family trust. By contrast, Naboth did not regard the vineyard which he owned as his *personal* property. He had inherited it from his family who had fought and worked for it, and he now held it in trust for another generation. The law of God protected his possession from compulsory purchase by a tyrannical king like Ahab. The attitude of Naboth enraged Ahab, for it stung his own conscience. The thwarted monarch went to his bed, refusing to talk or eat!

Jezebel's scheme – 'I will give you the vineyard.' Jezebel pandered to Ahab's sulking mood. She saw her opportunity and cunningly moved in. In the circumstances she realised that she could perpetrate a cruel murder and buy Ahab's allegiance into the bargain. She assured him that it would be an easy matter for her to obtain the vineyard. Ahab must have known this would not be possible without the use of wrong methods, but he turned a blind eye and waited for the desired object to be given to him. Disgust the children by explaining the terrible means Jezebel used to obtain the land. The conscientious, law-abiding Naboth was put to a cruel and ignominious death just to gratify a greedy man's desire. Jezebel used lies, cruelty and murder (vv 8-14). How many of us will tell lies, blame others and take things which are not ours so that we can have what we want?

Read verse 16 and note Ahab's cool and calm behaviour. This is typical of people after they have sinned. They suppress their consciences and behave as if they were good and honest. Then they try to enjoy the fruit of their wrong behaviour. Remind the class that mothers often suspect wrongdoing when their children behave unusually well and quietly! Ahab appeared calm, yet just below the surface his conscience was inflamed. We see this when Elijah appeared on the scene. The prophet did not speak a word before Ahab burst out – *Hast thou found me, O mine enemy?* (v 20.) How did he know that Elijah had come to rebuke him? This one sentence revealed his guilt.

So it is with men and women, boys and girls. Sometimes when a Sunday School teacher knocks on the door of a child, with a kindly invitation to attend God's house, they will lose their pleasant manner and rush off with all sorts of excuses. Adults, in conversation, will talk quite happily about politics, gardening, and many other things, but if anyone raises the subject of the faith, then all kinds of rude reactions are likely to occur. For all their bravado, people know deep down within them that they have sinned, and that they are running away and hiding from God.

God's justice for Ahab – 'I will bring evil on you.' Ahab and Jezebel imagined they had got away with cheating and killing Naboth, but God had seen, and had passed judgement. Elijah announced that Ahab, who had shown so little respect for his high and noble position as king, would have his privileges swept away (vv 21-22). For him and Jezebel the prophet's announcement was absolutely fair and just – *In the place where dogs licked the blood of Naboth shall dogs lick thy blood, even thine* (v 19). God judges all sin – including that of kings – and His judgements are just.

As we look back across our lives at all the wrong we have done, how we should tremble. Teachers could give examples. How many lies have we told? How often have we cheated in one way or another? How much energy and thought have we spent on getting what we want for ourselves? How unkind and hurtful have we been to others? What punishment would be just and fair for these and all our other sins? No wonder, then, the Bible describes a day when, at the return of the Lord Jesus, many will be terrified and attempt to hide from His wrath *(Revelation 6.16)*. Explain to the children that just because so many people 'get away' with wrongdoing in our lenient and immoral society, it does not mean that they will escape God's justice. Ahab did not, nor will they.

God's grace to Ahab. The last three verses of the chapter provide a wonderful example of grace – a word unfamiliar to modern children but of such importance in their appreciation of the character of God and His Gospel. Ahab was such a reprehensible character that no one will doubt that he deserved the punishment announced by Elijah. Yet at the twelfth hour, after Ahab had displayed some signs of possible remorse, the Lord showed him mercy and postponed judgement. Ahab did not deserve this kindness, yet God granted him mercy.

God's grace to us. Explain that this is what is meant by the Bible word *grace* – God's favour and kindness towards undeserving sinners. We do not deserve God's mercy – we have sinned in so many ways, with inward sins of pride, hatred, deceit, etc, and the sinful deeds mentioned earlier in the lesson. Yet, out of great love, the Lord God has offered a way of escape from the punishment we so justly deserve. Describe the atoning death of Christ on the cross of Calvary and the Gospel promises of pardon and transformation. No wonder the psalmist says: *The Lord is merciful and gracious, slow to anger, and plenteous in mercy (Psalm 103.8).*

Final judgement. Tell the class how Ahab and then Jezebel finally met a just death *(1 Kings 22.37-38; 2 Kings 9.30-37).* Ahab's remorse was only selfish and skin-deep, for he soon returned to his old way of life. Yet there is no kinder, more patient God than the Lord, to those who seek Him.

Visual Aid

VA 8 (see page 151) suggests using an outline of two hands, which will provide a simple but fascinating aspect to this lesson.

Sin – Suffering a Fatal Disease (122)

Naaman's Leprosy Cured

2 Kings 5.1-19

Aim: To use this Old Testament passage to show that sin is like a disease for which there is only one cure. We must forget our pride and go to the cross of Calvary, the only place where sin can be washed away.

Teachers' Introduction

This Old Testament event provides such a perfect Gospel illustration that it should enable us to explain the steps of faith and repentance in a very challenging way.

Lesson Outline

(1) A hideous and fatal disease (v 1). Describe this hero of a man, the kind of person we might all like to be. He was the chief officer in the Syrian army. (We use the more familiar and distinctive *AV* rendering 'Syrian' – rather than the 'Aramean' of modern translations.) The king of Syria liked and appreciated Naaman, his general, very much. He had earned the respect and honour of his nation by winning many victories in battle. Describe how all this was threatened by the four short words – *he was a leper (2 Kings 5.1).*

Explain that in those days this disease was very disfiguring and disabling and eventually fatal. In the months or years which led up to death, instead of drawing out sympathy, it would have caused Naaman's family and friends to feel repulsed by him as his body literally rotted away, and to avoid him. Because leprosy was infectious, sufferers were sent away from the rest of society. In Israel they were called *unclean.* Naaman would inevitably fall from power and esteem and would soon be an outcast.

Show how similar the disease of sin is. It attacks all classes of people, rich as well as poor, highly educated and very simple, young and old, and successful people as well as failures. Its symptoms are so like biblical leprosy. It gradually spreads and affects every part of us – our desires and thoughts, and our will. It steadily rots away our character. Worst of all, it makes us unclean and revolting in God's sight, and means that we must be outlawed from His presence now and in eternity. In other words the disease of sin leads to *eternal* death.

(2) An urgent search (vv 2-5). Describe how a man like Naaman must have searched for a cure. He knew he had only a short time before he would have to lose his post, leave his family, and abandon all the joys of life. Obviously he would have paid the best doctors to help, but all to no avail. So desperate was he that when a little captive Israelite maid offered a suggestion, he was willing to take it very seriously. Encourage the class to take the matter of their sin just as seriously. Show how mad it is to be complacent over such a killer-disease.

(3) The wrong 'doctor' (vv 6-7). Naaman was so ready to grasp at the possibility of a cure that he did not listen carefully enough to the advice of the little maid, and instead of going to see the prophet of Israel, he went to the king of Israel. He (and the king of Syria) had assumed that if any hope of a cure existed in Israel, it would be found in the palace. So Naaman set off laden with gifts and a letter for the king of Israel. How stunned he must have been when he found that these only enraged the monarch and led to fear of war. Explain that many people encounter the same problem when they seek a cure for sin. They imagine that they can pay for forgiveness by doing some good. The more they pay in good works, the more they expect to receive from God, just as some people expect more effective cures from expensive private doctors. But the Bible dismisses our best deeds as *filthy rags* and insists that the only Physician Who can cure sin is the Saviour.

(4) Wounded pride (vv 10-12). Naaman must have been perplexed and curious when directed to the prophet's house. But he was very annoyed when the prophet failed to appear, and sent a rather belittling message through his servant. Naaman had expected some dramatic cure to be performed, and by the prophet himself, in recognition of his high rank and dignity. He did not expect to be treated as a nobody. Yet it was implied that he was unclean and needed washing! Help the children to imagine the highly-charged atmosphere as he went to walk back to his chariot ready to order the long drive home.

Compare this with the reaction of most sinners when they first hear the Gospel. Many are too proud to accept the message that they are nothing but hopeless sinners in God's sight. They cannot take the truth that their good deeds are rotten in the sight of Heaven, and that their only hope is to acknowledge their failure, and to humbly ask the Lord to wash away their sin.

Many are deeply offended, refusing even to consider the offer of forgiveness.

(5) Listening to reason (v 13). Describe how Naaman's servants politely reasoned with him. As his anger died down and he was left, perhaps, to stare at the growing lumps of white, diseased flesh spreading to his hands and arms, he realised how foolish his attitude had been, and how unreasonable it was to object to such a simple prescription. Help the children to grasp the conflict which broke out in Naaman's heart. He knew that it was only pride which had prompted his reaction. Yet he found it hard to stamp on his pride in full view of his servants, not to mention the conquered Israelites. Naaman pictured in his mind the leper huts outside Damascus. That was where he would end up if he returned uncured. So this mighty man of valour buried his pride, and turned back to the River Jordan. There, in full view of his entourage, the humbled general obeyed the prophet's instructions exactly. Draw the obvious parallels. Urge your class to stop behaving like proud fools. Show them that they face a 'downhill' life in the grip of ever-growing sins; that they cannot afford to brush aside God's way of salvation.

(6) A wonderful cure (v 14). Picture the scene as Naaman lifted his body from the river the seventh time, and discovered his leprosy gone and his skin restored as new, with no scars or deformities left at all. Help the children to appreciate that God's way of washing away sin is just as effective and simple. We have to forget our pride, repent and trust the Saviour, as Naaman had to trust that washing in the Jordan. Anne Shepherd pictured such children:–

Because the Saviour shed His blood
To wash away their sin;
Bathed in that pure and precious flood,
Behold them white and clean!

(7) Restored and homeward-bound (vv 15-19). Encourage the class to enjoy the outcome of this incident. Naaman was now ready to meet Elisha as someone who believed in the true God, and he promised to worship and serve the Lord despite the difficulties in his homeland (where other gods were worshipped). Remind the children that any person truly saved by the Lord Jesus becomes His willing servant for life – no matter how difficult the circumstances. A real believer is a believer not only at Sunday School, but back at school the next day and in front of the family at home. Naaman was determined to pay his allegiance from now onwards to the God Who had saved his life and given him a new beginning. How much more do converted young people owe their allegiance and loyalty to the Saviour Who paid so dearly to wash their sin away!

Sin – Meeting Death (123)
The Shunammite's Son

2 Kings 4.8-37

Aim: To describe the tragic effect of sin and death on the soul, and to show that, just as Elisha restored the widow's son to life, so Christ is willing and able to raise our lifeless souls.

Teachers' Introduction

This lesson is another which compares sin with death. Its special feature is a particularly touching description of how the dead can be raised! May we, as teachers, be as anxious and patient as Elisha, so that we may breathe spiritual life into the children under our care.

Lesson Outline

A sudden death. Begin this lesson by announcing the heartbreaking news that a young boy who had begun the day strong and well had suddenly died. Help the children visualise the tragic scene. Our young people are often shielded from the reality and certainty of death, unlike their forebears who frequently mourned the death of young members of the family. To them the undertaker was a familiar figure. But now that most members of the community are largely protected from the sight of death, we can rightly bring it to our class's attention (but without undue emotionalism) by asking them to consider this event. Children are capable of looking at death objectively and of learning from it. Adults feel much more threatened and, as they get older, build a protective wall to isolate themselves from the subject.

Of a very special son. To make the tragedy even more painful, if that is possible, the young boy of Shunem was the much-loved child of an elderly father, and of a mother who had given up hoping for a child. Tell how the boy cried out in pain and was carried home by servants to his mother, in whose arms he died. The warmth of his body faded, his lips became silent and his ears unhearing. Never again would she welcome him home, watch him play, or put him to bed. Nothing could be done. It was no use calling a doctor. It was no use wondering if some other programme of events might have prevented the death. It was too late. Nothing could bring him back again. Remind the class that death is always a sad and horrible affair. The Lord God never intended that death should reign in our world. It was only as a result of sin that death entered the world *(Romans 5.12)*. Death is the ugly consequence of our sin.

A picture of spiritual death. Show that there is one aspect of death which can be helpful to us. *Physical* death can be a very dramatic picture of *spiritual* death. It can help us to understand that even while we are still alive physically, and brimming with energy, our *souls* may be dead. Draw parallels with the incident before us. The Bible teaches us that God, our heavenly Father, Who gave each one of us life, looks down on us kindly and looks for our affection, but instead He sees lifeless souls (just like the young boy's lifeless corpse). He listens for our prayers, but our lips are still where prayer is concerned.

When the boy was alive his mother loved to see him running about, active and talking, but once he was dead, she was filled with grief at the sight of his corpse. God made us for His glory and looks for signs of His own likeness in us. But instead of seeing kindness, truthfulness and purity, He sees pride, greed, lies and hatred. Viewed spiritually, we are grief-giving corpses. God planned that our lives would be worthwhile, fulfilling and useful, but sin has put an end to all that. Our souls are as cold as a dead body to God. Nothing He does for us, and no message

He sends us, seems to bring any response. We are dead in our trespasses and sins *(Ephesians 2.1)*. Help the children by this approach to see that the unbeliever's lifeless soul causes much pain and grief to his Maker and Father – just as the Shunammite's dead son did to her. Then say how this incident teaches that just as the Lord in this case raised a child's body, so He is able to breathe spiritual life into a dead soul. Draw comparisons:–

(1) His mother went urgently to Elisha. Describe how the mother, deeply shocked, could not accept her son's death. Instead of announcing the news (even to her husband), she laid his body in the little bedroom (set aside for the Lord's servant Elisha). Her boy had been born exactly a year after Elisha had promised that the Lord would send her a child. She felt very confused, and tormented. Had the Lord given her a son only to take him away again? She wanted to go to the prophet and tell him what had happened. Perhaps she wondered whether the Lord would give him the power to restore the boy's life, since He had given the child in the first place. Certainly we know that she went as quickly as possible to Elisha, about twenty-five miles away. Tell the class that in the really important matters of life and death, they must go to the Lord and His Word. Nowhere else will they find help. Fellow human beings are out of their depth in these affairs.

(2) The man of God came. Tell the class how Elisha sent Gehazi his servant ahead, but the mother refused to leave Elisha. She believed that only the Lord Himself, through His servant, could help now. We must believe that only the Lord can bring life to dead souls. Remind the class that you, as their teacher, cannot make them Christians, neither can the church nor the minister. Only the Lord God has this power.

(3) Elisha went to the boy. Describe how Elisha went into the bedroom where the body lay – cold and still. Point out that the Lord Himself must come to the soul of any boy, girl or adult before they can be born again. There is no way we can raise ourselves. We would never be able to make our way to Heaven. We would not even want to, because our souls (our spiritual part) are so dead!

(4) Elisha prayed. He acknowledged, that although he was a prophet, *he* could never raise the dead. Only the Prince of Life has power to do this, but Elisha was able to ask, just as we as teachers ask the Lord to give life and hope to our children.

(5) Elisha gave himself to the boy. Describe next how the prophet stretched himself upon the body, mouth to mouth, eye to eye, hands to hands. Tell the children that this reminds us of what was necessary before the Lord Jesus could grant life to our souls. It was not enough even for Him to give the word. He had to come down into our world and live amongst us. He had to come and take our sin upon Himself, and atone for it. He had to give Himself to us and for us.

(6) The boy's body became warm. As a result of Elisha's prayer and his giving of himself, warmth gradually began to flow into the boy's body. There was hope; the signs of life had begun to appear. Explain how pleased you are as a teacher when the first signs of *spiritual* life are seen in a class member. Perhaps someone begins to listen much more carefully, or to show an interest in Bible reading. Perhaps someone begins to pray seriously, and never misses a week at Sunday School unless it cannot be helped.

(7) Elisha was not content. He went downstairs and began to pace up and down. He was not satisfied, so he returned to the room and once again stretched himself on the child. Now real signs of life appeared. The boy sneezed seven times! And he opened his eyes! How glad Elisha was. He called Gehazi, who in turn called the mother. Soon she appeared at the door and was told by the prophet – *Take up thy son*!

We are not content until our young people are really converted. Genuine, new and spiritual life is vital. Nothing less is any good. Explain the great change of conversion, emphasising *spiritual life.* It would not have been any use at all for the dead boy only to have been preserved from rotting, or for him to have been given some kind of 'half-life', so that he breathed, but remained in a permanent coma. Real spiritual life is more than attendance at church, or vague belief. Emphasise this vital distinction.

(8) The boy awoke. Help the class imagine the boy opening his eyes and looking, first at Elisha, and then minutes later at his mother. Perhaps he did not realise it, but a moment ago, it was a certain 'fact' that he would never see them again, yet now they were gazing happily and fondly into his eyes. Tell the class how amazing it is when someone is converted and the soul begins to awaken – suddenly we understand so much more about our Saviour and we realise His love for us, and His mighty power and mercy. We grasp to what lengths He went to rescue us from the jaws of death.

Challenge the class as to whether they have ever had this wonderful experience. Assure them that although it may seem utterly impossible for the dead to live, yet with God nothing is impossible. Down the centuries of time the most unlikely people have been converted and brought to spiritual life by the Lord, Who will continue with this great work until the world ends.

Visual Aid

Provide a picture, or model, of the large house of Shunem with the little room built on the side for Elisha – sparsely furnished. This will provide a focal point for the children as teachers relate the events of the lesson. Headings (1) - (8) can be printed on cards and pinned up as the lesson proceeds.

Sin – Going to War with God (124)

The Syrian Army Attacks Elisha

2 Kings 6.8-23

Aim: To show that unbelievers are at war with God, for there is no 'neutral' position. To describe the grace of God in opening the way of peace at His own cost.

Teachers' Introduction

This lesson could well be described as a hidden gem. The events it records must be among the most fascinating found in the Bible, yet they are little known. Our task should therefore be an easy one. If we equate the Syrians (Arameans) with souls which are at war with God, then we can apply the principles which the Lord used to bring the enemy host under submission to illustrate the way of salvation.

Lesson Outline

(1) War breaks out. In today's lesson we read that the king of Syria was once again warring against the king of Israel. Surprise the class by suggesting that they also are involved in a deadly war! Explain that ever since sin came into the world men and women, boys and girls have been at war with God. Although He continues to sustain our world, granting people life and health, millions treat Him as their bitter enemy. They hide from Him and, whenever the opportunity arises, damage His kingdom. They break His laws and often even attack His people (those who believe in Him).

(2) An informer? Explain that on occasions the whole Syrian army would besiege Samaria, the capital of Israel, but our lesson today is more suggestive of guerrilla warfare. Describe the Syrian king's perplexity as he tried to account for the failure of his 'missions'. He could only conclude that there was an informer in their midst *(2 Kings 6.11)*. He was greatly frustrated that his carefully planned, top-secret raids were being thwarted. Wherever he pitched his camp, planning to trap the enemy, it was no use – the Israelites always avoided him. The missions were proving counter-productive, because instead of returning loaded with plundered wealth, his ranks were being reduced.

(3) No, God's prophet! It was one of his own men who informed him that Elisha the prophet was the cause of all the trouble. It was he who with deadly accuracy was able to predict from night to night the location of the Syrian force. Here we can remind the children that nothing can be hidden from God. However hard we scheme against Him and try to hide our plans and our sin from Him, He sees all. He knows our innermost thoughts. Wherever we are, whatever we do, God knows all about it *(Psalm 139)*.

(4) One against many! Once the king was certain that Elisha was responsible for spoiling his plans, he did not hesitate to instigate an all-out attack on this ageing, unprotected servant of God. However, he was obviously fearful of the prophet for the Bible tells us that – *therefore sent he thither horses, and chariots, and a great host (2 Kings 6.14)*. An entire 'armoured division' was sent to capture one man! Teachers can tell the children how so often the fury of the world (inspired by the devil) has been let loose on humble servants of God. (Men such as the apostle Paul, Luther, Wesley and Whitefield were often attacked by the civil powers or by great mobs.)

(5) Unseen forces. Elisha's young servant was terrified by this unequal match, but Elisha himself knew that all the power was with him. He realised that the Lord of Hosts had superior forces unseen by mortal eyes. He prayed that the Lord would enable his servant to see them too. Remind the class that it is naive only to believe in things seen with our ordinary eyes. Even in the physical world forces such as electricity are far more powerful than many which take on an obvious shape and form. Elisha's servant did not know that he was surrounded by a vast host of horses and chariots invisible to human sight, but mighty in power. In answer to Elisha's prayer, God enabled him to see them too.

Tell the children that our great desire is that God will enable them to *see* and believe in Him, Who, though unseen to mortal eyes, made the vast universe, the towering mountains and the mighty seas. His Word has stood firm and unmoved while generations of human beings have passed away. Has the Lord opened their eyes to Him, and His mighty power?

(6) The tables turned. In case Elisha's servant was in any doubt of God's power, he soon saw the mighty Syrian army (which he had so much feared) led meekly into the centre of fortified Samaria. Let the children imagine the pathetic sight, as this crack regiment followed Elisha. God had answered Elisha's prayer, and these proud soldiers were for the moment reduced to shuffling, blind captives. Use this point to warn the children that God will sooner or later humble all those who usurp His power and plot against Him. (The Lord Jesus made this clear in many of His parables, eg: *Matthew 21.33-41.*) Help the class to see how foolish it is to fight Him, especially when He is ready to do so much good to all who turn and submit to Him!

(7) Made to see. Being blinded and taken captive would have been bad enough for the Syrian officers, but imagine their horror when their sight returned and they discovered where they were. It was as if they found themselves trapped at the centre of a spider's web, with the spider just waiting to devour them! Perhaps they would have preferred not to see! When unbelievers first have their eyes opened they too often wish they were still blind. As they begin to see themselves as God sees them, ugly and perverted, and failures, they sometimes wish it were all a passing nightmare. Many children have been frightened when their spiritual eyes were opened so that they realised they were sinners in God's sight, deserving punishment. But wait . . .

(8) An undeserved feast. Our narrative takes another unexpected twist when, to the surprise and relief of the Syrian forces, instead of being massacred they found themselves seated at banqueting tables with *great provision* set before them *(2 Kings 6.23).* The prophet, for whom they had showed no pity, returned their hostility with mercy. He not only set them free, but proposed that they were given a great meal before they went. What a strange kind of war! What must these tough and vicious soldiers have thought of this generous gesture? We only know that having returned home they brought their raids to an end. Peace prevailed amongst them.

We have here another graphic illustration of God's grace to us. Once we have been reduced to seeing our sinfulness and our hopeless plight before God, He offers us free pardon and forgiveness. Instead of bringing down His sword of execution, He invites us to taste the benefits which the Lord Jesus has earned for us. Because Christ died for those who repent of their sin and put their trust in Him, they can be counted as members of His own family. Instead of treating them as enemies, the Lord is willing to call them *friends.*

(9) Peace restored. We have noted that after their merciful release the Syrian raiders ceased hostilities. The countries were now at peace. How glad the families of Syria must have been to receive back their husbands and fathers safe and well. No longer would they have to be parted. No longer would they have to live in a constant state of fear and anxiety, dreading the news of death from the battlefield. Now they could look forward to a period of prosperity and happiness.

Remind the children that the coming of the Saviour to our earth was announced by the angels to the shepherds in this way:– *Glory to God in the highest, and on earth peace, good will toward men (Luke 2.14).* His coming and His death mean that all who trust in Him can be reconciled to God and made one with each other – *he is our peace (Ephesians 2.13-19).* Urge your class to surrender to the Prince of Peace now. How terrible if they were to stubbornly hold out against Him until He returned as their Judge!

Sin – Refusing to Believe God's Promises (125)

Elisha's Promise of Plenty Kept

Read 2 Kings 6.24-33 to set the scene; 2 Kings 7.1-20 for lesson subject

Aim: To demonstrate vividly, by means of this fascinating but little-known Old Testament event, that unbelief in God's promises is both sinful and foolish. To convince the children that the Lord has great storehouses of blessing available for all who take His Word seriously.

Lesson Outline

Sadly, the children will be familiar with the sight of starving people on their TV screens. They may also have seen news coverage of people suffering the fear and privations of being under siege, trapped in a city where supplies of food have almost dwindled away, and where people are driven to survive on almost anything they can lay hands on.

(1) Starvation in Samaria. Explain that back in the days of Elisha this was the wretched condition of the people of Samaria. Though they had a massive city wall, when surrounded by the powerful army of King Ben-hadad of Syria, they began to starve. He reckoned that soon the people of Samaria would become so weak and emaciated they would not be able to fight. Then his troops would storm into the city to kill the men, rape the women, and collect up for themselves everything of value. So desperate was the situation that only the wealthiest citizens could afford to eat anything, and even they had to pay massive sums for items which normally a beggar would refuse. Some women were driven to the most desperate and horrible measures. Even the king was in despair, wearing sackcloth – an indication of his desperation.

Starvation of the soul. Encourage the children to be grateful that they are not among the world's starving. Urge them to be sympathetic and concerned about those so much worse off than themselves. Then show them that there are similarities between our society and the hungry people of Samaria. Explain that *spiritually* we also live in a starvation zone. Describe (in a way which is appropriate to the age of your class) some of the desperate measures which so many people are forced to take because their souls are short of spiritual food, and their lives therefore lack meaning, purpose and fulfilment. Some are so nervous that they cannot do without cigarettes. Others cannot live without alcohol, sometimes with terrible consequences for them and their families. Adults, desperate for friendship, enter relationships which often increase their own misery and deal further blows to their families. Some may seem to be enjoying life, but if we look below the surface we discover that they are paying a very high price for the pleasures which keep them happy. Many extra hours at work and highly stressful occupations are often the only means of funding the exotic holidays and dream homes paraded temptingly on television. And little children are often starved of affection and attention in the race for these shreds of happiness. (Members of the class whose parents are not Christians will be all too familiar with these situations. Others should be exposed to these facts and made to appreciate their own benefits.)

(2) Good news scorned. Tell how the king of Israel vented his rage on Elisha. But, instead of retaliating, the man of God made a very surprising announcement: *To morrow about this time shall a measure of fine flour be sold for a shekel (2 Kings 7.1).* Our children might expect to hear that the members of the king's court pricked up their ears, amazed to hear such news, even if it seemed too good to be true. After all, Elisha had often before been God's instrument for doing great and miraculous good, and desperate people usually clutch at any straw. But did the king's officer immediately send an expedition to check troop movements in the enemy camp? Did he seek clarification of this forecast from the prophet? No. He ridiculed the man of God and mocked his suggestion with great sarcasm. Repeat Elisha's words to this haughty doubter: *Behold, thou shalt see it with thine eyes, but shalt not eat thereof* (v 2).

Good news for us doubted. Draw parallels with our own situation. Remind the class that you often present them with the promise of good things. Eternal life, real joy and inward peace are blessings often spoken about. How do they react? Do they enquire earnestly? Do they consider thoughtfully? Or do they listen with deaf ears and shrug off the idea, granting God, His Word and His messengers no credibility? Do they treat God's promises with open contempt and ridicule?

(3) Plentiful food missed. Describe next what happened at twilight that very evening, when the Syrian camp, laden with food supplies and other items of great value, was deserted by the Syrian army (vv 6-7). Tent upon tent piled high with silver, gold, clothing, and endless bags of flour and barley, lay unprotected, ready for anyone to help himself! Yet no one came from within the city of Samaria, for no one had believed Elisha. Many lay dying within those city walls, when they could have been feasting. Some were shivering, when they could have been clothed warmly. Others were sorrowing, when they could have been celebrating the end of the siege. And all because they refused to accept God's message.

Heaven missed. How like them our generation is! People today could have happiness which is real and lasting! They could have peace without anti-depressants! They could have eternal security. But like those Israelites, they absolutely refuse to believe the Lord. Many would far rather believe the most obvious con-men and deceivers, than give any attention to the Bible. Others, like the dying people in Samaria, just believe what their godless leaders say, and accept their miserable existence without God.

(4) Four lepers make a discovery. The children may well ask – Did the food in the Syrian camp just rot while the people starved to death? No. Describe the four lepers, outcast and neglected, who were forced to beg outside the gate of the city, and who decided to approach the enemy camp not knowing that it had been deserted. They reasoned that they would die if they either stayed where they were, or if they tried to enter the city. They would also probably die if they approached the Syrian camp, but there was just a possibility that the enemy soldiers might take pity on them, and give them a chance to survive.

Tell how it was that these poor, pathetic lepers became the means by which the discovery of massive, free food supplies was made, and their availability communicated to Samaria (vv 8-15).

Spiritual riches discovered. Draw the obvious parallel with the provision of God's grace. It is when people have run out of optimism and confidence about how clever and capable they are, and how great their lives will be, that they may be moved to look for a source of help. The lepers found food and treasure, all provided by the power of the Lord. So we may find spiritual riches (describe some of the features of conversion) all provided freely by God for humble seekers.

(5) The lepers tell the good news. Draw the lesson to conclusion by relating the events that followed. At first the lepers helped themselves. But before long they were conscience-smitten, saying, *This day is a day of good tidings, and we hold our peace* (v 9). Quickly they returned to the city to pass the news to the king. (If time, mention his unnecessary scepticism and fears.) Before long, the people (those who were still fit enough) were swarming through the city gates, rushing towards the site where everything they needed, and much more besides, awaited their collection. Without sowing a single seed, barley was available in abundance. Without reaping a single plant, or milling an ear of grain, there was wheat in abundance. Soon the early collectors returned to the city gates where, just as Elisha had predicted, they sold a measure of fine flour for a mere shekel.

Christians must tell the Gospel. Remind any in your class who already know the Lord and have experienced His wonderful goodness themselves, that they have a duty, like the lepers, to convey the good news to others. Explain to the unbelievers in your class that you, as a teacher, see yourself like those lepers. You have made a great and wonderful discovery which you dare not keep to yourself. You once were threatened by the disease of sin, and despaired of life, and feared death. But now you have discovered the most wonderful Saviour Who has forgiven your sin and granted so many blessings that it is hard to describe them all. Perhaps the most amazing thing about it is that these blessings are all freely available for anyone, great or small, rich or poor, who will look for them.

(6) Unbelief brought death. One word of warning should be added before the lesson closes. It concerns the king's officer who ridiculed Elisha. As the prophet had declared, he lived to see flour and barley being sold for almost nothing at the city gate, but he tasted neither, for, as the people stampeded through the gates to obtain their first food for months, he was trampled to death. Tell the class earnestly that those who continue in wilful ridicule of God, opposing His messengers, will one day see the Lord Jesus and the benefits He waits to bestow, but will never experience them for themselves. Unbelief was the first sin, and it is the worst sin.

Revision (126)

Aim: To highlight from this series the various forms sin can take, and to remind the children from the incidents we have learned about, that sin is very common and very damaging. Having diagnosed the problem, we can remind them of different aspects of God's remedy.

Teachers' Introduction

We recommend that teachers use a visual aid to fix in the children's minds the following points derived from the lessons. The visual aid for the series suggested at the close of this lesson will be especially helpful in this lesson.

Lesson Outline

Remind the class of the lessons in the series, mentioning particularly the aspect of sin which each demonstrates. Those using the suggested visual aid should reveal the words that are written on the signposts, gradually building up a picture. Then encourage the children to recall the opposite Gospel truth along these lines:

(1) Elijah's warning to Ahab who had departed from the Lord and introduced Jerusalem to the heathen gods of his foreign wife, Jezebel, reminds us that: **SIN IS REJECTING GOD.**
(a) What unwelcome message did Elijah bring to the king?
(b) What will happen to children who turn away from the Lord?
(c) Where does the way back to God begin?
THE GOSPEL IS FINDING THE WAY BACK TO GOD.

(2) Elijah's challenge to the people of Israel as they assembled together with the Baal prophets on Mount Carmel reminds us that: **SIN IS PLAYING WITH OTHER GODS.**
(a) What did Elijah urge the people to stop doing?

(b) Why did they decide the Lord was the true God?
(c) Which gods are we tempted to serve instead of the Lord?

THE GOSPEL IS LEAVING THE WORLD'S SIDE.

(3) When King Ahab allowed his neighbour Naboth to be murdered so that he could have his vineyard, we saw that: **SIN IS WOUNDING THE CONSCIENCE.**
(a) What did the guilty Ahab say to Elijah when he saw him?
(b) Describe ways in which children today try to hide and forget their sin.
(c) Before we can ask the Lord Jesus to forgive us, what must we be ready to do?

THE GOSPEL IS FACING UP TO SIN AND SEEKING THE SAVIOUR.

(4) General Naaman's disfiguring and fatal leprosy reminds us that: **SIN IS A FATAL DISEASE.**
(a) What message did Elisha send to Naaman which made him very angry at first?
(b) What happened when he was persuaded to change his mind?
(c) What cure is there for the disease of sin?
(d) Where must we go to have our sin washed away?

THE GOSPEL IS BEING HEALED AND MADE NEW.

(5) A young boy died suddenly and lay lifeless on Elisha's bed. This reminds us that: **SIN BRINGS DEATH.**
(a) What was Elisha able to say to his mother after he had prayed and the Lord had granted the boy to live again?
(b) The Bible says that we are dead in sins. Who can 'awaken' us?
(c) What did the Lord Jesus promise to all who believe in Him?

THE GOSPEL IS RECEIVING THE GIFT OF ETERNAL LIFE.

(6) The Syrian army often made war with Israel and then came out to capture Elisha, which reminds us that: **SIN IS GOING TO WAR WITH GOD.**
(a) The Lord made the Syrian soldiers temporarily blind and Elisha led them into Samaria, but instead of ill-treating them what did he command the king of Israel to do?

(b) Do we have any good reason to treat God as an enemy? Has He done us any harm?
(c) Who came into this world to make peace between us and God?

THE GOSPEL IS ACCEPTING GOD'S PEACE.

(7) The starving people of Samaria did not believe Elisha when he brought good news to them, which reminds us that: **SIN IS REFUSING TO BELIEVE GOD.**
(a) When did Elisha promise that food would be available at the city gate at 'give-away' prices?
(b) What was the sin of the king's officer who scoffed at Elisha's prophecy?
(c) When people become Christians they first have to turn away from unbelief. Think of as many words as you can for the opposite of unbelief.

THE GOSPEL IS TRUSTING GOD'S WORD.

(8) Finally – **SIN LEADS TO HELL.**

Bring this lesson to conclusion by making this final and solemn point about sin. Explain that although some people seem to 'get away' with sin in this life (though most suffer as a result of sin even in this world), no sinner will ever be allowed entrance to Heaven. Instead they will be sent away from God and all His gifts and blessings for ever *(Revelation 21.8)*. That is why we raise these subjects so seriously. Only . . .

THE GOSPEL LEADS TO HEAVEN.

Point out that anyone who believes the Gospel and repents of sin, enters the road which leads to Heaven and to God. Plead with your class to change direction (use the visual aid to make this point) and join the highway which will lead them to the Saviour, and to the blessings He waits to bestow in this life, and in eternity.

Visual Aid

Cut out seven signposts (the old fashioned type, with arms pointing in opposite directions, as found at a road junction). These should be at least 10 inches tall, but the larger the better. Produce one such sign for each lesson.

On the arm pointing in one direction print the words which describe the aspect of sin highlighted in the lesson title. On the arm pointing in the opposite direction print the words which describe the opposite Gospel application. Eg: the first signpost will have the words – 'REJECTING GOD' pointing in one direction, and 'FINDING THE WAY BACK TO GOD' in the opposite direction.

As the series builds up, the signposts can be used to revise the main point of each lesson. It will be especially helpful for use in this revision lesson, providing a visual means of highlighting the chief lesson points and emphasising the contrasts between the pathways of sin and the Gospel.

(Pictures from the *Lessons for Life Bible Learning Course* sheets can be used in conjunction with this visual aid, providing a pictorial revision of the lessons, especially for younger classes.)

Series 16
Matthew's Gospel (Part I)
THE SAVIOUR COMES AND BEGINS HIS WORK

127 – God with Us

A child with a remarkable ancestry is born in Bethlehem. His mother is a virgin and His name means 'God with us'. Matthew proves from the Old Testament that all this points to the fact that Jesus was none other than the Son of God, born to be the Saviour of the world.

128 – The Wise Men and King Herod

Two completely opposite reactions to the coming of the Saviour raise questions for us. Whom do we most closely resemble – the earnest, open-minded travellers from the East who worshipped Christ, or the resentful, hostile King Herod who wanted to destroy Him?

129 – The Lord Jesus Is Tempted

Weak and weary, the Lord Jesus is approached by Satan with his subtle, malicious suggestions. But Christ withstands and defeats him. Do we handle the devil's temptations successfully? When tempted we should never forget that we have a sympathetic Saviour Who Himself has been tempted, and Who lives to represent us in Heaven, and to help His children in this battle.

130 – Jesus' Teaching – The Two Roads

At the start of His ministry the Lord outlines two courses which life can take. He shows that the *destination* is the most important consideration, and urges His hearers to take the path which leads to life, even though it is hard and unpopular.

131 – The Two Houses

One kind of person appears shrewd and successful, but the Lord describes such people as foolish. They hear His teaching but never act on it. Are we hoping to succeed in life without taking Christ seriously? Beware of the storms ahead!

132 – The Two Trees

With so many 'religions' around us, how do we know which to believe? The Lord Jesus gives some guide-lines. His illustration of trees and their fruit helps us to know whether or not we belong to Him.

133 – The 'Lord's Prayer'

If I want to return to God and find Him, what must I do? How should I ask Him to receive me? What should I pray for? The Lord's pattern prayer has all the answers.

134 – Jesus Heals a Leper

Not only was the Lord's teaching unique, but He alone could heal and restore very sick and deformed people at a word. A man badly affected by leprosy believes Jesus can heal him, and He does – completely and immediately. What can we learn from the healing?

135 – The Wheat and the Tares

Even unbelievers recognise that something has gone badly wrong with this world. In this parable the Lord Jesus, its Maker, outlines God's plan to put things right. It contains some warnings for unbelievers, and encouragement for believers.

136 – The Pearl of Great Price

It may seem hard to repent and leave behind our sinful ways, but once we find the Lord we look back at our old life and wonder what attraction it had – just like the pearl merchant who sold his entire stock, and was more than satisfied with his one, new acquisition.

137 – Walking on the Sea

At the beginning of this series we asked who Jesus was. The disciples who see Him walk across the storm-tossed waves are certain He is the Son of God, and they worship Him. Peter's experience provides a lesson on how to exercise faith.

138 – Revision

The people of our Lord's day wondered about His birth, marvelled at His miracles, and listened spellbound to His teaching. How have we been affected as we have heard of these things? Wonderful though these were, the Lord knew the chief purpose of His coming was to be put to death in Jerusalem.

Teachers' Introduction to the Series

So much of the literature for the young currently available on the life of Christ dwells almost exclusively on the 'story' aspect of His life. Many children have had illustrated stories of the Lord's life read to them alongside secular tales. Sadly, the effect is that they give sacred events as little credence as the lives of Cinderella or Rupert. Children are not surprised to hear that Jesus healed the sick, walked on the water, and even raised the dead. They expect such things in a story-book. Instead of being persuaded by these amazing signs that Jesus Christ was the Son of God, many think of Him as little more than a fictional character of bygone days.

Our purpose, therefore, throughout this series will be to emphasise that we are dealing with *history*, and carefully documented facts, not stories. We can point out that Matthew joined the Lord's band of disciples from early days and was an eyewitness of the majority of the events he records. He would have been in direct touch with 'reliable sources', such as the mother of Jesus, and other disciples, for information about events which he did not personally see. We want to convince the youngest child and the cynical teenager that Jesus of Nazareth really lived, and that everything recorded about Him actually happened. Only as we succeed will they begin to ask, along with the disciples who first witnessed these remarkable events, *What manner of man is this? (Matthew 8.27.)*

As we enquire into His unique birth, follow His victory over temptation, watch His amazing miracles, and listen to His parables, we shall give the children good reason, under the influence of the Holy Spirit, to believe that Jesus was the Christ, the Son of God, so that believing they may have life in His name (see *John 20.31*). Each lesson will have its individual emphasis, but this will be our overall objective. As the series opens with Matthew's account of the birth of the Saviour, we immediately pose the all-important question, 'Who was He?' Then, as the series closes, we draw together all the evidence which points to His divine nature. (Teachers should read through Lesson 138 and keep its aim in mind throughout the series.)

God with Us (127)

The Birth of Christ

Matthew 1 – 2.15; 4.12-16

Aim: To prove to the children that the baby born at Bethlehem was none other than the Son of God, Who came to be our Saviour.

Teachers' Introduction

This series opens with the incarnation. We quite deliberately begin this series with a lesson normally reserved for Christmas week. Dealing with it at an unusual time of the year will help us to convince the children that this is not a charming Christian legend, but historical fact. We shall follow Matthew as he traces the ancestry of this child, and the predictions concerning His birth.

Lesson Outline

Introduce the lesson as being about a unique birth in human history – the birthday which divided history into BC and AD. Despite this, it took place in very poor and humble circumstances. As we read about it in Matthew's Gospel we shall 'investigate' all the evidence so that we can answer the

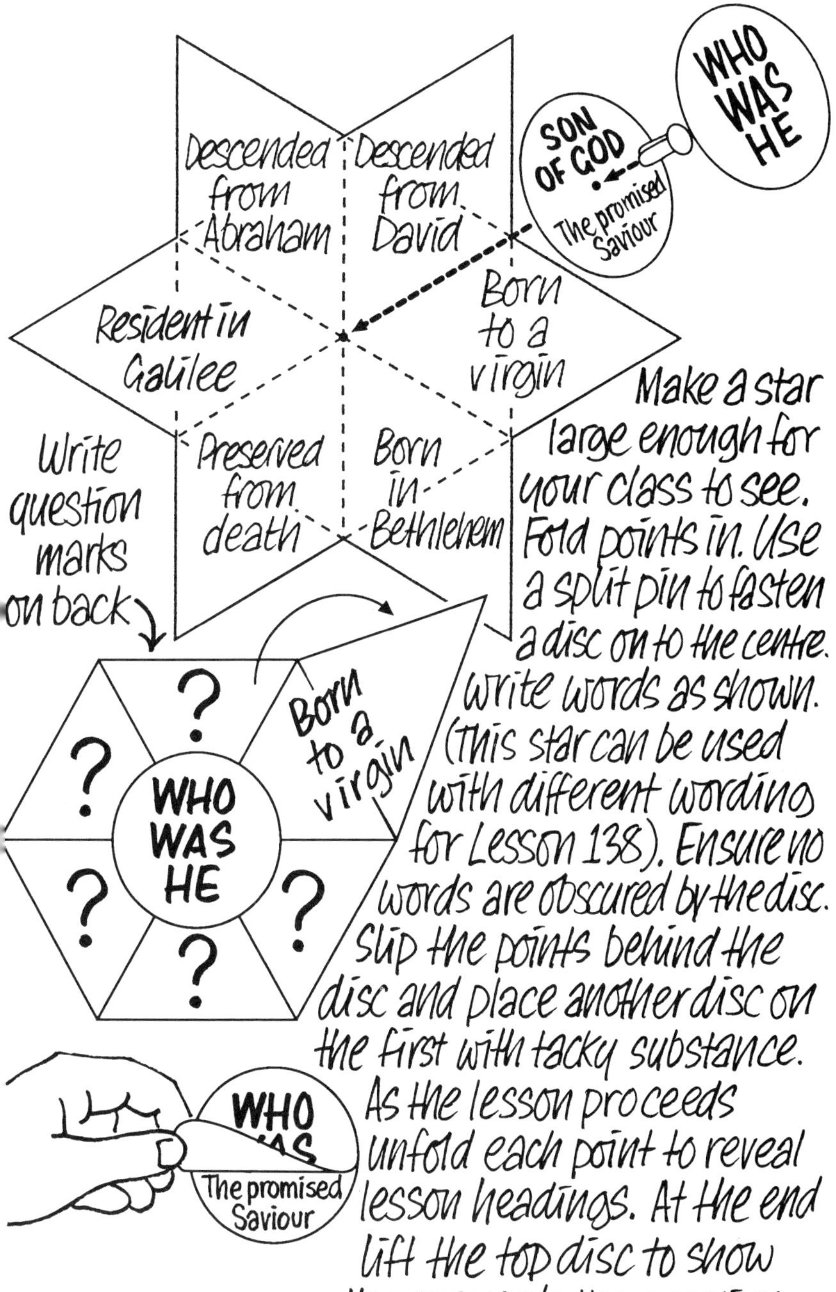

VA 10 – Visual Aid for use with Lesson 127 – 'God with Us'.

question – Who was this baby of Bethlehem? Was He just the son of a poor carpenter? Was He, alongside such names as Buddha, Mohammed and Socrates, one of the world's human leaders of a system of religion and thought, and nothing more? Or was He the Son of God, the second member of the Godhead, born to be our Saviour?

(1) Descended from Abraham. Interest the children by suggesting that we are all fascinated by our family history – who our great-grandparents were, where they lived and who they were descended from. Some people go to great lengths to find out! Show the children chapter one of *Matthew* with its family tree. Here recorded in detail are the forebears of this child, Jesus. One name stands out in particular: Abraham. Remind the class about the promises which God made to Abraham approximately 2,000 years before Christ's birth – that through a descendant of his, the whole world would be blessed *(Genesis 18.18* and *22.16-18).* Show how Matthew traces the family of Jesus right back to Abraham. (The older members of the class will be able to recognise other familiar names in the list.)

For many years it had seemed impossible that this promise to Abraham could be kept. However, we now know that it was through this member of Abraham's family, Jesus Christ, that God sent the whole world a Saviour. Through Him all the nations of the earth *have* been blessed in a remarkable way. Wherever the Gospel of Christ has been preached, lives have been transformed and society vastly improved. His coming has changed the course of human history.

(2) Descended from King David. Another name which stands out in the family tree, and which will be well-known to the children, is that of David. Remind them of God's promise to King David: *Thine house and thy kingdom shall be established for ever before thee: thy throne shall be established for ever (2 Samuel 7.16).* David died and by 586 BC his family had fallen from power when Zedekiah, his last descendant as king of Judah, was defeated by Nebuchadnezzar. Then Jerusalem and its Temple were destroyed. How could God keep this promise that kings from David's family would for ever reign? Through Christ –

Whose *spiritual* kingdom is still growing two thousand years later, and Who will reign eternally in Heaven. He alone fits this prediction.

(3) Born to a virgin. Tell the children simply how Matthew explains that Jesus had no earthly father *(Matthew 1.18-25)* for He was born of a virgin – the only time this has ever happened in history. (Older classes will be interested to note that these facts are confirmed by Luke, the doctor and respected historian, in his Gospel account.) Mary conceived Jesus because God's Spirit came to her, and the angel explained that her son would be called Emmanuel – 'God with us'. Joseph was very grieved when he found that his fiancée was expecting a child. He feared that she had been unfaithful. But the angel reassured him, and gave him the honour of acting as 'stepfather' to this unique child. This information makes it clear that Jesus was the second Person of the Trinity Who came down to live in this world as a human being, the Son of God *and* the Son of Man. Read verses 22 and 23 and show how Isaiah had prophesied these events 700 years before – that God would come in the person of a son born to a virgin *(Isaiah 7.14)*. Long-term as this prophecy was, it fitted perfectly this child born to Mary.

(4) Born in Bethlehem of Judea. *Matthew 2* records where Jesus was born. Although Mary and Joseph lived in the north, in Nazareth, events turned out surprisingly, and Mary's child was born in the far south, in Bethlehem of Judea (refer to the account in Luke's Gospel). Show that this in and of itself was a remarkable occurrence, because many years before, the prophet Micah *(5.2)* had predicted that a Ruler sent by God would begin His reign in the hearts of His people from this insignificant city of Judah. From this prophecy even the chief priests and the scribes knew that the Messiah would be born in Bethlehem *(Matthew 2.6)*, another event which confirms that this Jesus was none other than the promised Son of God.

(5) Preserved from death. Describe how King Herod, on hearing about this birth, became anxious about his throne and took terrible and unprecedented steps to kill the child. He ordered the destruction of all children under two years of age in Bethlehem – a measure which made him a hated ruler. (Next week's lesson will deal more fully with this incident.) This tragedy was predicted many years beforehand by the prophet Jeremiah *(Matthew 2.18* quotes *Jeremiah 31.15).* But because the Lord Jesus was the Saviour, He was divinely protected from Herod. Angels warned His parents, and they escaped to Egypt – another event which had been prophesied 700 years before Jesus was born (the end of *Matthew 2.15* is a quotation from *Hosea 11.1*).

(6) Resident in Galilee. Explain that most Jews would have expected their Messiah to live and reign in Jerusalem, but the prophet Isaiah had predicted that He would do much of His work in the lowly and despised region of Galilee. It was there that the Light would 'dawn' upon our dark world. Matthew records how Mary and Joseph, after their exile in Egypt, returned to their home in Nazareth of Galilee, and there the Lord grew up. (Luke tells us they visited Jerusalem once a year for the feast of the Passover.) When Jesus began His great work of preaching, He left Nazareth and settled in Capernaum which was also in the region (or county or state) of Galilee, the area specifically spoken of by Isaiah *(Matthew 4.12-16* quotes *Isaiah 9.1-2).*

These facts all point to one conclusion: that the child born to Mary in the Bethlehem stable was none other than the Son of God, the Saviour promised by God ever since Adam first sinned. The people of Bethlehem did not recognise Him but these details listed by Matthew assure us this was no ordinary baby. His ancestry, His unique conception, His birthplace and the events of His early years were all accurately predicted by God's prophets.

Mary asked the angel what she should call her son, and the answer was: *Jesus: for he shall save his people from their sins.* Ask the children questions which apply the lesson along these lines. Did you know that the Lord Jesus was God's Son, Who was deliberately sent into this sad world in order to die so that all who believe in Him might be saved? He did not die by accident, nor because evil men got the better of Him. He knew from before His birth that He had come to die. Have you repented of your sin, and given Him your heart and life?

Visual Aid

Use VA 10 (see page 197). The hexagon with its question, 'Who was He?' opens up into a star. Each point highlights one of the six headings of this lesson. Open the flaps at the appropriate moment, and at the conclusion reveal the answer to the question, 'The promised Saviour'. (This visual aid will be used again for Lesson 138 so it is worth making it carefully and strongly.) The children will be fascinated to see what lies beneath each question mark.

The Wise Men and King Herod (128)

Matthew 2.1-18

Aim: To enable the children to see that they fall into one of two categories. They are either for the Saviour, the category of the wise men, or, sadly, they are against Him, the category of King Herod.

Teachers' Introduction

Many children are familiar with the outline of events surrounding the birth of Christ, especially the visit of the wise men to Bethlehem. Instead of presenting this lesson in narrative-style, as at Christmas, we take a fresh approach which challenges the children's knowledge of the facts and requires a response.

Lesson Outline

Provide outline pictures of the wise men and King Herod. Ask the children what great historical event brought about the meeting of these men. Then ask the class to consider some of the differences between them in their behaviour towards the birth of Christ.

(1) Their investigations. (a) The wise men were thorough. Describe the wise men living many miles east of Jerusalem with little or no knowledge of the Bible, but deeply involved in the science of their day. Long before the age of telecommunications and computers, the sky provided a vast encyclopaedia of information. Travellers used it to chart their routes, and it provided the only reliable and internationally-accepted calendar and clock. The wise men may have come from ancient Persia or Arabia. They were Gentiles, and may have been astrologers, who struggled to find in the stars some indication of future events in the earth's history. Whatever their ideas in that fruitless field of study, they were astonished when they observed a uniquely magnificent star, new and low on the horizon, and they concluded that it indicated the birth of a great king. Though travel was difficult and dangerous in those days, they dropped all their studies in order to follow the star and search for the new-born king.

(b) King Herod was wilfully ignorant. His circumstances form a great contrast. Unlike the wise men, he lived in the land of the Bible, a land which was full of information concerning the birth of the Saviour of the world. A year before the wise men arrived in his land the great event had taken place and the Saviour had been born in Bethlehem only seven miles away from Herod's palace. His birth had been celebrated by angels and marvelled at by the local people *(Luke 2.13-18)*. Only eight days later, when He was brought to the Temple in Jerusalem, the arrival of this baby led to momentous words being said by godly senior citizens who lived close to the king's palace. *They* knew that He was God's promised Messiah. But Herod knew nothing about these events. He was not a man who respected God, believed the Scriptures, or watched out for the coming of God's promised Messiah. Though Herod lived in the land of the Scriptures, and so close to the birthplace of Christ, he knew nothing about His coming to earth.

Question 1. Turn the spotlight on to the class. Who do they most resemble? Are they like the wise men who, though they were disadvantaged Gentiles, took notice of the information they possessed and would not rest until they had found the Saviour? Do the children want to find God for themselves? Are they prepared to *seek diligently* for Him whatever the cost? Or are they more like King Herod? Do they have a Bible of their own, yet never search it for information about the way of salvation? Do they know others – perhaps parents or friends – who have been converted, yet never seek the Lord for themselves? Do they choose to ignore the Light of the world Who would bring knowledge and understanding of eternal issues to their lives?

(2) Their attitudes. (a) The wise men were determined and receptive. Remind the class that these men must have been disappointed when they reached the palace at Jerusalem to be told that the new-born king was not there. Indeed they must have sensed a somewhat hostile atmosphere. Their news was obviously not welcomed by the king, who was *troubled* by it. But they were not put off. As soon as they were informed that they had to journey a further seven miles, they set off, willing to search for the child amongst the lowly homes of Bethlehem, and then report back to Herod. The Bible records how they *rejoiced with exceeding great joy* when the star reappeared and led them without delay to their destination.

(b) King Herod was jealous and hostile. By contrast, Herod's attitude was sour and vicious, made hypocritical by a veneer of charm and concern. The history books tell us that Herod 'the Great' was a man who had used violence and dirty tricks to win and consolidate his kingly position – even 'liquidating' members of his own family who threatened his rule. The thought that his reign could be overturned by some new-born child was abhorrent to him. But he was cunning enough not to let it show when speaking to these noble visitors. Instead he feigned interest, hoping that the wise men's information would lead to the successful arrest and obliteration of this unwanted king. Children will readily picture this ogre of a man – but pass on quickly to the question:–

Question 2. What is *their* attitude to God's Son? Are they open to the good news of a Saviour? Are they ready to rejoice that their sins can be forgiven and overcome? Are they willing and glad to travel the extra mile, and suffer disruptions to their lifestyle, in order to meet the King of Heaven? Or do they more closely resemble Herod who did not want to hear the good news? Would they prefer to cling to life as they know it and refuse to consider anything different and better? Are they against God's messengers? Do they sometimes put on a false front, coming to Sunday School while they enjoy it, but refusing to really listen to the message and respond to it? Are they pleasant when they meet their friends and teachers, but obstinate and sullen towards the Lord?

(3) Their responses. (a) The wise men's appreciative worship. Help the children to picture the wise men as they at last ended their search. They had not been put off by the fact that the sought-after child was staying in a stable with His 'Dad', a lowly carpenter. This was not what they had expected, but the spectacular star convinced them that He was their King, and so they fell down and worshipped Him, presenting their rich gifts and treasures. They were not disappointed. Soon they received a heavenly message and were shown another, safer route home.

(b) King Herod's vicious enmity. In contrast, King Herod's attitude of petty stubbornness and deceit soon escalated into horrific sin. In his rage at being tricked he attempted the murder of the Lord's Messiah, but God prevented that. His fury led him to order the death of all children under two years old in Bethlehem and the surrounding area. It was one of the foulest crimes in recorded human history.

Our response. Point out to the children that unbelief always leads to worse sins. No one can ignore God through life and be unscathed by increasing sinfulness of heart and life. Without God all kinds of sin begin to grow and fester, and the Bible warns that the road of disobedience leads to destruction *(Matthew 7.13)*. Children and young people may like to imagine that they can live just as well without the Lord, but their attitude will soon lead to hatred and hostility towards God, and they will change from being indifferent towards their Maker to becoming His bitter enemies.

Urge the children, in closing, to follow the wise men – to seek the Saviour until they find Him. Assure them that if only they catch sight of the Lord Jesus' love to them in coming to Bethlehem and Calvary, they will not hesitate to fall down and worship Him, gladly giving Him their hearts and lives.

Visual Aid

The outline pictures of the wise men and Herod suggested at the beginning of the lesson will provide a focal point beneath which the three main sets of headings can be listed.

The Lord Jesus Is Tempted (129)

Matthew 4.1-11; Hebrews 4.15

Aim: To show the greatness and the kindness of the Lord Jesus in these traumatic events, and to urge the children not to allow Satan to turn them away from the One Who would be their Saviour and Friend.

Lesson Outline

Tell the class that after Jesus was baptised and the Father spoke from Heaven, saying, *This is my beloved Son,* He was taken into the bleak and barren wilderness to be tempted by Satan. Why was He tempted? Provide three answers:–

(a) We need a sinless Saviour. If the Lord were to die for our sins in our place, and make Himself an offering of perfect righteousness on our behalf, then He must be absolutely perfect and without any sin of His own. Even a child can see that if Jesus had an easy life and was never tempted, then Satan might rightly claim that He was not really qualified to be our Saviour. We shall see in this lesson how the devil came with all his craft, power and guile to tempt the Lord Jesus.

Satan knew what was at stake. If he lost this battle then millions of his human slaves and hostages would be set free, pardoned and enabled to go to Heaven, through the success of the Saviour. We shall see him tempting the Saviour in the most wicked ways. His suggestions were much more cunning and tempting than any suggestions he makes to us. But we shall see how the Lord Jesus resisted each temptation in turn. Remind the children that it is harder to resist temptation than to give in to it. (Give examples suitable for the age of the class – eg: when in trouble, is it easier to tell a lie, or to resist the temptation, tell the truth and face the consequences?) We should never think that because Christ was God it was easy for Him. It was because He was the Son of God that He (unlike all of us) was able to resist sin. But He was also truly man, and therefore the temptation was just as great as it is for us – far greater in fact. The cost of resisting Satan's suggestions went far beyond anything we could experience.

(b) We need a sympathetic Saviour. If the Lord was to be our Friend, our Mediator, and our great High Priest (our representative) in Heaven, then it was necessary that He should understand our trials and temptations. When someone suffers a terrible accident and loses arms or legs, or something similarly hard, that person finds the best help, comfort and guidance comes from a person who has suffered a similar hardship. Such a person *really* understands and identifies. Such a person more than anyone else can be a friend. As we read about the Lord Jesus under attack from the wicked one in the wilderness, we realise how much He sympathises with us. He came and took on a human body so that He might experience for Himself what it was to be tempted just as we are *(Hebrews 4.15)*.

(c) We need an example. From earliest childhood Satan comes to tempt, to lure us into sin, and to trap us. How can we escape his clutches? How can we resist his urgings? By going through this period of temptation, and by all His other teaching, the Lord Jesus has shown us the way. We learn from Him.

The temptations –

(1) 'Command that these stones be made bread.' Describe how Satan came to Jesus after He had fasted for forty days and was very, very hungry. (This in itself teaches how much the Lord Jesus was willing to humble Himself. How amazing that God, Who provides all creatures with their food, should so enter into a human body as to be hungry! Even children know what it is to be tempted in this way!) In this situation the Lord was strongly tempted to use His mighty power in His own interests and make bread from the stones around Him. (But how, as our 'champion' or representative, could He manifest *perfect* seeking after communion with His Father, and thus achieve perfect righteousness, if He yielded to the temptation not to take this seriously, and to think of His bodily appetites and comforts first?) However, instead of thinking only of His own comfort, what He wanted and how He could get it, the Lord used the Bible against Satan's evil suggestion – *Man shall not live by bread alone, but by every word that proceedeth out of the mouth of God.* He refused to use His mighty power selfishly, to satisfy His own hunger. Instead He continued to look to His heavenly Father, and obey Him, knowing that He, not Satan, would provide for *all* His needs.

Emphasise to older classes that this seemingly simple temptation had great implications for the Saviour. If He were to use His divine power to satisfy His own physical needs, then He could use that same power to do anything just to please Himself. He could for example use it to win the favour of the crowds. When He later turned five loaves and two fishes into food for five thousand He soon became enormously popular, so much so that the crowds wanted to make Him their king *(John 6.15)*. But unlike worldly heroes, He deliberately turned these crowds away making it clear that He had come to provide *spiritual* bread.

(2) 'Cast thyself down.' Describe how Satan next took Jesus to the Temple pinnacle and challenged Him to exploit His divine status by throwing Himself off its pinnacle, knowing that His heavenly Father had promised to keep Him in perfect safety. Chiefly, this suggestion was a temptation to live as a kind of superman, who would be immune from troubles and pains, able to escape them all. In other words it was a temptation to opt out of His gracious work as a Saviour Who would be humiliated, and would eventually take our punishment.

Perhaps also this dramatic escape would impress all who saw it, and the Lord's majesty would be seen and admired. How often Satan tempts all of us to be guided in our actions by what makes us feel good, and by what other people think of us. (Give examples.) How often we are told today that what matters is our self-esteem and self-confidence, and these will bring us success. This is the great lie of our present society. The older we get the more we are tempted to achieve the goal of personal success.

If there is time, point out that Satan cunningly quoted the Bible as he tempted the Lord. Warn the children that he keeps no rules of decency and fair play, and he has no respect at all for God, even twisting His words in his efforts to entice us into sin.

For His answer the Lord Jesus again used the Scriptures. However easy it would have been for Him to perform a sensational act of self-display, He refused, and set about His lowly task of winning the hearts of men and women by the means His Father had laid down. Later in Matthew's Gospel we shall see how Satan suggested to the Lord, through the lips of Peter, that He should opt out of going to Jerusalem and His death on the cross, and enjoy His popularity in Galilee, but once again Jesus refused to consider this suggestion.

(3) 'Fall down and worship me.' In this last temptation recorded by Matthew, Satan's audacity reached a climax. Only after offering Jesus an enormous prize, *the kingdoms of the world, and the glory of them*, did he slip in the suggestion that Jesus should fall down and worship him. Tell the class how Satan took Jesus to a high mountain top and showed Him all the wonders of the world and their glory. Notice that Satan did not show Him all the sin, the suffering, the fighting or the pain, but only the glory and the power which might be His. The Lord Jesus loved this world and had come to give His life for it. How typically deceitful of Satan to offer Him something which was not his to give anyway! But in His manhood the Lord Jesus was exposed to this most powerful temptation to pride and self-glory! 'Why serve the Father? Why do all this and go to Calvary only to share rule with the Father and the Holy Spirit? Come with me, and rebel, and You can have all this without any suffering on Calvary,' Satan seemed to imply.

Without any hesitation, the Saviour told Satan 'Be gone',

quoting the second commandment, *Thou shalt worship the Lord thy God, and him only shalt thou serve.* This ruled out the devil's suggestion once and for all, and the Lord – as truly man – became the first man to soundly and utterly defeat the temptation to pride and self-glory! How qualified He was to offer His perfect righteousness to earn Heaven for His people! How qualified He was to be a perfect atoning lamb for our sin!

At this point the devil left the Lord. Weary from His great ordeal, angels were sent to serve Him, until He was ready to leave Judea and return to Galilee where He began His great public ministry. We shall be hearing about some of His great miracles and teachings in the weeks ahead, so don't miss those lessons. As we close our lesson what can we learn from the temptations?

Jesus resisted the devil – and so should we. He did not listen for one moment to Satan's schemes. We, like the Saviour, should tell the devil to 'Be gone'. But instead we so often take Satan's suggestions seriously. We play with his ideas in our minds and give consideration to his promises. We lay ourselves open as he whispers that there is no God, or that one little sin will do us no harm. No wonder he defeats us as easily as he defeated Eve in the Garden of Eden. (Remember that she talked in an open, friendly way with the serpent, and so was beguiled.)

Encourage the children to follow the example of the Lord Jesus instead. Urge them to keep away from places, people and influences which are bad and against God. If God's Son refused to fraternise or hold a dialogue with evil, how much more should we! This is a particularly important point for children, for they are so easily influenced. Remind them, for example, that if they make friends with children who are unashamed liars, they will soon be made liars too. If they insist on going to godless parties, and later to pubs, they will soon follow immoral ways.

Jesus believed and obeyed God's Word – and so should we. On all three occasions the Lord quoted Scripture in answer to Satan's temptation. We too should love and learn the Bible. Any plan or idea which tells us to doubt the Bible and disobey its teachings must be wrong. The apostle Paul tells us that one of the most effective pieces of the Christian's armour is *the sword of the Spirit, which is the word of God (Ephesians 6.17).* Children who read the Bible daily are much less likely to be tricked into believing Satan's lies. (Eg: the theory of evolution is far less plausible to those taught to appreciate the greatness and glory of the Creator from *Genesis,* the *Psalms* and *Revelation.*)

Jesus refused to compromise – and so should we. He turned down Satan's suggestions immediately and completely. He did not compromise by committing just a small sin, such as turning a few small stones into bread. How easy it is for us to do a deal with Satan, and to half obey him, imagining as we do so that we are pretty good. We may be tempted to think, 'I won't give up believing in God, but I need not be a fully committed Christian.' Or, 'I go to Sunday School every week but I don't need to trust the Lord as *my* Saviour.' Or, 'I believe that Jesus Christ died on the cross for sinners like me, but why should I repent of all my sins and leave them behind?' No, if we are to find the Lord, we must seek Him with *all* our hearts *(Deuteronomy 4.29).*

'Tempted . . . yet without sin.' Make it clear that it is impossible for any of us to fully grasp all that the Lord Jesus went through as Satan tempted Him. We have only covered a tiny fraction of what these temptations involved, and we are amazed that the Lord Jesus should subject Himself to such a cruel experience. Nor was this the end of the Saviour's pains and temptations. After three years of ministry and buffetings from men and Satan, He finally submitted Himself to the death of the cross, the only means by which we could be released eternally from Satan's clutches. What amazing love to give Himself for us! Now, as a sympathetic Saviour, He lives to intercede for us before His Father's throne. When we feel ourselves buffeted by doubts and unbelief or drawn towards sin and wrongdoing, we can remember that the Lord Jesus is qualified and willing *to save them to the uttermost that come unto God by him, seeing he ever liveth to make intercession for them (Hebrews 7.25).*

Visual Aid

Pictures of a loaf of bread, the pinnacle of a tall building and a world globe will help to pin-point the three temptations. Key words can be printed beneath.

Jesus' Teaching – The Two Roads (130)

Matthew 7.13-14

Aim: To reason with the children about the two alternative ways of life and to show them the folly of ignoring the Saviour's directions.

Teachers' Introduction

The next three lessons group into a natural series drawn from Christ's 'Sermon on the Mount'. His teaching on the two roads, the two houses and the two trees fits usefully together to provide clear guidance for the children as they face the great issues of life.

VA 11 (see page 213) provides basic pictures which can be enlarged and elaborated to illustrate the main points of each lesson, and to provide a graphic summary of all three. Teachers should look at this before beginning these lessons.

Lesson Outline

Remind the class (with the aid of the map suggested in Lesson 93) that the Lord Jesus had returned to Galilee and begun His great work. Large crowds gathered to see and hear Him *(Matthew 4.23-25)*. What did He teach them? What made His words so memorable and unique? In the next few weeks we shall be learning some of the lessons that He taught. Today's lesson is about two roads.

Roads – their main purpose. Armed with visual aids which can include road maps, pictures of scenic views, traffic jams and road accidents, we begin by pointing out the most basic fact – that what matters most about a road is where it leads. Help the children picture themselves driving towards a roundabout or fork in the road. The large signboards at the opening of each road will not indicate what type of road lies ahead (whether it has two or three lanes, is surfaced with asphalt or chippings, or whether it passes through scenic countryside), neither will they advertise the restaurants and other facilities to be found alongside the road. They will simply indicate the names of the towns to which the road leads – London, Glasgow, etc. Other details are only of secondary importance.

The roads of life – where they lead. Aim to surprise the children by immediately pointing out that the one thing most children and adults do not consider when setting out on the great journey of life is their destination. How silly! How risky! Ask them what they would think of their parents if, when they set off on the family holiday, they simply drove along the nearest, most attractive-looking road, without having a clue where it was going. They would rightly regard this as idiotic. Yet many people set out on the greatest journey of all, the journey of life, without stopping for a moment to consider which path they should take. The Lord Jesus challenged them to consider the alternatives very seriously.

Suggest that we now return to the days of the Saviour, before cars were invented, and when roads were rather primitive. People walked long distances and used animals, carts and sometimes (for the noble) carriages for travel. The Lord pictured people coming to a crossroads where they would have to choose which of two roads to take.

(1) The popular road. Outline its features which included:–

(a) A wide gate. This road had a wide gateway which was easy for animals, carts and people to pass through. There was no toll to pay, no bolt to unlock, no narrow gate to pass through or stile to climb.

(b) A broad road. The road itself was broad, with plenty of room to rove from side to side, talk to fellow travellers, and manipulate carts, carriages, ponies, baggage, etc. This road was also easy to walk or ride along, being smoothed down and flattened by the tramping of many travellers.

(c) A crowded road. It was a busy route and one could enjoy the company of the crowds which travelled in both directions.

Unfold applications during lesson. ↑ Fold here.

VA 11 – Visual Aid for use with lessons on 'The Two Roads', 'The Two Houses' and 'The Two Trees'.

There would be inns and other places to stop for refreshment and entertainment. Once when Jesus was twelve, His parents had taken Him along the Jerusalem to Nazareth road. The party of friends and relatives was so large that they had not missed their boy for almost a whole day. This tells us just how busy such roads could be.

The unbeliever's life. In His mind's eye the Lord Jesus pictured men and women, boys and girls being drawn to a way of life which had many parallels with this kind of road or pathway.

(a) The open way. This is a way of living which is easy to get into. It has no 'gate'. It is the way of the crowd, where children and others just follow everyone else without bothering to think. There are no standards or conditions to meet before setting out upon it. It is popular with all kinds of people.

(b) The easy way. It represents a style of living which means that people can do whatever they like and have complete freedom from God's commands. Conscience does not bother them, or righteousness, or the Lord. A good time is all that matters along this road of life. What does it matter if they lie or cheat from time to time? Is there a God Who watches and sees their pride and deceit growing? They cannot see Him, and assume He does not exist. If anxiety crosses their mind about the future they quickly turn to some form of exciting diversion (their games, their music, their day-dreams) and soon forget their worries. More thoughtful people get keyed up about politics or environmental issues, but even these brush aside the Lord and His warnings.

(c) The crowded way. Help the children to identify this road as the one which most people take today. They follow the latest trends and current views presented at school or on the television. They believe whatever they hear, preferring to stay with the majority. They refuse to do any personal thinking, and do not trouble to ask any questions about life.

Once the class begins to see the point, turn their attention to another, almost unnoticed, road:–

(2) The unpopular road. Describe the second road with its main characteristics which included:–

(a) A small gate. It had to be entered by a narrow gate, which meant that anyone wishing to take this path had to stop, put down the animals or goods they were carrying, and manipulate the bolt. Even when it was opened, the gate was so narrow that people could pass through only one at a time.

(b) A narrow road. The path was narrow because it was less used. Perhaps thistles and briars at times invaded the track. Narrow paths are associated with hilly terrain, with steep climbs and routes round the sides of mountains. This was a difficult road, requiring determination, effort and boldness.

(c) A lonely road. By comparison with the broad way, this road was taken by far fewer people, and often it could be a lonely road. But the views were better, and when people met up, they had much more in common, and more to talk about.

The believer's life. This second road described by the Lord can be used to picture:–

(a) Christ – the Gate. Believers do not simply follow the crowd. They stop and consider their life's policy (because God's Spirit is working in their hearts). They come to the Lord in repentance, and they experience conversion. The Saviour is the *gate* to this new life – explain the way in which Calvary is the gateway to the Christian life. (Elsewhere, the Lord called Himself 'the Door'.) This is the most wonderful gate – the 'gate of grace'. One might expect that the gate guarding the path to eternal life would be heavy and forbidding, and capable of being opened only by perfect people who deserve Heaven. On the contrary, it is a gate of mercy, which swings open to welcome all who trust in Christ. Why then is it a narrow gate? First, because we must come to Christ one by one, repenting and seeking for ourselves. We cannot go through this gate in groups. Secondly, because, though it should be the most popular, it is the least popular. People will avoid the gate which opens only if they repent and yield to Christ.

(b) Christ – the Way. Once on the narrow pathway, we find that it also stands for Christ! In other words, He is personally as close to all who follow Him as a road is close to someone walking upon it. Christ is like a road to us. A road *upholds* us (eg:

our feet cannot sink into mud or quicksand); a road *guides* us safely (for it will not change its route!); and a good road *uplifts* us (by taking us through beautiful scenery and interesting places). The Lord does all these things for Christians, and makes Himself known to them.

(3) The destination. In addition, and supremely, we return to the original point. Hold the children's attention by asking the *chief* reason for the Lord Jesus urging His listeners to take the second path despite its unpopularity and difficulties – its destination. Which route are we on? If the broad way, then are we ready to change roads? Why should we? Let us put the question in the spirit of the illustration. Given the chance of speeding along a modern motorway in a high-performance car with the radio on and the sun-roof open, who would stop, get out and exchange such a ride for one on a bicycle, pedalling up a steep and lonely mountain track? Ask the class to think carefully. There are some circumstances which would encourage many sensible people to quit the motorway:–

(a) Danger ahead! Suppose they could see a seven-mile traffic jam ahead, or a grey wall of fog (with flashing lights warning of a traffic accident ahead) in which they might be involved in horrible carnage and receive injuries that would leave them in a wheelchair, would they still want to speed ahead on the motorway? Would they possibly consider it better to get off the motorway as fast as possible, whatever the alternative? This was the point that the Lord was making. Where is your life leading? Are you are speeding towards trouble and failure, and then your eternal punishment, banished from God? No wonder He issued this warning!

(b) A far better destination. Before closing, remind the class of the possible destination of the narrow pathway, first in the illustration, then in the spiritual realm. Suppose some climbers reach the top of the narrow, uphill path and find themselves overwhelmed by the magnificent view, the clear air and the warm welcome by their best friends into a beautiful and comfortable hotel where delicious meals and exciting pastimes are waiting to be enjoyed. Would not this make all the difference?

The destination is far more important than the route. The journey would have lasted only hours, but the destination was a place where a long stay would be enjoyed.

Draw parallels with the heavenly home which the Lord Jesus has promised to all who believe and follow Him. It is a perfect, happy, lasting and secure home, protected from all sin and sorrow by the Lord God Himself. Close by urging your class to think carefully about where their lives will lead them.

Visual Aids

In addition to using VA 11 (see page 213), provide a picture of two roads, one a wide, well-used road (possibly a modern motorway), the other a narrow, uphill path. Place printed headings on the appropriate roads as you describe the pros and cons of each.

The Two Houses (131)

Matthew 7.24-27; Luke 6.46-49

Aim: To show the nature and importance of true repentance, and the necessity of faith in the Lord Jesus as the foundation of the Christian life. To describe the disaster which befalls those who try to build their lives without God's Word.

Lesson Outline

Wise or foolish? Surprise the children by explaining that the Lord Jesus divided people into two categories – those whom He called *wise*, and the rest whom He classed as *fools*. Discuss the meaning of this second word. A dictionary says: 'A person who lacks sense or judgement. A person who is made to appear ridiculous. An idiot.' Today children are often encouraged to view people who hold Christian beliefs and values as foolish. Jesus was able to demonstrate by a simple illustration in words, that it is those who despise and ignore His teaching who are foolish and unwise. Urge the children to listen carefully to His assessment of the two men who each built a house. Explain that in the land where the Saviour lived it was quite common for families to build their own houses.

(1) The wise man's house. (a) Finding a good site. Eastern children would listen as their parents discussed the suitability of a parcel of ground for their new home. Their father would be anxious to know how far down he would have to dig in order to find a layer of rock or firm ground on which he could build the foundation of the house.

(b) Preparing the ground. Having chosen the site the family would all lend a hand in its preparation, removing the topsoil and digging deep into the ground. All loose and sandy soil, and especially all roots and other remains of vegetation, had to be cleared away. It was easy to get impatient at this stage and wonder why such a tedious and costly operation was necessary. A wise father would insist that this was all done, and for a good reason. A house would sink slightly into the ground before long if it had been built on top of unstable, loose soil, containing rotting material. Then the walls would subside and crack, and eventually the house might collapse. Even worse, heavy rain or floods might wash away the loose soil, causing the house to fall suddenly.

(c) Building on a solid foundation. Once they had found something solid on which to fix the house, the walls could be firmly built, and windows, doors and roof followed quickly. Before long the family could move their belongings in.

The believer's life. Ask the children to work out in their minds what the Lord's illustration teaches. What do we have to remove from our lives before we can seriously begin the Christian life? What did the rock and the foundations stand for?

(a) The site of repentance. Show that repentance is pictured in the preparation of the ground. How can we ask the Lord to receive our lives, and be our Saviour and Lord, if we keep deliberate sins hidden just under the surface? The Lord warned His hearers that it was no good listening to Him with approving smiles if they had no intention of acting on His words. We must give up the sins of lying, stealing, hatred, selfishness and pride. The 'spade' of the Holy Spirit must disturb these sins, taking them out of us as we truly repent of them. This is indeed a painful experience, but it is essential. Ask your children if they have felt truly sorry about their sin. Have they experienced the tears of shame and regret? Have they really longed for the Lord to take away their sin and give them a new start to life? Repentance is pictured by the act of digging out the rotten, unstable soil.

(b) The solid ground of faith in the Lord Jesus. Alongside repentance, coming to Christ means placing one's entire trust in Him. This is perfectly pictured by the solid rock on which the walls of the house should be built. Explain how Calvary is the solid ground and basis of salvation. There the Lord perfectly and eternally put away the punishment of our sin. The person who trusts *his own* good works as the means of pleasing God and earning Heaven, builds his hope upon crumbling, weak ground, or moving sand. Christ is the Christian's only hope and rock.

(c) The foundation of God's Word. This is a solid rock for our lives. We need to have a certain and reliable source of information about God, what He is like, what He will do, how we may find Him, how we may please Him, and so on. People have many different opinions – but they are mere speculation. To build our lives upon these would be building on crumbling ground! They may all be wrong! Then where is the solid, reliable source of information about the soul? The Bible is the only foundation.

(2) The foolish man's house. (a) No survey. Turn quickly to the other man who was building his house nearby on the first piece of land available. He did not care that he was building on sand. His house went up very quickly.

(b) No preparation. He spent much more time on getting ornate decorations and up-to-date furniture. Imagine the family of the wise man looking on dismayed as the foolish man held a house-warming party for all his friends – even before their own foundation was finished! Probably the wise man's children wondered why their father had wasted so much time worrying about digging down to the rock layer.

The unbeliever's life. (a) No repentance. The foolish man pictures the person who builds his life without worrying about the 'foundation' – being converted to Christ. He hears about this teaching, but does nothing about it. Ask if there could be a child present who falls into this category – proud of coming to Sunday School, familiar with the Gospel, sometimes complaining of being bored in the lesson, yet having no intention of repenting or looking to the Lord for salvation.

(b) No security. The person who ignores God sometimes *seems* to leap ahead in life, filling life with pleasures and possessions, and receiving much admiration and applause. But unseen, beneath ground level, there is no foundation. Many people have an unseen, missing part – their soul is not saved!

(3) A storm. Now explain *why* Jesus classed such people as fools. Describe what happened. Suddenly a storm thundered down. Rain and wind beat against both houses, and the fool's house collapsed, while the wise man's house stood firm. Now the family of the wise man respected their father's insistence on a strong foundation.

The storms of life. Challenge your class by informing them that their attitude to the Lord Jesus and His words will sooner or later be put to the test. Explain that life is never a 'walk-over'. Storms will soon beat against them. Suggest the kinds of trials which everyone can expect. Temptations to sin come like recurring squalls or storms. Alongside come other storms, such as the breakup of families, failure in examinations, illness, betrayal by friends, financial worries, redundancy (which has brought many a sportsman and actor to the brink of ruin and despair). Finally, at the very end, comes the fear of death. Explain that these things put everyone to the test. Show your concern as you warn of these dangers for those who reject the Gospel. There are countless proud, godless people whose self-confidence and competence to handle themselves has collapsed in the face of these situations. They have had no heavenly Friend to turn to, no rule of God to guide them, and no Saviour to shelter them from Satan's wiles and schemes and to strengthen them when the storms of life and death appear.

Wise or foolish? Urge your class to respect Christ for confronting men and women with these great issues. Help them to admire Him for the wonderful simplicity of His illustration – no one could ever say it is too difficult to understand! Encourage all to be wise and to hear and do all that the Saviour taught.

Visual Aid

Draw a simple outline of two houses. As the lesson proceeds fix on the appropriate headings, eg: 'No survey', 'No preparation', etc.

The Two Trees (132)

Matthew 7.15-23; see also Matthew 23

Aim: To prepare children for the fact that there are many false professors of religion who may influence their views, and thus to follow the Lord's example in warning the vulnerable. To encourage the children to test their own profession.

Teachers' Introduction

Even the youngest child needs to be warned of the dangers of life. From earliest days parents take care to prepare their children, using even nursery stories that feature evil characters as well as good. The Lord here warns His disciples of *counterfeit* Christians, and it is part of our duty to warn our children against being influenced by those who claim to be Christians but who have no real experience of the Lord.

Adults as well as children are confused when they hear so many different groups claiming to be Christian. They see numerous denominations and sects and these become an excuse for them to throw up their hands and refuse to consider the Gospel at all. We must show them what is distinctive about authentic Christianity, and point them to the Lord Himself. Discovering true religion is not as hard as they imagine. Who are some of the *false* Christians whose views affect our children?

(1) There are many RE teachers in schools who teach liberal theology and who pour scorn on biblical faith. They often tear the Bible to pieces in class. Such teachers represent Christianity

as little more than a moral code. (Unfortunately, it is necessary for teachers to warn young believers against choosing religious studies as a subject for school examination, because the Bible is examined according to the cynical, critical, destructive prejudice of nineteenth-century liberalism. Discredited as it now is, it remains the dominant influence in school religious education.)

(2) There are many unbelieving clergy and ministers who are given time on television to deny the virgin birth, resurrection, etc, and whose religion is obviously lifeless.

(3) Television evangelists are now well publicised, and it is clear to most people that their interest in religion has more to do with making money and showing off than winning souls. Older children may have heard of recent cases of these men being involved in fraud, adultery, etc. (With the coming of universal, satellite television programmes, this group, unfortunately, is set to increase.)

(4) The new stream of 'worldly Christians', some of whom may be known to our children, will distort their perceptions of Christianity. They will hear that one or two pop stars or other show business personalities are 'Christians', and notice their complete identification with the culture of the age.

In addition, this lesson provides the criteria (five 'Marks of Grace') by which children can test themselves and their own standing in God's sight.

Lesson Outline

True and false Christians. Remind the children that many people today speak about God at school, at home, at church and on television. Jesus warned that not all such people really belong to God. He said some religious teachers are false teachers *(Matthew 7.15)*. They put themselves across as God's servants or ministers (they may even wear parsons' robes, etc), but many are not in touch with God at all. When the Lord came to earth there were leaders of the Jewish church who behaved in a highly religious way, wore special clothes, said prayers in public places, and were known as Pharisees. Yet the Lord Jesus said that they would not go to Heaven *(Matthew 5.20)*. Similarly it is possible for us to pretend we are Christians when we are not.

How can we tell a true Christian? We cannot go by what people claim, and we must not be taken in by superficial appearances. The Lord has given a test for us to use. He said, *Ye shall know them by their fruits (Matthew 7.16).*

Look for the fruit. Experts can often tell you the name of a tree even in winter, when it has no leaves, but most people know from the fruit. This is a certain test, because a thorn cannot bear grapes, neither a thistle figs. Is someone a true Christian? Am I a true Christian? Do I have the character of a Christian? What should my *fruit* or behaviour and works look like?

(1) A repentant person *(Luke 3.8).* Everyone who is a true Christian has repented humbly of their sin, and trusted in Calvary for salvation. And they go on being sorry for their sins and asking God's forgiveness, and by His help striving to overcome them and get them out of their lives. Children who used to lie, stop lying when they become Christians. Bad tempers are controlled. Swearing and blaspheming cease. Christians do not become perfect immediately, but a new hatred of sin is noticeable and pronounced. If a Christian finds he is doing something wrong, or bad conduct is pointed out to him, instead of being proud and offended, he is humble and wants to put matters right. Repentance is a sure sign of a real Christian.

(2) A changed person *(2 Corinthians 5.17).* Another sure fruit is a new nature. Not only does the bully become kind, and the selfish person begin to think of others, but a new attitude to life takes over. The new Christian puts the Lord first, and serves Him, and wants to be His follower.

(3) A Bible-believing person *(Acts 2.42).* A real convert is seen from his new love for the Bible. He realises it is God's perfect, infallible Word, from which the Lord will speak to him and teach him. If we come across religious people who do not believe the Bible to be God's inspired Word, and who regard it as a collection of myths and legends, and criticise or ignore its teaching, we can be sure they are not true Christians. They fail this test. Also, if we hear of people who claim to believe the

Bible, but take no notice of the things it commands, then they are probably not true Christians.

(4) A praying person *(Romans 8.15).* Real Christians speak to their Lord, and God hears and answers. Every day they draw near to the Lord, praising Him, asking His forgiveness for their sin and asking His blessing for other people and for their own lives. In any emergency, they pray to the Lord. In any success, they praise Him. Children can easily see that those ministers who recite prayers on the television – looking all around as they do so – are not really praying at all. How can they be real Christians?

(5) A loving person *(1 John 3.14).* Here is another test for a true Christian. Truly converted boys and girls have their closest friends amongst Christians and they look forward to being with other believers. They feel a special bond, and are able to talk about the Lord, and their experience of His blessing. But also, their concern and feeling covers relatives and friends who are unconverted. Jesus called His first disciples to be *fishers of men.* All true Christians long to bring others to the Lord Jesus and the Lord blesses their efforts. Do you want your friends to know the Lord Jesus? Do you invite them to Sunday School?

Drawing conclusions. A true church is one where the members work and pray so that many others will come to know and love the Saviour. If we see a church where the minister is not concerned about the souls of men, women and children, however beautiful the church building may be, we should doubt if it is a *true* church.

One day the truth will come out about everyone – whether we are real Christians or not. We may be able to pretend to other people that we are, but there is Someone Who knows the truth already, and that is God. We cannot fool Him. He sees into our hearts. One day He will judge all of us, and then everyone will know the truth. Those who have been false Christians will be destroyed like the bad tree, but those whose lives bring forth fruit for the Lord Jesus will be eternally blessed *(Matthew 7.19).* There is no need for any member of the class to fear that judgement, for the Lord is ready to forgive and change any who call upon Him.

Visual Aid

Provide a cut-out tree and five large fruit. Print the five 'Marks of Grace' used in the lesson on the fruit. As you cover these points 'hang' the fruit on the tree. At the close of the lesson, or during the subsequent lesson, briefly revise and test this group of lessons by using VA 11 (see page 213).

The 'Lord's Prayer' (133)

Matthew 6.8-15

Aim: To show how the 'Lord's Prayer' can be used as a prayer of repentance by those ready to end their rebellion and find peace with God.

Lesson Outline

Remind the class that, before conversion, we are all enemies of God. We have rebelled against our heavenly Father and taken a journey to a 'far country'. Any message or approach from Him has been pushed aside and ignored by us, or met with a hostile attitude, hardened resistance and even bitter hatred in our hearts. Show that all children, before conversion, harbour one or other of these two sinful attitudes to the Lord. Help your class to face this fact.

Ending hostilities. At the end of any war there have to be peace talks and negotiations. Similarly when battle-weary sinners return to the Lord they need to know the terms of surrender, the right approach. It may be that some children have listened carefully to previous lessons and now find an earnest desire to make their peace with God. Perhaps the Lord has fired His arrows of conviction into their souls, whilst at the same time drawing them to Himself with the cords of love. The question then arises – How can they best approach God? What should they say? Is God willing to spare such guilty, daring rebels? What kind of prayer should they pray?

A mediator. Remind them that the Bible speaks of the Lord Jesus as a mediator, a go-between. He is the best person to advise us and He has left us the perfect peace plan. It is plain and clear, short and simple and has been used down the centuries as a pattern of prayer for returning sinners. Any children wanting to know exactly how they can become Christians should listen with great care.

(1) 'Our Father.' Picture wounded soldiers receiving the surrender terms from a victorious enemy with fear and apprehension. Imagine them trembling as they start to read the opening phrases of the document which they expect to be crushing and humiliating. Share their profound relief and joy as they discover that their enemy addresses them as members of his family now returning, and welcomes them. We too can rejoice that the Lord Jesus taught His disciples that they could address almighty God as, 'Our Father'.

These words remind us that although we have wandered far from the Lord, yet He is still our Maker – as the Bible puts it – *It is he that hath made us, and not we ourselves; we are his people, and the sheep of his pasture (Psalm 100.3).* Despite our sin and shameful behaviour He is willing to have us back. In fact, He is ready to meet us and take us home because we are too poor and weak to make the journey ourselves *(Luke 15.20).* Instead of herding us into prisoner-of-war camps awaiting execution, He is willing to prepare a great feast to celebrate our return! All children seeking the Lord should go immediately to Him encouraged by these wonderful words and trust their souls to their Father in Heaven.

(2) 'Which art in heaven.' The only condition for our return and restoration to the heavenly family is that we cut all ties with our old master, the devil, and recognise that God's realm is quite different. The Lord is holy, lifted up, and pure, and if we want to be with Him we must be prepared to be made like Him. We must be willing to discard our old uniform of lies, selfishness, hatred, etc and put on the righteous robes provided by our Saviour.

(3) 'Hallowed be thy name.' The first matter to be put right is our attitude to God Himself. Before conversion we have had all kinds of wrong attitudes. Sometimes we have spoken of God as if He just did not exist, and perhaps His name has been insultingly used in blasphemy. Now we must come using that great name with awe and reverence, knowing that it belongs to the One Who holds our eternal future in His hands and Who was willing to suffer that we might live.

(4) 'Thy kingdom come.' Just as surrendering troops must lay down their arms and sign papers of loyalty and obedience as they become citizens of the conquering country, so all those who desire to enter the kingdom of God must be willing to be ruled and schooled by the Lord. They must leave behind resistance (whether open or sullen) to His laws and gladly accept His ways.

(5) 'Thy will be done.' They will be issued with a new rule book, the Bible, which must govern all future belief and behaviour. Unlike their former administration, it is honest, helpful and infinitely wise. They must want to do God's will, and be guided by Him.

(6) 'Give us this day our daily bread.' Our new King has promised to provide all our daily needs so long as we put His kingdom first in our lives *(Matthew 6.33)*. Unlike Satan, who makes many alluring promises and cruelly breaks them all, the Lord keeps His word and provides generously for His subjects, not only with respect to earthly needs but with rich provisions of joy, peace and eternal life. Every day He invites us to come to Him with a shopping list of all our needs and then He delights to grant us more than we could ever have asked or thought *(Ephesians 3.20)*.

(7) 'Forgive us our debts, as we forgive our debtors.' As we approach His throne room for an audience with the great King our greatest need is that of forgiveness. We must recognise that we do not deserve forgiveness, and we dare not even ask for it unless we truly mean every word. The Lord looks for a change of heart. *He* knows if we mean what we say. If we pretend to Him to be sorry for sin, but all the time prefer to go on living like rebels and worldlings, then He will not forgive us.

(8) 'Lead us not into temptation, but deliver us from evil.' Once we have come to know the Lord, we certainly do not want to fall back to our old ways. Therefore we pray that the Lord will keep us faithful to Him, and hold us through strong temptation. But even as we come to the Lord asking for conversion, we must realise that this is to be for life and then for eternity.

(9) 'For thine is the kingdom, and the power, and the glory, for ever.' Help the children picture the scene as a surrender document is signed and sealed. The defeated party looks at their new ruler, surveying the face of the king who for so long has been their enemy. When they see for themselves the superior power, strength and glory of the conqueror they wonder why they have struggled against him for so long. Battle-weary, they gladly place themselves in his safe and powerful hands. Assure the children that if they return to the Lord, lay down their resistance, and surrender their lives to Him, they too can rest their souls safely in His keeping, knowing that His power and glory will protect them eternally, and that His kingdom will stand secure for ever.

Application. Ask if any child still wants to remain part of Satan's rebellion against God – to be ordered about by him, used as a pawn by him, and finally taken by him to hell. Surely not! Urge the members of your class to make sure that they are among the great host of men, women and children who can confidently address God as 'Our Father', and gladly mean every one of the words of this wonderful prayer given to us by the Lord Jesus Himself. Encourage them to learn it, and better still to use it as a pattern prayer.

Visual Aid

Provide a picture of a walled city with a defeated army at its gates ready to surrender, also a peace document (a scroll) from the king bearing the words of this prayer. Teachers may like to begin the lesson with the words covered and then uncover each phrase as they teach it.

Jesus Heals a Leper (134)

Matthew 7.28 – 8.4; see also Mark 1.40-45

Aim: To see the injurious effects of sin, pictured in the Bible as a disease, from which we need to be delivered.

Lesson Outline

Describe the atmosphere as Jesus came to the end of His teaching on the mountain. A large crowd had been listening to Him. They were used to sitting through boring sermons given by their religious leaders, but this was different. Instead of hiding their yawns, and feeling great relief at the close of the preaching, they went away deeply impressed and thoughtful at the things which the Lord had said. Matthew tells us that they were *astonished* at His teaching. Unlike the scribes who had learned their religion from dry-as-dust professors, the people realised that Christ spoke with authority, as One Who knew God and His ways directly. Some began to realise that Jesus was no ordinary person. Many began to believe that He was at least a great prophet sent by God. We know that, in fact, He was the Son of God sent to teach us the way back to God.

Words proved by deeds. But Jesus not only taught with God's power and authority, He also acted. He performed countless amazing miracles on all kinds of needy people to demonstrate to those who were willing to listen that He was indeed God's Son, the Saviour of the world. This example of the Lord's healing miracles shows His power over one of the most unpleasant diseases known to mankind. Explain that such healing miracles not only proved that the Lord was Who He claimed to be, but they also serve as 'parables' of His power to heal our spiritual disease, and to restore our souls.

Leprosy. Tell the class what a tragic disease leprosy was. (It has reared its ugly head in many parts of the world over the centuries with different symptoms, but we concentrate on the strain familiar in New Testament times.) Its worst features were:–

(a) It was infectious and therefore its victims had to be isolated from the rest of society.

(b) It was greatly disfiguring – it led to dry, scaling skin, loss of nails and hair, and eventually the shrinking of bones and gums, causing the leper to look hideously deformed.

(c) Although leprosy sufferers could live for many years in gradual decline, the disease was usually fatal.

The Lord's great kindness. Describe the condition which afflicted the leper who came to Jesus. Mark tells us that Jesus had compassion upon him – indicating something of his sorry condition. Most people would have been so horrified by the sight of this poor man that they would have turned away.

Our ugly condition. Surprise the class by suggesting that in the sight of the God we are probably even more repugnant than the leper. That man was disfigured by ugly physical sores which were not of his doing, but we, in God's sight, are polluted and disfigured by the guilt of sins which we have willingly and knowingly committed. Imagine what a deliberately lying heart must look like to the holy God. Imagine what a proud thought must seem like to the Lord Who is pure, or how a display of evil temper must appear. In His sight all selfish and greedy thoughts are vile, and we who are full of these things must revolt Him. Yet because of His mercy He does not turn away from us. Instead, the Son of God came from Heaven to give His life on Calvary's cross in order to restore us.

Next we look at the way in which the leper approached the Lord. We need to be saved from our disease of sin before it drags us down to hell. What better could we do than follow the leper's example:–

(1) He came to Jesus. He saw his great need, and his horrible condition, and he desperately wanted to be made clean and well. Do we? Or will we wait until the X-rays of Heaven declare our case to be irreversible on the day of judgement? Urge the children to go quickly to the great Physician of Souls while there is time, asking Him to make them clean, and to take away all their ugly sin-stains.

(2) He worshipped Jesus. The leper must have heard Jesus speaking. He knew that He had already performed miracles on many sick people. (It may be necessary to explain that, unlike modern 'faith-healers', Jesus' cures were instant and lasting, and they were performed on people with the most severe illnesses, such as blindness, deafness, and paralysis. Also, He never failed. He raised the dead and commanded even nature to obey Him.) The leper had heard about the power of the Lord, and he wanted to know more. He fell down and worshipped Him. Do we? Many people, when they hear about how Christ rose from the dead, and how He has transformed the lives of millions of believers, respond with scorn, and refuse to believe and acknowledge Him as God. Are we like this? Do we think that we are doing the Lord a favour by coming to Sunday School, instead of realising that it is only because of His amazing grace and mercy that we can hear about Him at all? Try to convince the class that if only they knew Who they were learning about, they too would fall silent, listen and worship.

(3) He trusted Jesus. What a simple sentence the leper addressed to the Lord, yet how much it tells us about his thoughts: *If thou wilt, thou canst make me clean.* This leper truly believed that the Lord had the power to do what no other person could do – heal him. Do we believe that the Saviour can forgive our sins, change our lives and renew us, or are we full of doubts and misgivings? The leper's only doubt was his own unworthiness. He wondered if the Lord would want to use His divine power to benefit such a worthless, hopeless case. That should also be the way we feel. Soon he heard those wonderful words of Jesus, *I will; be thou clean*, and he felt that touch – a touch which meant more than words could say to a leper, an 'untouchable' – and instantly he felt cured and well. How simple! Yet how powerful! And how immediate!

Close by urging your class to consider this matter earnestly.

There is no doubt that the Lord Jesus is willing to save – why else did He endure the agony of Calvary? His love for us is in no doubt, why then do we hesitate? Is it that we forget how sick we are? Is it that we are too proud to 'kneel' and ask? Is it that we believe Satan when he puts doubts into our minds, instead of believing the Lord? We should wait no longer. We should go to Christ and ask for forgiveness and new life, but we must mean this prayer with all our hearts.

A testimony. Soon the leper was on his way to the authorities to 'register' his healing and announce his return to normal living. Explain to the class what a glad day it will be when they are able to say that they have been to the Saviour and received His forgiveness, and that they are now ready to enlist in His service day by day.

The Wheat and the Tares (135)

Matthew 13.24-30 and 36-43

Aim: To teach the children how God, the Creator, views our world and ourselves. To show them the urgency and importance of seeking the Saviour before it is too late.

Teachers' Introduction

In the parable of the Wheat and the Tares the Lord gives a divine assessment of our planet and the history of the human race – its earliest times, its problems and its end. He touched upon the time of creation, the Fall and final judgement, and all in the space of fifteen verses. Yet the genius of this parable is that these great truths are expressed in a simple picture, easily understood by the smallest child, and at the same time challenging to the most intelligent minds. Indeed this parable is calculated to shock the hearers into considering the eternal destiny of the soul in a way which no amount of lecturing could ever do. Whereas it is often best with older classes to present the application of the parable alongside each stage of events, we suggest that in this case the meaning should be kept until *after* all the events have been unfolded.

A 'green' topic. By teaching children to see the world as God sees it, this parable provides a Christian perspective on environmental issues with which modern children are constantly bombarded at school and by the media. It reminds us of the first and most vital factor – that this world is a 'field' belonging to the Son of Man, and the tragedy of human corruption and condemnation towers above the problems of the environment.

Lesson Outline

The parable. Interest the class by announcing that this lesson involves agricultural sabotage. Explain that espionage, insider-dealing, cheating, fraud and malicious spite have existed down the ages, and are nothing new. In Bible times, before modern-day industries had been established, money was chiefly invested in agriculture. Tell the parable vividly. A farmer sowed good seed in his field, investing a large amount of capital. An enemy sowed tares amongst it (while the farmer slept) and went away. The farm workers noticed two 'crops' growing (one good, one bad) where there should have been only one. The farmer realised that the tares were the work of an enemy, and that to uproot the weeds at this stage would destroy the crop. Therefore, he would leave both to grow together until harvest, then destroy the weeds while saving the crop.

Its meaning. Tell the class (especially older classes) that this is not your own interpretation, because the Lord Himself explained very carefully the meaning of this parable.

(1) The farmer and field. The farmer or sower is the Son of Man (the Lord Jesus) and the field is the world. This world belongs to God Who made it. The first man and woman who were made were described by Him, along with all creation, as *very good (Genesis 1.31)*. Explain that it is at this first, vital point that so many people go wrong. They assume that the world belongs to them, not God, and that they have the right to govern it themselves. They forget that, *The earth is the Lord's, and the fulness thereof; the world, and they that dwell therein (Psalm 24.1)*. Every adult and every boy and girl was made by the Lord to love, obey and serve Him.

(2) An enemy. Tell how, as the farm workers in the parable discovered that the wheat was riddled with weeds, so we, as we look at our world, discover that something has gone badly wrong. It is certainly not *very good.* As we grow up and experience life for ourselves, we realise how wrong and bad things are. There is war, famine, suffering and injustice wherever we look. Our own lives are spoilt by greed, lies, pride, hatred, selfishness, etc. The scientists tell us that mankind is in danger of damaging the planet's ecosystems irretrievably through greed and exploitation. What has gone wrong? What explanation did the Lord give for the problem?

Turn back to verses 28, 38 and 39. Jesus' verdict was, *An enemy hath done this* (v 28), and then the enemy is named as *the devil* (v 39). Remind the class that it was the devil who persuaded the first man and woman to turn away from God and disbelieve Him and disobey Him. Since that moment, which is called the Fall, our world has been chaotic. And throughout time Satan has done his utmost to sabotage the human race, bringing the population of the world to unbelief and rebellion. By God's great mercy, millions of people have turned to Jesus Christ, and come to know Him and walk with Him. But throughout the world there are also millions who have nothing to do with the Lord, and who try to choke out the church. Satan has invented all kinds of religions and philosophies to lure people away from believing in the one true God, their Maker and Lord. So there is unhappiness and chaos and poverty and even war as people kick against the Lord's wisdom and counsel.

(3) God's plan. Like the workers in the field of the parable who asked about destroying the tares, we might ask why God does not destroy all falsehood, atheism, and all unbelievers. The answer given by the Saviour in the parable teaches that God is waiting to gather a great crowd of believers from every nation on earth, from every period of history, adults and boys and girls, into His kingdom. Had He immediately rooted out sinners and destroyed them, we would have never benefited from His grace and love. God allows the world to continue. He leaves the field (the world) undisturbed, so that believers and unbelievers live side by side. We see sin flourishing all around, but we also see God's saving love reaching out and bringing people to salvation. Sometimes it is hard for Christians to struggle against the ungodly all around them. Often unbelievers seem to do so much better than believers – just as weeds seem to flourish in a garden.

(4) The day of harvest. But the Lord warned that this was only a temporary arrangement. Men and women may dismiss God and even persecute His people, but the day of harvest draws nearer. The Saviour described the day when He would send His angels and they would divide everyone into two groups. All those who believe in Christ and trust in His atoning death will be gathered in to spend eternity in God's kingdom. But those who continue in unbelief and disobedience will be sent to punishment. Just as weeds are dug up and burned, so unbelievers will be removed and punished for ever.

Show how reasonable and just God's judgements are. Weeds are burnt so that they cannot proliferate and do further damage. The Lord Jesus particularly condemned those who caused others to disbelieve (stumbling-blocks) and those whose behaviour affected others (lawless people). God does not desire the death of sinners, but if they adamantly refuse His gracious invitation, and ignore His willingness to convert and transform their lives, He is left with no alternative. Urge your class to join those who seek the Saviour, who repent and accept His rule in this world however difficult, and who look forward to the great day of harvest.

All the world is God's own field,
Fruit unto His praise to yield;
Wheat and tares together sown,
Unto joy or sorrow grown;
First the blade, and then the ear,
Then the full corn shall appear:
Lord of harvest, grant that we
Wholesome grain and pure may be.
(Henry Alford)

The Pearl of Great Price (136)

Matthew 13.45-46

Aim: To show the great desirability of our magnificent, all-surpassing Saviour, and the impact which finding Him has upon us.

Lesson Outline

Comment to your class on the age-old fascination of 'collecting'. Explain that there are famous collections of paintings and antiques as well as of popular items such as stamps, football pictures and dinky toys. Point out that there is a sense in which the whole of life is a collection. Most families keep a photo-album – the collection of a lifetime's memories and achievements. What is your life's collection of memories and achievements going to be like? What will its value be?

Finding quality pearls. Introduce the class to this merchant who searched for pearls in order to sell them to wealthy clients. Why should people be interested in buying and collecting pearls?

(1) Very rare. Real pearls are found in oyster shells gathered from the sea bed by strong and experienced divers. In ancient times these men had to dive underwater for long periods (without breathing-masks) in order to collect as many shells as possible. Other skilled workers opened the shells in such a way that the hidden pearls within would not be damaged. Only on rare occasions is a really 'perfect' pearl discovered. Small wonder pearls are highly prized!

(2) Very beautiful. Pearls are not showy or garish, but they are most exquisite. Unlike precious metals such as gold and silver, which need to be refined and expertly handled to decorate some other item, or diamonds which need to be cut and shaped before their beauty is apparent, pearls are naturally and immediately beautiful. Their unusual kind of gentle beauty makes the smaller pearls unusually suited for use in clusters or strings, and the larger pearls have a unique lustre and depth.

(3) Very costly. Because of their rarity and beauty, real pearls are highly priced. In centuries gone by they were owned and worn only by kings, queens, members of the nobility, and other immensely rich people. Merchants who traded in pearls moved in high society.

The merchant's collection. Return to the merchant who had built up a fine stock of valuable pearls. No doubt he travelled widely to obtain such a collection. Point out that in those days travel was far more difficult, costly and dangerous than today. Perhaps the merchant knew different languages in order to deal with those, in different lands, who acquired the best specimens. All his efforts were worthwhile if he was able to secure for his rich clients a choice selection of this much-desired jewel.

Our collection. Tell the class that the merchant pictures us. We are collectors of the 'pearls of life'. What are the 'pearls' that we are collecting? What pearls do we treasure, and boast of? What do we pay dearly for, with our efforts and desires? Are we looking for the pearls of entertainment, or of sporting achievement? Are we gathering the pearls of a beautiful home, a collection of videos, success in exams, or qualifications in a particular career?

The pearl of great price. Describe how one day the pearl merchant came across a pearl which was more valuable and more beautiful than any he had ever seen, and he was overcome with astonishment. It was so perfect, so large, and of such a magnificent texture and lustre, that it was clearly worth more than all his other pearls put together. As he gazed at this stunningly beautiful pearl, it made all his other pearls seem small, flawed, and comparatively valueless. He realised that he must obtain this pearl.

The greatest Pearl of all. In this special pearl the Lord was picturing the *kingdom of heaven,* of which He is the King. Though He did not compare the pearl directly with Himself, it is nevertheless a description of Him – for His kingdom is a reflection of His own glory. Show the children how a pearl resembles the Saviour and His rule:–

(1) He is absolutely genuine. The Lord Jesus is like a perfect pearl. He is no fake. He is truly and genuinely God. He is the perfect Truth, and He never misleads or tricks us.

(2) He is unique. Like that one pearl for which the merchant exchanged all, there is only one Saviour. The Lord Jesus was the *only* person Who was both God and man. He came to this world, was tempted like us and yet, unlike any other person, He lived a perfect life. He alone could buy the gift of eternal life for us by dying in our place on the cross.

(3) He is precious. The Lord Jesus is precious because of Who He is – the eternal, all-powerful, all-knowing God. He is precious because of His kindness and love, and because of His works. He suffered willingly to take away the punishment of sin. No amount of money could buy pardon, but the suffering of our Saviour purchases our freedom. No wonder that He is precious to every true believer!

(4) He is enduring. The Lord Jesus is the source of everlasting life and He offers this life to all who believe. Just as real pearls can be distinguished from mock pearls by the fact that their beauty never fades (teachers may be able to show children a string of paste pearls with scratched and flaking surfaces), so Christ never loses His power to save us. His love never fades, nor are His promises ever broken. To be a disciple of Christ is to know a joy and gladness which survives throughout life and extends on to eternity.

(5) He transforms. A pearl necklace can transform a woman's appearance. She may have only simple clothing, but with a string of pearls around her neck her appearance takes on a touch of beauty, even majesty. The lives of poor, needy, sinful failures take on a new lustre and worth when the Lord Jesus comes to adorn their lives. Think of John Newton who had a reputation for being a foul-mouthed sailor, but who, after conversion to Christ, penned the words – 'How sweet the name of Jesus sounds in a believer's ear,' together with many other beautiful hymns. Adorned by the Lord, his life brought much

sweetness and light to the world of his day. (Eg: he was influential in the abolition of slavery and the promotion of the first missionaries.)

A huge exchange. Describe how the merchant probably gazed upon this pearl with divided emotions. He longed with all his being to buy the pearl. But then he considered its enormous cost, and realised that he would have to sell his entire stock and possessions to raise the necessary money. Was he prepared to part with a lifetime's work for the sake of only one pearl? Would he see all that he had worked for go, for this supreme pearl?

Show that we sinners are faced with a similar decision. Jesus warned, *Whosoever doth not bear his cross, and come after me, cannot be my disciple.* And – *Strait is the gate, and narrow is the way, which leadeth unto life, and few there be that find it.* And – *If any man will come after me, let him deny himself, and take up his cross, and follow me.* We have to ask – Are we prepared to give up our sins, our ambitions, and our pride in order to gain Christ? And are we prepared to put Him first in our lives – ahead of everything else? Can we happily go along with the apostle Paul, who said, *What things were gain to me, those I counted loss for Christ (Philippians 3.7)*?

Completely satisfied. Turning back for the last time to the pearl merchant, describe the moment when he gathered up all his pearls and goods and set off to sell all. Maybe he felt a few pangs of regret as he saw them carried away, but only for a moment. Soon he was on his way to collect *the* pearl, and as soon as he saw it again, any misgivings faded away fast. It surpassed all his expectations. In comparison his old pearls seemed like paste. He looked back horrified that he had ever considered them worth keeping when the opportunity to obtain this pearl was within his grasp. As he looked at it, he began to appreciate its perfection, its shape, its beauty. He felt he could gaze at it for ever.

A precious Saviour. At this moment, the teacher will want to tell the class with personal conviction, that this is how all true Christians feel when they relinquish the world and all its fleeting, tawdry pleasures and values, and find Christ, the Pearl of greatest price. The Queen of Sheba said after her visit to see King Solomon and his glory, *I believed not the words, until I came, and mine eyes had seen it: and, behold, the half was not told me (1 Kings 10.7)*. Explain this is how all Christians feel about the Lord Jesus once they have found Him. The apostle Paul spoke of the *excellency of the knowledge of Christ Jesus my Lord (Philippians 3.8)*. Peter wrote, *Unto you therefore who believe he is precious (1 Peter 2.7)*.

Sum up this lesson in the words of an old hymn which is still fresh and challenging:

And must I part with all I have,
My dearest Lord, for Thee?
It is but right, since Thou hast done
Much more than this for me.
(Benjamin Beddome)

Visual Aid

Teachers should cultivate the habit of collecting pictures which will one day be useful in their Sunday School work. Those who have collected pictures of pearl-divers, advertisements featuring pearls, etc, will now be rewarded!

Walking on the Sea (137)

Matthew 14.13-33

Aim: To use two extraordinary events from this period of Christ's life to prove His deity, and to sympathetically help those who are still beset by doubts.

Teachers' Introduction

We conclude this series with two of the most remarkable miracles performed by Christ, miracles which brought home to the disciples His divinity in a manner beyond dispute. Matthew's account of these events is very straightforward and factual. Avoiding 'story-book' style, we must reflect the literal, authentic ring of his record, so that our hearers respect it as true history. Rather than showing the class pictures from Bible story-books, show the children up-to-date pictures and photographs of shipwrecks and heavy seas. Remind those who live inland that the sea is still very powerful and destructive. Point out that, despite our technological advances and ability to build enormous ships of great tonnage, we still cannot guarantee safety for those who travel on the high seas. The lifeboat service still answers hundreds of calls for help around our shores every year from vessels large and small.

Lesson Outline

Remind the class of the question which we posed at the beginning of this series: Who was He? Ask the children to consider these events, unique in the history of mankind, recorded by a 'civil servant', Matthew, who was probably an eyewitness. Help the children to visualise the huge crowd that had followed the Lord to seek His help (on a day which had started as a day of rest for Him). The Lord was too kind to send such a persevering crowd away disappointed, and spent most of the day healing their sick and teaching them.

As the day drew to a close the crowd were to witness an even more extraordinary and significant miracle. Instead of taking up His disciples' suggestion that they should be sent away to nearby villages to buy food for themselves, He miraculously multiplied five loaves and two fishes so that the entire crowd could be fed – a demonstration of His unique and divine power. No mere human being before or since has done such a thing. John tells us that the crowd saw the political possibilities attached to such mighty power, and were about to take Jesus by force to be their king *(John 6.15)*. It was only because the Lord insisted that His kingdom was *spiritual* that they later became disenchanted and turned away.

An extraordinary night. The feeding of the vast crowd is enough to answer our question – Who was He? – and to prove that He was the Son of God. But before the disciples reached home they were to have this confirmed yet again. Explain that in order to disperse this great and enthusiastic crowd, Jesus ordered His disciples to take to their boat and proceed ahead of

Him to the opposite shore. Meanwhile He retreated to the mountain alone to pray. Describe vividly the events that followed:–

(a) When a considerable distance from the shore (John speaks of twenty-five or thirty furlongs – three or four miles), a violent storm blew up, battering the craft and frightening the disciples (despite the fact that several of them were used to storms on the Sea of Galilee).

(b) At the fourth watch (ie: between 3 – 6 am) the Lord came towards them walking on the sea.

(c) Their understandable reaction to the sea-walking figure was one of fear and alarm. They could only assume they were seeing a ghost.

(d) Peter's impulsive response to Christ's reassurance was to ask the Saviour to command him to come to Him on the waves.

(e) Peter's brave start was followed by his failure, when he allowed the howling wind to frighten him and shake his faith in the Lord's power.

(f) Christ immediately responded to his desperate call, then rebuked him.

(g) They arrived safely back in the boat and the wind immediately died down.

(1) What does this event teach about the Lord? Ask the class to think carefully. Had they been present, what would they have thought as the boat drew safely to the home shore? The answer is – that He was certainly God's Son. Would they not agree that the person they had just seen walking on the sea and calming it into submission must be none other than its Maker, come to earth in a human form? No one else before or since has ever demonstrated such power over one of earth's most powerful forces, the sea. Only the Maker and Designer of the laws of nature could so easily overrule them.

(2) What does this event teach about His character? Ask the class to notice *how* the Lord used His great power. Never did He use it for selfish gain or power. Instead He used it to help and comfort His friends. He did not leave them alone to wrestle with the wind, but left the relative security and shelter of the mountainside and stepped on the raging foam, making His way to their storm-tossed boat. His immediate concern, when they became alarmed, was to reassure them that it was He, and to set their fears at rest, and give them at the same time a further proof of His divine nature.

Remind the class that this is typical of the Lord Jesus. He is not lofty and cut off from our trials. He is the Saviour Who came to live amongst men and women, and to give His own life that they might be rescued, ransomed and saved. He did it all for us. Illustrate this point by giving an example of someone who 'comes to the rescue'. Eg: stranded on the hard shoulder of a motorway on a cold, wet night, what an unexpected but welcome relief it would be if someone drew up alongside, got out of their car, opened their tool kit and, in spite of the drenching rain, set about changing your punctured tyre – and all in a cheerful frame of mind! Suppose you later discovered that this person was the Minister of Transport. How surprised you would be. This is a poor illustration – but it may help children understand the love and kindness of the Lord.

(3) What does this event teach about conversion? (a) When the disciples realised it was the Lord, Peter's immediate reaction was to ask Christ to enable him to walk out to Him, and the Lord invited him – 'Come!' Remind the class that this short word was often spoken by the Lord to all kinds of people in need. He, the great Maker of the universe, by Whose power we all exist, invites us to *come* to Him. He also enables us to do so, as He did Peter. Christ calls us to put our trust in Him, and He grants us the faith to do so. Like Peter we should set out boldly as soon as we hear the Lord's call.

(b) Emphasise to the class the uniqueness of the miracle, that an ordinary man like Peter should walk on water, defying the laws of nature, even in the middle of a great storm. Everything that Christ did, He did for a purpose. This was done to help us realise that what Christ does in our lives is *miraculous*. When He calls us to come to Him, it is so that He can change us in a way no power on earth can do.

A guilty, sinful person is forgiven – something that only God has the power to do, because Christ has taken the punishment of sin for those who trust in Him. Secondly, character is changed, something which all the world's best surgeons could not do for a person. The violent, mean man becomes kind and generous, while rude, cheating young people are completely different. What amazing changes! Nothing like this can be done by human power. Thirdly, *spiritual* life is given – almost like a telephone line to Heaven and a power cable from Heaven at the same time! With this new life, believers love the Lord, have new power over sin, and speak to Him in prayer.

(c) Now remind the children how Peter was scared by the wind howling around him, so that his faith failed and he began to sink. Suggest that young people, anxious to come to Christ, often find themselves scared by Satan who hurls the winds of temptation and doubt across their path. Their friends at school may sneer at their interest in Christ, and the pull of temptation to join in sinful talk, immoral viewing or harmful and time-wasting pastimes, may seem overwhelming. Being constantly bombarded in science lessons, by television programmes, and by so many other sources, with the theory of evolution (when in fact it is scientifically flawed) and pressured to do away with God, they find belief in a Creator severely shaken. Doubts are hurled at them from all directions by a scornful, scoffing world. Like Peter they may feel themselves sinking into sin and doubt, and fear that they will never reach the Lord.

What did Peter do when he began to sink? He cried out to the Lord to save him. Urge your class to do the same. Encourage them to look to Christ however strong and powerful the forces arrayed against them. He is still mighty to save and help, but without Him they can do nothing. Immediately on hearing their earnest cry, the Saviour will stretch out His mighty hand and take hold of them, and bring them to certainly find Him. (In Peter's case He took Peter to the tossing boat and calmed the elements.) He will never abandon those who call out to Him for help and salvation. His power is undiminished.

A new day. Soon the disciples had all their doubts and

unbelief removed and were worshipping their Lord saying, *Of a truth thou art the Son of God* (v 33). Assure the class that once they have been truly saved by the Lord they will be ashamed of their former doubts and be determined only to serve the great and wonderful Saviour Who is now their dearest Friend and their constant Guide through life.

Visual Aid

Provide up-to-date pictures of heavy seas, shipwrecks, ocean storms, etc, to set the scene.

Revision (138)

Who was He? – The Son of God, the Saviour

Aim: To prove from these lessons that Jesus was none other than the Son of God born to be our Saviour. To urge our children to review the amazing facts they have learned, draw the obvious conclusions and carefully reconsider their own response to them.

Lesson Outline

Return to the question asked in the first lesson of this series – Who was He? Who was Jesus of Nazareth? What reasons do we have for believing that He was the Son of God? Ask the children to recall the many remarkable facts and events we have covered in recent weeks which vindicate Jesus' claim to have come from Heaven. Suggest to the children that they consider how astonished they would feel when, for the first time they heard about a child being born who had no human father, and whose birth was surrounded by other highly unusual events. What would they think if they heard of – or saw – this person, as an adult, performing amazing sign-miracles in full view of thousands of people?

Ask the children to recall some of the other events covered in the series which point to the fact that Jesus was the Son of God. Even Nicodemus, from the party of Pharisees (a group normally most hostile towards Christ), said that no one could do such signs unless God was with him. *We* believe that no one could do such signs unless He was God Himself appearing as a man. Show the children the visual aid (see below):

(1) Born of a virgin. Ask the class to remember the time when an angel had to appear to Joseph, the carpenter of Nazareth, to assure him that the child expected by Mary, his fiancée, had been conceived by the Holy Spirit. The angel gave instructions that Joseph should marry Mary and prepare for the birth of her wonderful son. Ask the class the meaning of the two names given to the child before His birth, Jesus and Emmanuel. Remind them that the prophet Isaiah had spoken of Emmanuel, and His birth to a virgin, seven hundred years previously. Ask the class which other unusual events around the birth of Jesus are recorded by Matthew (the wise men and the star). Help them see the significance attached to them. Turn this portion of revision to account by explaining why the Lord needed to be born as a babe.

(2) Resisted all Satan's temptations. Remind the class that, following Jesus' baptism when a voice from Heaven had affirmed, *This is my beloved Son, in whom I am well pleased*, Jesus was led into the barren wilderness country. After forty days and nights of going without food, He underwent a period of intense pressure and temptation. Yet He refused to be moved by the threats and bribes of the devil, who attempted to get the Lord to alter His plan and purpose in life. Ask the class to remember some of the suggestions Satan made, and the Lord's firm answers. Remind the class *why* it is so comforting to us to see that Christ would not consider Himself, but stuck to His plan. (Because of His great love towards us, He would not be deflected from dying for us. His perfect and wonderful character shines through. And without this, how could He make a *perfect* offering of Himself to earn our salvation?)

(3) Healed the sick. Next, remind the class that the Lord healed thousands of people from a wide variety of physical, nervous and spiritual diseases, usually instantly and always permanently. In this He was observed by thousands of eyewitnesses, many of whom were educated men and women (such as Matthew and Luke, the doctor). Ask the children about the particular example of healing which we have studied in the series. Ask them to imagine the effect which would have been made on them, had they been present to see the badly disfigured leper returning home, his flesh completely restored to normal at the command of this Jesus. Help them consider the impact which would have been felt by any unprejudiced observer, of the immediate and complete healing of so many sick, disabled, blind, deaf and epileptic people. His divine power and nature were certainly proved beyond doubt.

(4) Spoke with great authority. In this series of lessons we have listened to the teaching of the Lord. Depending on the age of the class, ask questions which help them to appreciate the unique teaching of the Saviour. Though spoken two thousand years ago, His teachings, expressed in never-to-be-forgotten stories of everyday life, are still renowned and remembered around the world, even by young children. They are so simple and easy that the simplest person can follow them, and yet the greatest brains never exhaust their meaning and significance. No other person has ever had his words so widely publicised and studied. No other teaching has been commented on and written about more than the Lord's. The Bible itself is the world's best seller, and the books published about the Bible are impossible to count. No literature has had anything like the influence upon so many people of the world, for so long a time.

Remind the class of the reaction of the crowds who first heard the teaching of Jesus. They were *astonished at his doctrine: for he taught them as one having authority, and not as the scribes (Matthew 7.28-29)*. No wonder that thousands gathered wherever Jesus went, to hear Him speaking.

(5) Taught the way to Heaven. Remind the class how the Lord's pattern prayer shows a repentant sinner *how* to return to God. Ask what the *pearl of great price* stood for and question the children about the price the merchant was prepared to pay for it. Speak about the two ways of life described by Christ in His illustration of the two roads. Who else can help them on such a vital topic as the saving of the soul? Politicians, entertainers and sports personalities are mostly 'all at sea' when it comes to the really important issues.

(6) Walked on the sea. Remind the class about the Lord's feeding of the 5,000 with only five loaves and two fishes! Point out this is not like modern faith-healers who cannot prove a single healing to the doctors! Refer to the Lord's walking on the sea, and calming the raging storm at a word. Who could doubt His divine nature after witnessing such mighty power? Remind the class that the disciples present were deeply shaken by what they had seen, and were frightened. Their reaction was to worship Him, saying, *Of a truth thou art the Son of God (Matthew 14.33)*. Urge your class to do the same.

Conclusion. Having given these great reasons for believing that Jesus was indeed the Son of God, go on to ask why He came. Ask why God's beloved Son should leave His wonderful home in Heaven to visit this sin-sick and hostile world. Close the lesson with the heart of the Gospel.

Remind the class that however convincing the proof of Jesus' divinity is, and however touching the message of His work on Calvary for us, vast numbers of people refuse to admit that they need a Saviour. They just will not face up to the danger they are in. Urge the children to be amongst those who *believe that Jesus is the Christ, the Son of God; and that believing . . . have life through his name (John 20.31)*.

Visual Aid

Teachers can reuse the visual aid prepared for Lesson 127 (see VA 10, page 197). They should replace the original six points with the six headings of this lesson.

Lessons for Life, books 1-4

Lessons for Life 3 is the third to be published of four books of Sunday School lessons designed to cover a four-year syllabus. Each book follows the same format, consisting of lessons which have proved successful in Sunday Schools over many years, now revised by the author. The contents of each book are as follows:–

Lessons for Life 1 (lessons 1-46)

Miracles Demonstrating Jesus' Power (Mark's Gospel – Part I)
The Lord's saving power seen in His power over nature, death, the devil, human need and illness (5 lessons)

In the Beginning (Genesis – Part I)
The truth about God, creation and the fall, with the earliest salvation testimonies (6 lessons)

Opposition to Jesus (Mark's Gospel – Part II)
Examples of key sins – prejudice, pride, hardness, hate, etc – seen in the Lord's opponents, and to be repented of by all (6 lessons)

Highlights from the Conversion and Preaching Journeys of Paul (Acts – Part I)
Evangelistic lessons from the life (and converts) of the apostle (8 lessons)

God's Great Plans (Genesis – Part II)
Character studies from Abraham to Joseph showing the power and goodness of God towards His people (12 lessons)

The 'I AM' Sayings of the Lord Jesus (John's Gospel)
Exalting the Saviour through His own great metaphors – the Living Water, the Bread of Life, etc (9 lessons)

Lessons for Life 2 (lessons 47-92)

The Christian Pilgrimage – Salvation from Sin's Slavery (Exodus – Joshua – Part I)
The journey from Egypt to Sinai (8 lessons)

People Who Followed Jesus (Luke's Gospel – Part I)
Christian conversion and its chief characteristics (11 lessons)

The Christian Pilgrimage – Pictures of Salvation and Heaven (Exodus – Joshua – Part II)
The journey continues from Sinai to Jordan (6 lessons)

Gospel Appeals in the Saviour's Parables (Luke's Gospel – Part II)
Teaching the consequences of sin and the only way of escape (11 lessons)

Judgement and Deliverance (Joshua – 1 Samuel)
Examples and warnings for all, from Rahab to Saul (10 lessons)

Lessons for Life 3 (lessons 93-138)

Gains and Losses in Following Jesus (Mark's Gospel – Part III)
Repentance, faith and conversion, and their alternatives (8 lessons)

Great Differences (1 Samuel – 2 Chronicles)
Contrasts drawn from the lives of David and Solomon to illustrate conversion and the believer's privileges (12 lessons)

Early Reactions to the Apostles' Message (Acts – Part II)
Various categories of hearer and the Holy Spirit's work in their lives (6 lessons)

Sin and Its Cure (1 and 2 Kings – Elijah and Elisha)
The nature of sin and its punishment, with God's remedy graphically presented (8 lessons)

The Saviour Comes and Begins His Work (Matthew's Gospel – Part I)
A chronological account of the life and teaching of the Lord highlighting His attributes and saving purpose (12 lessons)

Lessons for Life 4 (lessons 139-184 – in preparation)

The Word of God (Amos to Jeremiah)
The Bible authenticated in history and in transformed lives

The Life, Death and Resurrection of the Lord Jesus (Matthew's Gospel – Part II)
Continuing the chronological account of the life and teaching of the Lord

Character Studies from Daniel, Ezra and Nehemiah
The transforming work of grace and its dramatic results

How God Fits Us for Heaven
The steps of salvation explained from Romans and applied to young people today

The Lord's Ten Great Commandments
The 'schoolmaster' to lead us to Christ and the way of safety and fulfilment

Lessons for Life Sunday School Aids

Lessons for Life users may wish to use the take-home leaflets to accompany the lessons each week. These are entitled: *Lessons for Life Bible Learning Course.* They feature an outline picture for colouring by children, questions and a hymn verse related to the lesson, and suggested passages for personal Bible reading for the ensuing week.

Sunday School hymn sheets, and chorus and verse sheets, for hanging or mounting are also available. (These can also be obtained on A4 sheets for those who wish to have their own enlarged copies made locally, or who wish to have overhead transparencies made.) Other helps, such as visual aid materials, are also in course of preparation. Enquiries concerning take-home leaflets, hymn sheets, and news of other materials should be made to:–

Lessons for Life, Metropolitan Tabernacle,
Elephant & Castle, London SE1 6SD.

Other Wakeman Trust books of special relevance to Sunday School ministry

Lessons for Life 1
Lessons for Life 2
Jill Masters

each 207 pages, paperback

Each containing 46 lessons for the first and second years of the four-year lesson scheme.

The Necessity of Sunday Schools
In this Post-Christian Era

Peter Masters & Malcolm H. Watts

112 pages, paperback

A clarion call for the unique effectiveness of *evangelistic* Sunday Schools operated on a large scale. This book offers invincible proof that the Bible sanctions and commands child evangelism of the kind represented by vigorous Sunday School outreach. The authors contend that there is no need for Sunday School numbers to fall, or for Schools to close. Christians should take a 'total neighbourhood responsibility' for the rising generation. Here is real stimulation and encouragement for the opening or enlargement of Sunday Schools, along with counsel and help for workers.

Men of Destiny
Men of Purpose
Peter Masters

172 and 167 pages, paperback, illustrated

Youth leaders and Sunday School teachers will appreciate for illustration the 25 outstanding testimonies contained in these volumes of great Christian biography.

Men of Destiny:

Tsar Alexander Pavlovich *(The tsar who defeated Napoleon)*
Lieut 'Birdie' Bowers *(Scott's 'bravest man' in the Antarctic)*
Sir James Simpson *(The discoverer of anaesthetic chloroform)*
Alves Reis *(The counterfeiter who nearly owned his country)*

Joshua Poole *(The story of 'Fiddler Joss', drunkard turned preacher)*
Viscount Alexander of Hillsborough *(A leader of the House of Lords)*
John Newton *(The transformed slave trader)*
Jean Henri Dunant *(Founder of the International Red Cross)*
Martin Luther *(The ex-monk who led the Reformation)*
Bilney, Tyndale & Latimer *(Three heroic English martyrs)*
Alfred the Great *(The king who organised England)*
Lieut-General Sir William Dobbie *(World War II hero of Malta)*

Men of Purpose:

Michael Faraday *(Father of electrical science)*
Henry J. Heinz *(Founder of the food empire)*
Félix Mendelssohn *(A composer with a spiritual journey)*
Lord Radstock *(Whose missions brought conversions to Russia's aristocracy)*
James Clerk Maxwell *(Father of modern physics)*
Philip P. Bliss *(The hymnwriter who won countless souls)*
Fred Charrington *(The brewer who renounced a fortune)*
Lord Kelvin *(Britain's greatest scientific inventor)*
James Montgomery *(A poet who ran away from God)*
Sir John Ambrose Fleming *(Inventor of the radio valve)*
Daniel Defoe *(The founder of journalism and great novelist)*

These books are available from Christian bookshops, or from the publisher:

The Wakeman Trust, 5 Templar Street,
London SE5 9JB.